VISUAL QUICKSTART GUIDE

# PHP FOR THE WORLD WIDE WEB

Larry Ullman

 Peachpit Press

Visual QuickStart Guide
**PHP for the World Wide Web**
Larry Ullman

## Peachpit Press
1249 Eighth Street
Berkeley, CA 94710
510/524-2178
800/283-9444
510/524-2221 (fax)

Find us on the World Wide Web at:
http://www.peachpit.com

Peachpit Press is a division of Addison Wesley Longman

Copyright © 2001 by Larry Ullman

Editors: Nancy Davis, Rebecca Gulick
Technical Editor: Cliff Vick
Production Coordinator: Lisa Brazieal
Compositor: Owen Wolfson
Cover design: The Visual Group

ISBN 0-201-72787-0

9 8 7 6 5 4
Printed and bound in the United States of America

Printed on recycled paper

*For Jessica, Gina, and Rich,
with gratitude for all of their
love and support.*

## Special thanks

Many, many thanks to everyone at Peachpit Press for their assistance and hard work, especially: Marjorie Baer, Nancy Davis, Rebecca Gulick, Lisa Brazieal, Nancy Aldrich-Ruenzel, and Kate Reber.

My appreciation to Bruce Bowden for his emendations and for being such a fuddling, irrefragable polyhistor.

Thanks to Rasmus Lerdorf and the entire PHP community for developing, improving upon, and supporting such wonderfully useful technology.

# TABLE OF CONTENTS

# INTRODUCTION

The World Wide Web can be a mysterious place. New technologies are created and implemented, often with little or no documentation and support. Faced with acronyms that represent systems that change on an almost daily basis, one easily becomes overwhelmed.

One example of this has been the growth in what is referred to as *open source* software: programs freely available to both distribute and improve upon. The most popular open source model is the Unix operating system, and Linux in particular. However, while these open source programs create stable and very useful products, they can be unfortunately difficult to learn. The lack of beginner's manuals and easy-to-follow guides keep these powerful technologies from being as popular as they deserve to be. PHP, an open source Web scripting language, is another wonderfully utilitarian tool that, despite its value and general ease of use, has been daunting to pick up, until now.

This book is intended to help you learn PHP, giving you both a solid understanding of the fundamentals and a sense of where to look for more advanced information. While not a comprehensive programming reference, this book does provide the knowledge you need to begin building dynamic Web sites and Web applications using PHP today.

# What is PHP?

PHP originally stood for "Personal Home Page" as it was created in 1994 by Rasmus Lerdorf to track the visitors to his online resume. As its usefulness and capabilities grew (and as it started being utilized in more professional situations), it came to mean "PHP: Hypertext Preprocessor." (What the definition basically means is that PHP handles data before it becomes HTML—which stands for HyperText Markup Language.)

According to the official PHP Web site, found at www.php.net (**Figure i.1**), PHP is a server-side, cross-platform, HTML embedded scripting language. This may sound like a mouthful, but it's fairly straightforward and meaningful when broken down into its parts.

First, *server-side* refers to the fact that everything PHP does occurs on the server (as opposed to on the *client*, which is the Web site viewer's computer). A server is simply a special computer that houses the pages that you see when you go to a Web address with your browser (e.g., Netscape Navigator or Internet Explorer). I'll discuss this process in more detail later in the chapter (see *How PHP Works*).

When we declare that PHP is *cross-platform* we are indicating that it can be used on machines running Unix, Windows NT, Macintosh, OS/2, and other operating systems. Again, we are talking about the *server's* operating system, not the client's. Not only can PHP run on almost any operating system, but, unlike with most other programming languages, your work can be switched from one platform to another with very few or no modifications whatsoever. Naturally you can develop PHP on any operating system, too, just as you can HTML.

**Figure i.1** At the time of this book's printing, this is the current appearance of the official PHP Web site, located at www.php.net. Naturally this should be the first place to look for most of your PHP questions and curiosities. It contains the latest edition of the PHP manual with other user comments added, as well as links to more resources.

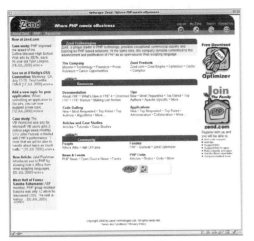

**Figure i.2** This is the home page of Zend, creators of the programming that is at the heart of PHP 4. Detailed information on the latest version of PHP can be found here.

To say that PHP is *HTML embedded* means that it can be put within your HTML code— HTML being the code with which all Web pages are built. Therefore, the actual programming of PHP can be only slightly more complicated than hand-coding HTML.

Finally, PHP is a *scripting language*, as opposed to a *programming language*. This means that PHP is designed to do something *only after an event occurs*, for example, when a user submits a form or goes to a URL (Uniform Resource Locator—the technical term for a Web address). Programming languages such as Java, C, and Perl can write stand-alone applications, which may or may not even involve the Web. The most popular example of a scripting language is JavaScript, which commonly handles events that occur within the Web browser, and is somewhat similar to PHP, although it is a client-side technology. Another way to refer to the different types of languages is to use the term *interpreted* for languages such as PHP and JavaScript, which cannot act on their own, and *compiled* for those like C and Java, which can.

PHP is currently in Version 4.0 although, as this version is relatively new, many servers are still running Version 3.x. This book will discuss PHP 4 specifically, but the differences between the two versions are insignificant as far as programming is generally concerned. The majority of the benefits in the new version are found in its improved performance. More information about PHP 4.0 can be found at www.zend.com, the minds behind the core of PHP 4.0 (**Figure i.2**).

WHAT IS PHP?

# Why Use PHP

Put simply, PHP is better, faster, and easier to learn than the alternatives. When designing Web sites, your primary alternatives to PHP are: simple HTML; CGI scripts (Common Gateway Interface, commonly, but not necessarily written in Perl); ASP (Active Server Pages); and JSP (Java Server Pages). JavaScript is not truly an alternative to PHP (or vice versa) as JavaScript is a *client-side* technology and cannot be used to create HTML pages in the same way that PHP or CGI can.

The advantage PHP has over basic HTML is that the latter is a limited system that allows for no flexibility or responsiveness. Visitors accessing HTML pages will see simple pages without any level of customization or dynamic behavior. With PHP, you can create exciting and original pages based upon whatever factors you want to consider (for example, the time of day or the user's operating system). PHP can also interact with databases and files, handle email, and do many other things that HTML cannot.

Webmasters learned a long time ago that HTML alone will not produce enticing and lasting Web sites. To this end, server-side technologies such as CGI scripts have gained widespread popularity. These systems allow Web page designers to create Web applications that are dynamically generated, taking into account whichever elements the programmer desired. Often database-driven, these advanced sites can even be updated and maintained more readily than static HTML pages.

So the question is: Why should a Web designer use PHP instead of CGI, ASP, or JSP to make a dynamic Web site? First, PHP is both faster to program in and faster to execute than CGI scripts. I won't get into too much detail on the execution of these various processes (or open up a debate on the subject) but suffice it to say that compared to full programming languages, PHP is much easier to learn and use. People—perhaps like you—without any formal programming training whatsoever can be writing out PHP scripts with ease after reading just this one book. In comparison, ASP requires an understanding of VBScript, and CGI requires Perl (or C), and both of these are more complete languages, and, therefore, more difficult to learn.

Second, PHP was written specifically for dynamic Web page creation, whereas Perl (and VBScript and Java) were not, inferring that, by its very intent, PHP can do certain tasks faster and easier than its alternatives. I would like to make it clear, however, that while I'm suggesting PHP is definitely better for certain things (specifically those it was created to do) than CGI or ASP, PHP is not a better programming language than Java or Perl as they can do things PHP cannot.

My final argument for learning PHP is that once you do, and as its popularity continues to grow (it is already being used on nearly three million Web sites), you will find yourself well ahead of the learning curve on this, the latest "next big thing" in the world of Internet technology.

**WHY USE PHP**

# How PHP Works

PHP is a server-side language, which means that the code you write in PHP resides on a host computer that serves Web pages to Web browsers.

When a visitor goes to a Web site (www.DMCinsights.com, for example), your Internet service provider directs your request to the server that holds the www.DMCinsights.com information.

The server reads the PHP code and processes it according to its scripted directions. In this example, the PHP code tells the server to send the appropriate Web page data to your browser in the form of HTML (**Figure i.3**). In short, PHP is creating an HTML page on the fly based upon parameters of my choosing, and the server, therefore, contains no static HTML pages.

This differs from an HTML-generated site in that when a request is made, the server merely sends the HTML data to the Web browser and there is no server-side interpretation occurring (**Figure i.4**). Hence, to the end user's browser there may or may not be an obvious difference between what home.html and home.php may look like, but how we arrived at that point will be critically altered. The major difference is that by using PHP you can have the server *dynamically* generate the HTML code. For example, different information could be presented if it is Monday as opposed to Tuesday or if the user has visited the page before or not. Dynamic Web page creation is what sets apart the less appealing, static sites from the more interesting and, therefore, more visited, interactive ones.

The central difference between using PHP and using straight HTML is that every thing PHP does, it does on the server and it then sends the appropriate information to the browser. This book covers how to use PHP to send the right data to the browser.

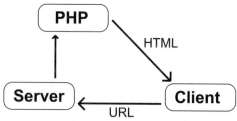

**Figure i.3** This graphic demonstrates how the process works between a Client, the Server, and a PHP module (an application added to the server to increase its functionality) to send HTML back to the browser (albeit in very simplistic terms). All server-side technologies (ASP, for example) use some sort of third-party module on the server to process the data that gets sent back to the client.

**Figure i.4** Compare this direct relationship of how a server works with basic HTML to that of Figure i.3. This is also why HTML pages can be viewed in your browser from your own computer since they do not need to be "served," but dynamically generated pages need to be accessed through a server which handles the processing.

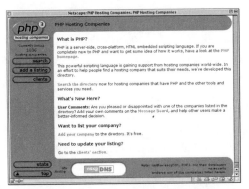

**Figure i.5** Through PHP's home page (Figure i.1) or directly you can access hosts.php.net, a site where you can search through the ISP's who offer PHP on their servers.

# What You'll Need

The most important requirement for working with PHP—since it is a server-side scripting language—is access to a PHP-enabled server. Considering PHP's popularity, it is most likely that your ISP (Internet Service Provider) or Web host has this option available to you on their servers. To be sure, you will need to contact them to see what technology they support. As of this writing, over one thousand ISPs and Web hosts provide PHP support (**Figure i.5**).

The other option you have is to install PHP on your own server—commonly just a machine running Windows NT or Linux, with the necessary Web server application installed. (For example, Apache is a free Web serving application for Unix and NT systems, or you could use Personal Web Sharing with Windows.) Brief information on installing PHP is available in Appendix A, *Installation and Configuration*. If you are up to the task of using your own PHP-installed server, you can take some consolation in knowing that PHP is available for free from the PHP Web site (www.php.net) and comes in easy-to-install packages.

The second requirement is almost a given—that you have some sort of text editor on your computer. NotePad, WordPad, SimpleText, and similar freeware applications are all sufficient for your purposes, while BBEdit, WordPerfect, Word, and other commercial applications offer more features that you may appreciate. If you are accustomed to using a graphical interface (also referred to as WYSIWYG—What You See Is What You Get) editors like Dreamweaver or GoLive, you can consult your manual to see how to program within that application.

*continues on next page*

WHAT YOU'LL NEED

Third, you will need some method of getting the scripts you write in your text editor to the server. If you are working directly on your own server, you can simply save the scripts to the appropriate directory. However, if you are using a remote server with your ISP or Web host, you will need an FTP (File Transfer Protocol) program to send the script to the server. Another option is to telnet to the remote server and use an editor such as Vi or Pico to write your scripts directly on that machine.

From you this book only assumes a basic knowledge of HTML, although the more comfortable you are handling raw HTML code *without* the aid of a Web creation application such as Dreamweaver, GoLive, FrontPage, or PageMill, the easier the transition to using PHP will be. Every programmer will eventually turn to an HTML reference at some time or another, regardless of how much he or she knows, so I would encourage you to keep a good HTML book by your side. One such introduction to HTML coding is Elizabeth Castro's *HTML for the World Wide Web: Visual QuickStart Guide*, also by Peachpit Press.

Previous programming experience is certainly not required, although it may expedite your learning, as you will quickly see numerous similarities between, for example, Perl and PHP or JavaScript and PHP.

**WHAT YOU'LL NEED**

**Script i.1** Better text editors will automatically put in line numbers for you as you work. You should never put these in yourself!

```
1   <?php
2   print ("Hello, World!");
3   ?>
```

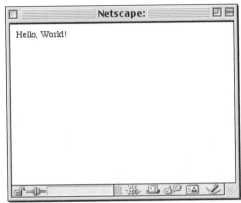

**Figure i.6** This is the view you will see of the browser window. It will not make any difference whether you use Netscape Navigator or Internet Explorer (or something else) on Macintosh, Windows, Linux, or any other operating system for the purposes in this book.

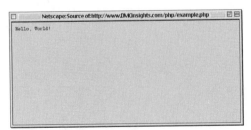

**Figure i.7** By selecting "Page Source" from the View menu in Netscape or "Source" from the View menu in Internet Explorer, you can see the HTML that the browser received. In this case, it only received the text "Hello, World!"

# About This Book

In this book I have attempted to convey both the fundamentals of programming with PHP and some of the more advanced features you may end up using, without going into overwhelming detail. I have used the following conventions to do so:

The step-by-step instructions will indicate what coding you are to add to your scripts and where. The specific text you should type will be printed in a unique type style to separate it from the main body text. Example:

```
<?php print ("Hello, World!"); ?>
```

The PHP code will also be written out as its own complete script as I go and will be numbered by line for reference (**Script i.1**). You should not insert these numbers yourself, as it will render your work inoperable. I recommend using a text editor that automatically displays the line numbers for you, as this will help when debugging your work (see Chapter 14, *Debugging*).

In these blocks I will also highlight in red the particular parts being discussed in the step-by-step instruction section to draw attention to new or relevant material. Likewise, where appropriate, sections of the browser window will be marked (**Figure i.6**). One last view you will see in this book is that of the HTML source itself (**Figure i.7**), accessed in Netscape Navigator through the View > Page Source menu or in Internet Explorer through View > Source. The difference is insignificant between these two particular figures, but understand that **Figure i.7** displays the text the browser receives and Figure i.6 demonstrates how the browser interprets that text. Using PHP, we will create the text that is sent to the browser.

*continues on next page*

**ABOUT THIS BOOK**

Since the column in this book is narrower than the common text editor screen, sometimes lines of PHP code printed here have to be broken up where they would not otherwise break in your editor. A small gray arrow indicates when this kind of break occurs. For example:

```
<HTML><HEAD><TITLE>First PHP Script
→ </TITLE></HEAD><BODY>
```

You should continue to use one line in your scripts, or else you will encounter errors when executing. (The gray arrow is not used in scripts that are numbered.)

While demonstrating new features and techniques, I will do my best to explain the why's and how's of them as I go. Hopefully between reading about and using a function you will clearly comprehend it. Should something remain confusing, though, this book contains a number of references where you can find answers to whatever questions you may have (see Appendix C, *PHP Resources*).

Because of the nature of how PHP works, please also understand that there are essentially three views of every script: the PHP code itself; the code that gets sent to the browser (mostly HTML); and what the browser displays to the end user. I will show as much of these three views as possible, depending upon space constraints, with priority given to the PHP itself.

# Companion Web Site

While reading this book, you may also find it helpful to visit the *PHP for the World Wide Web: Visual QuickStart Guide* Web site, located at www.DMCinsights.com/php. There you will find every script in this book in action and available in a downloadable form. However, I would strongly encourage you to type out the scripts yourself in order to become more familiar with the structure and syntax of PHP. The site will also include a more detailed reference section, with links to numerous useful Web pages for you to continue learning PHP. In addition, the site will include an errata section listing any mistakes made in this text.

## Questions, comments, or suggestions?

If you have a PHP-specific question, there are newsgroups, listservs, and various question-and-answer sections available on PHP-related Web sites for you to turn to. These are discussed in more detail in Appendix C, *PHP Resources*. You can also direct your questions, comments, and suggestions to me, via e-mail, at: php@DMCinsights.com.

COMPANION WEB SITE

# GETTING STARTED WITH PHP

1

Learning any new programming language should always begin with an understanding of the syntax you will use, and that's what we'll explore in this chapter. I will primarily cover the fundamentals, but will also include some recommendations that will improve your work in the long run. Failure to follow the rules of syntax is an all-too-common cause of errors in your code.

By the end of this chapter you will have successfully written and executed your first PHP scripts.

# Basic Syntax

In order to create your first PHP page, you will start off exactly as you would if you were creating an HTML document from scratch.

There are two main differences between a standard HTML document and a PHP document. First, PHP scripts should be saved with the .php extension (e.g., index.php). Second, you wrap your PHP code with the <?PHP and ?> tags to indicate what is PHP as opposed to what is HTML.

## To create a new PHP script on your computer:

1. Open a text editor such as SimpleText, WordPad, or whichever application you prefer.

2. Choose File > New to create a new, blank document.

3. Type <HTML> <HEAD> <TITLE>First PHP → Script</TITLE> </HEAD> <BODY> (**Script 1.1**).

   You can put each element or element group on its own line to make it neater.

4. Type <?PHP on its own line.

5. Press Return to create a new line and then type ?>.

6. Type </BODY></HTML>.

7. Choose File > Save As. In the dialog box that appears, choose Text Only (or ASCII) for the format.

8. Choose the location where you wish to save the script.

9. Save the script as first.php.

**Script 1.1** This is the most basic structure of an HTML document, with the PHP tags inserted into the body section. All PHP scripts must use some form of the PHP tags in order for the server to know what to process as PHP. Anything within those brackets gets treated as PHP, while everything outside of them gets sent to the browser as standard HTML.

```
1    <HTML>
2    <HEAD>
3    <TITLE>First PHP Script</TITLE>
4    </HEAD>
5    <BODY>
6    <?PHP
7    ?>
8    </BODY>
9    </HTML>
```

## ✔ Tips

■ Check with your ISP to learn which file extensions you can use for PHP documents. For this book you will use .php, although you may be able to use .phtml instead. Servers still running PHP version 3 commonly use .php3 as the default extension. A file extension tells the server how to treat the file: file.php will go through the PHP module, file.asp is processed as ASP, and file.html is a static HTML document.

■ You can also check with your ISP to see if short tags (using <? and ?> instead of <?PHP and ?>) or ASP tags (<% and %>) are acceptable. Programs like Macromedia Dreamweaver can work better with PHP pages if you use ASP tags.

**Script 1.2** Since we will save this as a different file, we also changed the HTML title line when we added the phpinfo() function.

```
1    <HTML>
2    <HEAD>
3    <TITLE>Test PHP Script</TITLE>
4    </HEAD>
5    <BODY>
6    <?PHP
7    phpinfo();
8    ?>
9    </BODY>
10   </HTML>
```

# Sending Data to the Browser

Now that you have created your first PHP script, it's time to make it actually do something. As discussed in the introduction, PHP tells the server what data to send to your Web browser. For starters, you will use the phpinfo()function to create our data. This function, when called, will send a table of information to the Web browser itemizing the specifics of the PHP installation on that particular server.

### To add the phpinfo() function to your script:

1. Open your first.php script in your text editor, if it isn't already.

2. Put your cursor between the PHP tags (<?PHP and ?>) and create a new line by pressing Return).

3. On the new line, type phpinfo();.

4. Change the title of the page by replacing **First** with **Test** in line 3 of the HTML (**Script 1.2**).

5. Save your script as test.php.

Every statement within PHP code must end with a semicolon (;). Forgetting to do so is a common cause of errors. You can put multiple statements on one line, with each separated by its own semicolon. For the sake of clarity, however, I would not recommend it.

A statement in PHP is an executable line of code, like print() or phpinfo(). The semicolon concluding these lines are the equivalent of telling PHP to go ahead and execute the command. Conversely, comment lines, the PHP tags, control structures (conditionals, loops, etc.), and certain other constructs I'll discuss in this book do not merit a semicolon. Each

*continues on next page*

of these aspects of PHP do not do anything in and of themselves so much as dictate the circumstances for the statements to follow. That is to say: the PHP tag only indicates that PHP code is to follow; comment characters render text moot, and so forth. Thus, in general, a semicolon concludes a specific action, while no semicolon is required for constructs that create conditions.

## ✔ Tips

- For better or worse, PHP is rather liberal when it comes to case sensitivity of built-in functions like `PHPINFO()`. `PHPinfo()` and `PHPINFO()` will net the same results. Later in the book (for example, Chapter 2, *Variables*) you will see examples of instances where the word case will make a crucial difference. HTML, in contrast, is entirely case insensitive.

- `Phpinfo()` is an example of a built-in function which comes standard in PHP. To learn more about functions and how to create your own, see Chapter 9, *Creating Functions*.

- You will find it handy to have a copy of the `test.php` file around. You can use this to check the PHP capabilities of a new server or see what features are supported, such as databases, GIF building, etc. You can also use this file to experiment with different extensions and learn which ones the server will process correctly and which it will not.

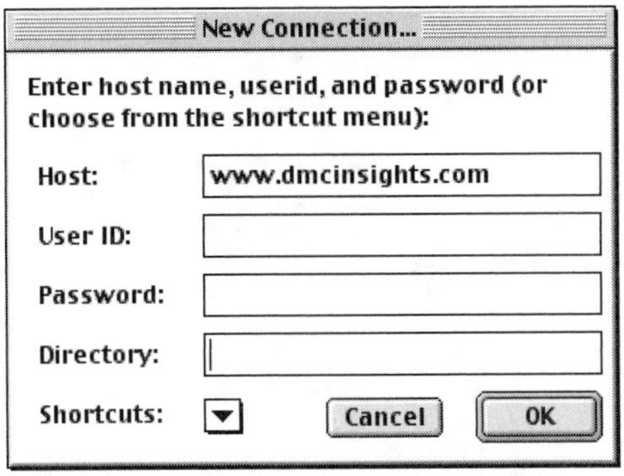

**Figure 1.1** Fetch is a popular FTP application for the Macintosh, although there are others. Enter in your username and password that the ISP or Web host provided to you. If you know the directory where the files are to be stored, you could enter that here as well.

# Testing Your Script

Unlike HTML, which can be tested on your own computer using a Web browser, in order to see what the output of your PHP script will look like, it needs to be saved to a PHP-enabled server. If you are working directly on a server, the script is already there once you've saved it. If you are creating your script using a text editor on your home computer, you will need to use FTP (file transfer protocol) to place it on the server. Your ISP or Web host should provide you with FTP access. You will also need an FTP application such as Fetch (for the Macintosh) or WS_FTP (for Windows).

### To FTP your script to the server:

1. Open your FTP application.

2. Connect to the server, using the address, username, and password provided to you by your ISP or Web host (**Figure 1.1**).

3. Find the proper directory for your HTML pages (e.g., www/ or htdocs/).

4. Save your script (test.php) to the server. (As a rule, most FTP applications save transferred pages to the server with the same filename you are using for those files on your computer. If your particular FTP program gives you the option to specify the filename, use test.php.)

*continues on next page*

TESTING YOUR SCRIPT

## To test your script in the browser:

1. Open your favorite Web browser.

2. Enter the URL of the site where your script has been saved. (In my case, this is `http://www.DMCinsights.com/php.`)

3. Add `/test.php` to the URL.

4. Press Return. The page should load in your browser window (**Figure 1.2**).

The `phpinfo()` function displays the system information for the PHP module installed on your server. It's handy for testing a new PHP installation, determining which PHP extensions are usable, and recording what PHP features are supported.

## ✔ Tip

- Some text editors, such as BBEdit, have built in FTP capability, allowing you to save your scripts directly to the server.

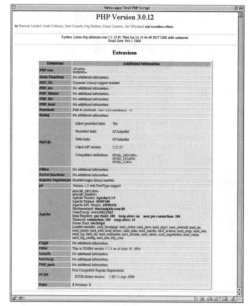

**Figure 1.2** If you see the text `phpinfo();` then either PHP is not installed correctly or the extension you used (.php in our case) is not treated as a PHP file.

**Script 1.3** By putting the print statement between the PHP brackets, we have the server send the *Hello, world!* greeting to the browser. It's the same as if we had put *Hello, world!* within the HTML code.

```
script
1   <HTML>
2   <HEAD>
3   <TITLE>First PHP Script</TITLE>
4   </HEAD>
5   <BODY>
6   <?PHP
7   print ("Hello, world!");
8   ?>
9   </BODY>
10  </HTML>
```

Netscape: First PHP Script

Hello, world!

**Figure 1.3** If your script has been executed correctly, your browser should look like this (not very exciting, but it works).

# Sending Text to the Browser

PHP would not be very useful if all you could do was see what PHP features were installed. What you will use it to do most frequently is to send information to the browser in the form of plain text and HTML tags. For this, you will use the `print()` function.

## To print a simple message:

1. Open `first.php` in your text editor.

2. Put your cursor between the PHP brackets and create a new line by pressing Return.

3. Type `print ("Hello, world!");` (**Script 1.3**).

   Printing the phrase *Hello, world!* is the first step most programming references teach you. Even though it's a trivial reason to use PHP, I'll abide by the convention for demonstration purposes.

4. Save your script.

5. Upload your script to your server and test it in your browser (**Figure 1.3**).

*continues on next page*

## ✔ Tips

- There are different functions you can use to send text to the browser including echo() and printf(). Echo is virtually synonymous to print, so it will not be discussed in any more detail. I will cover printf() in Chapter 13, *Creating Web Applications*.

- You can use print() with or without the parentheses but you must always use the quotation marks, e.g., you could have typed print "Hello, world!"; While we'll use parentheses in this book to further separate out printed statements, most programmers do not use them. My suggestion is to find a style that you like and stick to it.

- Failure to use an opening or closing quotation mark or parenthesis or neglecting to include the required trailing semicolon for every statement are common causes of errors when using the print() statement. If your script is not executing properly, check these items first.

**Script 1.4** By using the print function, you can send HTML tags along with your text to the browser, where the formatting will be applied.

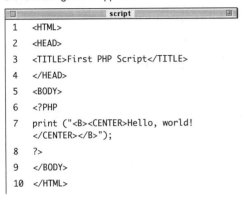

```
1   <HTML>
2   <HEAD>
3   <TITLE>First PHP Script</TITLE>
4   </HEAD>
5   <BODY>
6   <?PHP
7   print ("<B><CENTER>Hello, world!
    </CENTER></B>");
8   ?>
9   </BODY>
10  </HTML>
```

**Figure 1.4** Our new version of the script, with a little more decoration and appeal. Any HTML tag can be sent to the browser from PHP; just be sure to follow HTML conventions (use closing tags, for example).

# Sending HTML to the Browser

As those who first learned HTML were quick discover, viewing plain text in a Web browser leaves a lot to be desired. Indeed, HTML was created in order to make plain text more appealing and useful. Since HTML works by adding tags to text, you can use PHP to send HTML tags to the browser, along with our other data.

### To send HTML to the browser using PHP:

1. Open your first.php script in your text editor.

2. Edit the "Hello, world!" text in line 7 by adding bold and center tags to read print ("<B><CENTER>Hello, world!</CENTER> → </B>"); (**Script 1.4**).

3. Upload your script to your server and reload the page in your browser (**Figure 1.4**).

### ✔ Tip

■ HTML tags which require quotation marks (e.g., <FONT COLOR="#000000">) will cause problems when printing from PHP, since the print() function uses quotation marks as well. To avoid complications, you *escape* the quotation marks using the backslash (\). In our example, the statement you would use is print "<FONT COLOR=\"#000000\">";. By escaping a quotation mark within your print() statement, PHP will print the mark instead of interpreting it as either the beginning or end of the print statement itself. I will cover many examples of escaping throughout this book.

# Using White Space in PHP (and HTML)

As those who hand code HTML understand, white space (blank lines, tabs, and other extra spaces) in your code can help maintain an uncluttered programming environment while not affecting what the viewer sees in the browser. By inserting blank lines between sections of code, placing nested elements one tab-stop in from their predecessor, and by spacing out code, a script will look more organized, making it easier to initially program and later debug. Thus, judicious use of white space in your work is highly encouraged and can be utilized in both your PHP and the resulting HTML.

Remember that there are three areas of Web development this book considers: the PHP scripts, the data that the PHP sends to the Web browser (mostly in the form of HTML), and how the Web browser interprets or displays that data. I'll briefly address the issue of white space for each of these.

When programming your PHP, you should understand that white space is generally (but not universally) ignored. Any blank line (whether it be just one or several in a row) is completely irrelevant to the end result. Likewise, tabs and spaces, are normally inconsequential to PHP.

HTML code outside of PHP (**Script 1.4**, lines 1–5), can be spaced out just as you would within the PHP, but to address the layout of the HTML actually generated by PHP (**Script 1.4**, line 7), you will need to use special characters.

**Script 1.5** When we add blank lines we will not affect the appearance of the page in our browser but it does make our code more readable. For each \n we include in our print statement, another break will be inserted into our HTML source (not to be confused with <BR> which will create a return in how the browser displays the HTML).

```
1    <HTML>
2    <HEAD>
3    <TITLE>First PHP Script</TITLE>
4    </HEAD>
5    <BODY>
6    <?PHP
7
8    print ("<B><CENTER>Hello, world!
     </CENTER></B>\n");
9
10   ?>
11   </BODY>
12   </HTML>
```

**Figure 1.5** Our page still looks the same in the browser with the new line as it did without it, since \n is not an HTML tag and the blank lines in the PHP code (lines 7 and 9) do not get sent to the browser.

## To change the spacing of your PHP and the data sent to the browser:

1. Open first.php in your text editor.

2. Insert a new line before and after the print command by pressing Return at the appropriate places.

   The new lines within the PHP serve only to add focus and clarity to our script.

3. At the end of the print command (now on line 8), add \n, within the quotation marks (**Script 1.5**).

   The \n character combination sends a command to the Web browser to start a new line in the HTML source. Think of it as the equivalent of pressing the Return key.

4. Save your script, upload it to your server, and view it with your browser (**Figure 1.5**).

While the above series of steps can make your PHP and HTML more readable, remember the additional white space will not affect the appearance of your page in the Web browser (Figure 1.5). To do that you must use HTML tags (the code to create a space in your browser is   and the HTML equivalent of pressing Return is <BR>).

*continues on next page*

**USING WHITE SPACE IN PHP (AND HTML)**

## ✔ Tips

- One exception to the rule of immaterial white space in PHP would be extra spaces within a print statement, resulting in extra spaces being printed to the browser. However, HTML largely ignores white space as well.

- To see what code was sent to the browser, use the "View Source" or "View Page Source" feature built into all browsers. You will quickly be able to tell the difference between using a new line and not using a new line (**Figures 1.6** and **1.7**). While it may be hard to appreciate the benefits of white space on a twelve-line script, this will become more significant as your scripts become larger and more complicated.

- There is a school of thought that recommends condensing your HTML code into the tightest possible package by eliminating all superfluous spaces. The thinking behind this is that you will increase the download speed of the page once you are no longer transmitting extra spaces. While the notion is not without merit, doing so is not conducive to practicing and learning.

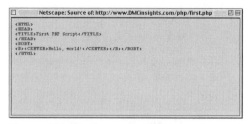

**Figure 1.6** Viewing the source of a Web page is a good way to determine where a formatting problem may exist. This is the source code from our script before we added the \n and blank lines.

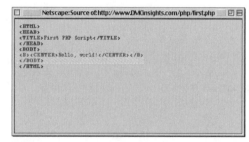

**Figure 1.7** The \n we put into our print statement separates the "Hello, world!" line from the other HTML tags. When sending more complicated HTML code to our browser, using new lines helps simplify the look of the source.

**Script 1.6** By putting either `//` or `#` in front of a single line of code, that line will no longer be processed by the server.

```
                    script
1   <HTML>
2   <HEAD>
3   <TITLE>First PHP Script</TITLE>
4   </HEAD>
5   <BODY>
6   <?PHP
7
8   // print ("<B><CENTER>Hello, world!
    </CENTER></B>\n");
9
10  ?>
11  </BODY>
12  </HTML>
```

**Figure 1.8** With the print command commented out, the page looks just like it would if the print command were not there. Since the server never processes the print command, the browser never receives the *Hello, world!* text.

# Adding Comments to Your Scripts

Every programmer eventually figures out that making notes to yourself is a lifesaver when you inevitably need to return to a project to tweak, copy, or fix some code months later. Adding these notes, or *comments*, to your work helps remind you of what you were thinking at the time, which is not always so evident months later. The computer itself ignores these comments when processing the script. PHP supports three methods of adding comments.

There are two ways to comment out one line of code—by putting either `//` or `#` at the very beginning of the line you want ignored. You can also use `//` or `#` to begin a comment at the end of a PHP line like this:

```
print ("Hello."); // Just a greeting.
```

## To comment out one line of code:

1. Open the `first.php` script in your text editor.

2. On line 8, before the print command, type `//` or `#` (**Script 1.6**).

3. Save your script, upload it to the server, and view the page in your Web browser (**Figure 1.8**).

    If it worked right, you should not be seeing anything in your browser. Don't be alarmed—it's no mistake! The browser did not print "Hello, world!" because the PHP never told it to, on account of the `//` or `#` you added.

Using /* before and */ after a section of code, you can have the server ignore anything from a single word to several lines.

## To comment out multiple lines of code:

1. Open the first.php script in your text editor.

2. Delete the # or // before the print() command.

3. Anywhere before the print() command on line 8 but after the initial PHP tag (<?PHP) on line 6, type /*.

4. Anywhere after the entire print() command on line 8 (i.e., after the semicolon) but before the closing PHP tag (?>) on line 10, type */ (**Script 1.7**).

5. Save your script, upload it to the server, and view the page in your Web browser (**Figure 1.9**).

**Script 1.7** Although it may seem like a superfluous use of /* */ to comment out one line of code, there is nothing wrong with doing so, and we will still get the same results as if we had used // or # (Figures 1.8 and 1.9).

```
1   <HTML>
2   <HEAD>
3   <TITLE>First PHP Script</TITLE>
4   </HEAD>
5   <BODY>
6   <?PHP
7   /*
8   print ("<B><CENTER>Hello, world!
    </CENTER></B>\n");
9   */
10  ?>
11  </BODY>
12  </HTML>
```

**Figure 1.9** It makes no difference which convention you use to comment out your script as long as you use them properly: // and # for one line and /* */ for any number of lines. (This will be the last image of absolutely nothing that I put in this book, I promise!)

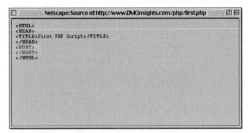

**Figure 1.10** Compare the code here to that before we commented out the print command (Figure 1.7) and you'll see that the PHP code never gets to the browser. HTML code that has been commented (using <!-->) still appears in the source code but is not interpreted by the browser.

**Figure 1.11** If your text editor color codes your code, it makes programming a lot easier. Here BBEdit puts commented code in gray, indicating that that particular code is inactive.

## ✔ Tips

- You can comment out just one line of code (as in our example) or several using the /* and */ method. With // or # you can only ever negate one line at a time.

- Different programmers prefer to comment code in different ways. The important thing is that you find a system that works for you and stick to it. Those who also do JavaScript programming will most likely use // and /* */ as these are the same in both languages. Perl programmers are more familiar with the # method.

- Note that you cannot use HTML comment characters (<!- and ->) within PHP to comment out code. You could have PHP print those elements to the browser, but in that case you will be creating a comment that appears in the HTML source code on the client's computer (but not in the browser window itself). PHP comments never make it as far as a user's computer.

- As text commented out within PHP is not sent to the browser (**Figure 1.10**), it makes this a good place to leave notes that only the programmer will ever be able to see.

- More advanced text editors such as BBEdit will use colors to indicate which code is commented out and which code is not (**Figure 1.11**). This can be very helpful when working on large scripts.

# VARIABLES

In the last chapter you used PHP to send simple text and HTML code to a Web browser—in other words, something for which you don't need PHP at all! Don't worry, though, as this book will teach you how to use the `print()` statement in conjunction with other PHP features to do truly useful things with your Web site.

In order to make the leap from creating simple, static pages to dynamic Web applications and interactive Web sites, you need to be able to handle data, for starters. What you will use to accomplish this are variables. Variables are an important concept and an essential tool for PHP, as well as JavaScript, Java, Perl, or any other programming language.

Variables allow you to temporarily store and manipulate data. They give any programming language its true power. Understanding what a variable is, the types of variables that a language supports, and how to use variables is critical to your work. This chapter will discuss the fundamentals of variables used by PHP, while Chapters 4 through 6 will cover what you can specifically do with the different types of variables.

# What are Variables?

A variable is best thought of as a container for data. Once data has been stored in a variable (or, put differently, once a variable has been assigned a value), that data/variable can be altered, printed to the Web browser (when I say *printed*, it may help to think of it as *sent*, but it's the `print` statement that does the sending, so either term is appropriate), saved to a database, e-mailed, and so forth.

Variables are, by their nature, flexible: you can put data into a variable, retrieve that data from it (without affecting the value of the variable itself), put new data in, and you can continue this cycle as long as is necessary. But, variables in PHP are also temporary: they only exist— that is, they only have a value—while they are used within a script. Once you are in a new page, those variables cease to exist, unless you pass them along to the new page, which I'll discuss in the next chapter (*HTML Forms and PHP*).

**Script 2.1** It is always better to include too many comments than too few because what seems obvious at the time of initial programming may not be so understandable when you go back in months later.

```
1    <HTML>
2    <HEAD>
3    <TITLE>First PHP Script</TITLE>
4    </HEAD>
5    <BODY>
6    <?PHP
7    /* This page prints a simple greeting. */
8    print ("Hello, world!");
9    ?>
10   </BODY>
11   </HTML>
```

# Variable Syntax

In PHP, all variables begin with a dollar sign ($), followed by the variable name itself. This name must begin with either a letter (A–Z, a–z) or the underscore (_), followed by any number of letters, underscores, or numbers, used in combination or not. You may not use spaces within the name of a variable. Instead, the underscore is commonly used to separate words in a variable name.

Keep in mind that variables are case-sensitive. Consequently, "$variable" and "$Variable" are two different constructs, although it would never make sense to use two variables with such similar names. One should quickly get into the habit of creating variable names that make sense on their own, as well as using comments to indicate the purpose of variables (**Script 2.1**). These habits will reduce errors and make revisiting your work less taxing. For example, "$FirstName" is more useful than "$FN" and putting in a comment that details what a variable's purpose is will make your work abundantly clear. In fact, you may decide that "$first_name" is a better variable name than "$FirstName" because there are no capital letters to get right and the words are separated for clarity. No matter how you decide to name your variables, the most important thing to remember is that whatever convention you use, be consistent. This will help you avoid making trivial errors in your programming.

Unlike some other languages, in PHP you neither have to declare what a variable is (to declare a variable is to assign it a type—I'll cover variable types in *Types of Variables*) nor initialize it prior to first use (to initialize a variable is to create it). With PHP, a variable exists and is defined the first time you use it.

# Types of Variables

In this book, I will cover three broad categories of PHP variable types: numbers, strings, and arrays.

Technically speaking, PHP breaks numbers down into two types: "integers" and "floating-point" (or "double-precision floating-point" or "doubles"). But for our purposes we will refer to both of these as just "numbers." Due to the lax way PHP handles variables, it will not affect your programming to group the two categories of numbers into one all-inclusive membership.

PHP also makes use of a variable type referred to as "objects," but that is a far more complicated topic than we can discuss in an introductory book. To learn about objects and how to use them, see Appendix C, *PHP Resources*. Once you are more comfortable with PHP, you may find that learning about objects will greatly facilitate your coding, as object-oriented programming (OOP) is a powerful timesaver.

## Numbers

I've combined the two types of numbers— integers and floating-point—into one group for ease of learning. I'll discuss the difference between the two briefly.

The first type of numbers—integers—are the same thing as whole numbers. They can be positive or negative but include neither fractions nor decimals. Numbers which use a decimal point (even such as "1.0") are floating-point numbers. You must also use floating-point numbers to refer to fractions, since the only way to express a fraction within PHP is to convert it to its decimal equivalent. So "1 1/4" would be written as "1.25".

Examples of valid integer values include:

1
1972
-1

Examples of valid floating-point values include:

```
1.0
19.72
-1.0
```

Since we will refer to both as numbers here, any of the above would be considered valid number values.

Examples of invalid number values would include:

```
1 1/4
1972a
02.23.72
```

The fraction is invalid as it contains two unusable characters: the space and the slash (/). The second item is invalid as it uses both numbers and letters, which is acceptable for the name of a variable, but not as the value of a number variable. The third example is invalid since it uses two decimal points. If you need to refer to one of these values for some reason other than to perform calculations on them, you can assign them as strings.

## Strings

A variable is a string if it consists of characters (some combination of letters, numbers, symbols, and spaces) enclosed within either a pair of single (') or double (") quotation marks. Strings can contain any combination of characters, including other variable names.

Examples of valid strings values include:

```
"Hello, world!"
"Hello, $FirstName!"
"1 1/4"
'Hello, world! How are you today?'
"02.23.72"
"1972"
```

*continues on next page*

Notice how in the last example you took an integer and made it into a string by putting it within quotes. Essentially the string contains the characters "1972" whereas the number is equal to 1972. It's a fine distinction and one that will not matter in your code, as you could perform mathematical calculations with the string "1972" just as you could with the number.

Examples of invalid string values include:

```
Hello, world!
"I said, "How are you?""
```

The first example is invalid as it is not within either single or double quotes. The second example is tricky. You will have problems assigning that value to a string because once PHP reads the second quotation mark, it assumes that the string ends there and the continuing text will cause an error.

Then how do you use a quotation mark within a string you may wonder? Just as discussed in Chapter 1 when using the `print()` function to create HTML, you can *escape* the quotation mark by putting a backslash (\) before it. By changing this string to "I said, \"How are you?\"", you have told PHP to include those two quotation marks as part of the value of the string, and not treat them as the string opening or closing indicators. So while any combination of characters can be included in a string, special characters must be escaped to print correctly. Along with the double quotation mark, you should also escape the apostrophe or single quotation mark ('), the backslash(\), and the dollar sign ($).

## ✔ Tips

■ The benefit of using double quotes over single quotes with strings is that a variable's value will be printed out using the former but not the latter. If you use single quotes, the line `print 'Hello, $FirstName!';` will result in `Hello, $FirstName!` being printed instead of, say, *Hello, Larry!* (assuming `$FirstName` has been assigned the value of `Larry`). If you escape the dollar sign within double quotes (`print "Hello, \$FirstName!";`) you will once again print the name of the variable and not it's value (here, `Hello, $FirstName!`).

■ In Chapter 1, *Getting Started with PHP*, I demonstrated how to create a new line by printing the \n character. Although escaping a quotation mark prints the quotation mark, escaping an "n" prints a new line, escaping an "r" creates a carriage return, and escaping a "t" inserts a tab into your code.

## Arrays

I will cover arrays more thoroughly in Chapter 6, *Using Arrays,* as they are more complicated than either numbers or strings, but I'll introduce them briefly here. Whereas a string or a number will at most contain one value, an array can have a number of values assigned to it. You can think of an array as a list of values. In other words, you can put multiple strings and/or numbers into one array. You can even put multiple arrays into an array!

### ✔ Tip

■ A standard array in PHP composed of strings and numbers (also known as an "indexed" or "vector" array) is what Perl also calls an array. By creating an array that consists of arrays, you can create the PHP equivalent of a Perl "hash," also called an "associative" or "multi-dimensional" array. In PHP, we refer to both types of arrays—single- or multi-dimensional— as simply "arrays."

TYPES OF VARIABLES

# Assigning Values to Variables

I mentioned in the beginning of this chapter that you do not need to initialize or declare your variables. So how do you give them value in your scripts? You assign a value to a variable, regardless of the variable type by using the equal sign (=). Therefore, the equal sign is called an *assignment operator*, as it assigns the value on the right to the variable on the left. You will learn about the various types of operators throughout the next several chapters.

For example:

```
$number = 1;
$floating_number = 1.2;
$string = "Hello, World!";
```

For better or worse, because variable types are not locked in (PHP is referred to as a "weakly typed" language, as is JavaScript), they can be changed on the fly:

```
$variable = 1;
$variable = "Greetings";
```

If you were to print the value of $variable now, it would print out "Greetings."

## ✔ Tips

■ You'll learn about assigning values to arrays in Chapter 6, *Using Arrays*.

■ You can set the variable type by *casting* it upon first use (casting a variable is similar to declaring it, where you formally establish its type). The syntax for doing so is:

```
$number = (integer) 5;
$string = (string) "Hello, World!";
```

To be honest, there is little merit in doing this, but it is an option, if you would prefer to stay more consistent with other programming languages you use.

# Predefined Variables

There are two reasons you will want to understand the concept of predefined variables: 1) because they have their own uses in your programming; and, 2) so that you don't inadvertently create a variable with the same name.

Predefined variables are a special type of variable that the Web server application (for example, Apache), the Web server operating system (Solaris or Windows NT), or the PHP module itself uses. The first two categories are also referred to as "environmental variables." There will be some inconsistencies among servers as to what predefined variables exist, so use your test.php script (discussed in Chapter 1) to see which are in use on your machine (**Figure 2.1**).

Examples of a server's environmental variables are: HOSTNAME (how the server refers to itself), and OSTYPE (what operating system the server is running).

Examples of Apache's environmental variables are: DOCUMENT_ROOT, which indicates where the files are stored on the server; and HTTP_USER_AGENT, which details the browser and platform of the person viewing the page.

The PHP_SELF variable is the most commonly used PHP variable and is equal to the name of the current page. In Figure 2.1, the PHP_SELF variable indicates that the page being viewed is test.php.

## ✔ Tip

- Although it's not likely, creating a variable within a page with the same name as an environmental variable will cause peculiar results, so being aware of the existing variable names ahead of time makes your debugging easier. As you can tell from the list of environmental variables produced by our test.php script (Figure 2.1), simply by not using all capital letters as a variable name, you minimize the chance of a conflict.

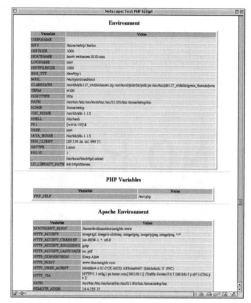

**Figure 2.1** Another great use of the test.php script is to check to see which environmental and PHP variables exist and what their settings are.

# HTML FORMS

# AND PHP

3

Perhaps the most common use of variables is in conjunction with HTML forms. Web sites utilize forms to register and login users, to receive feedback, for online shopping, and for many other purposes. Even the most basic site will find logical reasons to incorporate them.

Frequently, programmers create CGI scripts in Perl to handle the data created by these forms, but the same results can be achieved more easily using PHP. Unlike CGI scripts, where you have to write a segment of code that will extract the information sent by the form, PHP has a nice method of built-in support for receiving data from an HTML form without the need of any parsing.

This chapter will cover the basics of creating HTML forms and how that data is transmitted to your PHP script. Those who are new to the topic of forms may want to refer to an in-depth HTML resource for more detailed coverage of the topic, considering their importance in the field of Web site design.

HTML FORMS AND PHP

# Creating a Simple Form

For your HTML form you will create a feedback page that takes the user's first and last names, e-mail address, and comments. You'll need to create the necessary fields with this in mind.

### To create an HTML form:

1. Open your text editor and create a new document:

   ```
   <HTML><HEAD><TITLE>HTML Form
   → </TITLE></HEAD><BODY></BODY>
   → </HTML>
   ```

2. Between the body tags, add the opening and closing <FORM> tags:

   ```
   <FORM ACTION="HandleForm.php">
   → </FORM> (Script 3.1).
   ```

   The <FORM> tags dictate where a form begins and ends. Every element of the form must be entered within these two lines. The ACTION attribute tells the server which page (or script) will receive the data from the form.

3. Save the page as form.html.

4. After the opening FORM line (line 6) but before the closing FORM tag, press Return to create a new line.

5. Now begin adding your form fields by typing:

   ```
   First Name <INPUT TYPE=TEXT NAME=
   → "FirstName" SIZE=20><BR>
   ```

   Follow a consistent naming convention within your form by giving each field a logical and descriptive name. Use letters, numbers, and the underscore (_) when naming fields. As you work, keep track of names you use for each field (**Script 3.2**).

**Script 3.1** Every HTML form begins and ends with the <FORM> </FORM> tags. When hand-coding forms, take care not to forget either tag. Also be sure to direct the form to the proper handling script with the ACTION attribute.

```
script
1   <HTML>
2   <HEAD>
3   <TITLE>HTML Form</TITLE>
4   </HEAD>
5   <BODY>
6   <FORM ACTION="HandleForm.php">
7   </FORM>
8   </BODY>
9   </HTML>
```

**Script 3.2** Any combination of input types can be added to your form—just ensure that all of them are within the <FORM> tags or else those elements will not appear. As a stylistic suggestion, laying out these input elements within a table can give your form a more professional—and more useable—appearance.

```
script
1    <HTML>
2    <HEAD>
3    <TITLE>HTML Form</TITLE>
4    </HEAD>
5    <BODY>
6    <FORM ACTION="HandleForm.php">
7    First Name <INPUT TYPE=TEXT
     NAME="FirstName" SIZE=20><BR>
8    Last Name <INPUT TYPE=TEXT
     NAME="LastName" SIZE=40><BR>
9    E-mail Address <INPUT TYPE=TEXT
     NAME="Email" SIZE=60><BR>
10   Comments <TEXTAREA NAME="Comments"
     ROWS=5 COLS=40></TEXTAREA><BR>
11   <INPUT TYPE=SUBMIT NAME="SUBMIT"
     VALUE="Submit!">
12   </FORM>
13   </BODY>
14   </HTML>
```

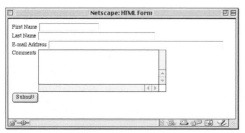

**Figure 3.1** If you have typed in your form correctly, it should look like this in your Web browser. Make sure that you close the form and include the submit button within it.

Last Name <INPUT TYPE=TEXT NAME=
→ "LastName" SIZE=40><BR>

Add the <BR> tags to make the form look cleaner when viewed in the Web browser.

E-mail Address <INPUT TYPE=
→ TEXT NAME="Email" SIZE=60><BR>
Comments <TEXTAREA NAME="Comments"
→ ROWS=5 COLS=40></TEXTAREA><BR>

A TEXTAREA gives the user more space to enter in their comments than a TEXT field would. However, with the TEXT input you can limit how much information the user can enter, which you cannot do with the TEXTAREA. When creating your form, choose input types appropriate to the information you wish to retrieve from the user.

**6.** On a separate line, type

<INPUT TYPE=SUBMIT NAME="SUBMIT"
→ VALUE="Submit!">

The VALUE of a SUBMIT type is what will appear on the button itself in the Web browser. You could also use "Go!" or "Enter," for example.

**7.** Save your script, upload it to your server, and view it in your browser (**Figure 3.1**). (Since this is an HTML page, not a PHP script, you could view this in your Web browser directly from your computer.)

*continues on next page*

CREATING A SIMPLE FORM

## ✔ Tips

■ In this example you created your form by hand-coding the HTML, but you can do this in a Web page application (such as Dreamweaver or GoLive) if that is what you are more comfortable with.

■ Note that you used the HTML extension (.html) here as you created a standard HTML page (not necessarily a PHP page). You could have used the PHP extension and achieved the same results, even though there is no actual PHP utilized. (Remember that in a PHP page, anything not within the PHP brackets—<?php and ?>—gets treated like HTML.)

■ Although I didn't do so here, I would recommend that most forms, especially more involved ones, also have a Reset button, created with the code:

```
<INPUT TYPE=RESET NAME=RESET VALUE=
→ "Reset">.
```

■ Be careful to make sure that your ACTION attribute correctly points to an existing file on the server or else your form will not be processed. In this case, we are indicating that the HandleForm.php file is within the same directory as the form.html page.

# Using Get or Post

The experienced reader will notice that we are missing one thing in our initial <FORM> tag, namely adding a METHOD attribute. This attribute tells the server how to transmit the data from the form to the handling script. I omitted it earlier because the topic merits its own discussion.

There are two choices you have with METHOD: GET or POST. I suspect that most HTML coders are not entirely clear on the distinction and when to use which. In truth, for the most part it won't make much difference (especially as you first begin using them) as either will generally get you the results you need.

The difference between using GET versus POST is squarely in how the information is passed from the form to the processing script. The GET method will send all the gathered information along as part of the URL. The POST method transmits the information invisibly to the user. For example, upon submitting your form, if you use the GET method, the resulting URL will be something like:

```
http://www.DMCinsights.com/php/
→ HandleForm.php?FirstName=
→ Larry&LastName=Ullman.
```

Whereas using the POST method, the end user would only see

```
http://www.DMCinsights.com/php/
→ HandleForm.php.
```

*continues on next page*

When choosing which method to use, you may want to keep in mind these three factors: 1) with the GET method you are limited as to how much information can be passed; 2) the GET method publicly sends the input to the handling script (which means that, for example, a password which is entered in a form becomes viewable by anyone within eyesight of the Web browser, creating a larger security risk); and, 3) a page generated by a form that used the GET method can be bookmarked while one based upon POST cannot be.

In this text, I will use POST for handling forms, mostly to distinguish from a technique I will use where the GET method theory adds capabilities to your Web site (see *Inputting Data Manually*). Either method will successfully pass along the data from the form and the final decision for which method you use should be based upon any mitigating factors in your form and whether or not the resulting page should be bookmark-able.

### To add a method to your script:

1. Open form.html in your text editor.

2. Within the initial <FORM> tag, add METHOD=POST (line 6, **Script 3.3**).

3. Save the script and upload it to your server.

4. View the source of the page to make sure that all the required elements are present (**Figure 3.2**).

**Script 3.3** It is up to you whether to use the GET or POST method as long as you remember to use one of them. With experience you will determine when it makes sense to use one rather than the other, but it is more of a finesse than function issue.

```
                          script
1    <HTML>
2    <HEAD>
3    <TITLE>HTML Form</TITLE>
4    </HEAD>
5    <BODY>
6    <FORM ACTION="HandleForm.php" METHOD=POST>
7    First Name <INPUT TYPE=TEXT
     NAME="FirstName" SIZE=20><BR>
8    Last Name <INPUT TYPE=TEXT
     NAME="LastName" SIZE=40><BR>
9    E-mail Address <INPUT TYPE=TEXT
     NAME="Email" SIZE=60><BR>
10   Comments <TEXTAREA NAME="Comments"
     ROWS=5 COLS=40></TEXTAREA><BR>
11   <INPUT TYPE=SUBMIT NAME="SUBMIT"
     VALUE="Submit!">
12   </FORM>
13   </BODY>
14   </HTML>
```

**Figure 3.2** By viewing the source of a page, you can see why something will work and why it won't. As with all programming, subtle changes can make all the difference.

**Script 3.4** By taking the value of the NAME="Name" element in your HTML form and adding a dollar sign, you create a variable that contains the value of what the user entered in that corresponding form field. This is true whether the HTML input type is TEXT, TEXTAREA, or a SELECT menu and is one of the reasons why PHP is so great for handling HTML forms (compared to, say, CGI scripts, which require parsing code).

```
script
1   <HTML>
2   <HEAD>
3   <TITLE>Form Results</TITLE>
4   <BODY>
5   <?php
6   /* This page receives and handles the data
    generated by "form.html". */
7   print "Your first name is $FirstName.<BR>\n";
8   print "Your last name is $LastName.<BR>\n";
9   print "Your E-mail address is $Email.<BR>\n";
10  print "This is what you had to say:<BR>\n
    $Comments<BR>\n";
11  ?>
12  </BODY>
13  </HTML>
```

# Receiving Data from a Form in PHP

You've created your form. Now you need to write the HandleForm.php script, which will receive and process the data generated by the form.html page. Here is where the true simplicity of PHP is demonstrated.

## To create the HandleForm.php script:

1. Open your text editor and create a new document.

   ```
   <HTML><HEAD><TITLE>Form Results
   → </TITLE><BODY><?php /* This page
   → receives and handles the data
   → generated by "form.html". */ ?>
   → </BODY></HTML>.
   ```

   This is the standard format for a PHP page (**Script 3.4**). We added the comment to tell us the purpose of the script. Even though the form.html page indicates where the data is sent to (via the ACTION attribute), we ought to make a comment here indicating the reverse.

2. Create a new line after the comment but before the closing PHP tag. Type

   ```
   print "Your first name is
   → $FirstName.<BR>\n";.
   print "Your last name is
   → $LastName.<BR>\n";
   print "Your E-mail address is
   → $Email.<BR>\n";
   print "This is what you had to
   → say:<BR>\n $Comments<BR>\n";
   ```

3. Save your script as HandleForm.php.

4. Upload your script to the server, making sure that it is saved within the same directory as form.html.

*continues on next page*

**5.** Test your script in your Web browser (**Figures 3.3** and **3.4**).

The point of this exercise is to demonstrate how easily you can transfer data from an HTML form to a PHP page. The PHP script will store the data in corresponding variables, so $FirstName takes on the value of what the user inputted into the field labeled *FirstName* (you take the name of the field in the HTML, add a dollar sign, and then you have the variable with the corresponding value). The transfer is automatic and, unlike CGI scripts, no parsing is necessary.

### ✔ Tips

- Another benefit to using PHP to handle HTML forms is that data is automatically escaped in transit. For example, if *I thought "form.html" was too simple!* was entered as the comment, the $Comments variable will be equal to *I thought \"form.html\" was too simple!* so that it may be printed without complication (**Figure 3.5**).

- If you wanted to pass a preset value along to your script, use the HIDDEN type of input within your HTML form. For example, the line <INPUT TYPE=HIDDEN
  → NAME="ThisPage" VALUE="form.html"> inserted between the FORM tags would create a variable in your handling script called $ThisPage with the value of "form.html". Similarly, by telling PHP to
  print ("<INPUT TYPE=
  → HIDDEN NAME=\"FirstName\"
  → VALUE=\"$FirstName\">");
  you can extend the life of the $FirstName variable by passing its value along.

- Although you can have the same file both display a form and handle the form's output using PHP, it does make your scripts unnecessarily complicated and difficult to debug. In the interest of simplicity, we will use a separate file, aptly named HandleForm.php.

**Figure 3.3** Whatever the user enters into the HTML form will be printed out to the Web browser by the HandleForm.php script (see Figure 3.4).

**Figure 3.4** This is another application of the print statement discussed in Chapter 1, but it does constitute your first dynamically generated Web page. Later chapters will cover how to manipulate the data received as well as how to send it in an e-mail or enter it into a database.

**Figure 3.5** PHP will automatically escape special characters entered into HTML. This is helpful when sending data back to the browser (as in this example where the quotation marks would interfere with the print() statement if not for being escaped) and when entering it into databases.

**Script 3.5** Instead of coding the page to automatically say "Hello, World!" or "Hello, Larry!" we have made the page dynamic by printing out the value of a variable instead. Now, as that value changes, so will the resulting page.

```
                    script
1   <HTML>
2   <HEAD>
3   <TITLE>Using Variables</TITLE>
4   <BODY>
5   <?php
6   /* This page may have numerous lines of
    code containing the following print
    statement. */
7   print "<H2> <CENTER> <B> Hello, $FirstName.
    </B> </CENTER> </H2> <BR>\n";
8   /* This page may have more code after the
    print statement we are focusing on. */
9   ?>
10  </BODY>
11  </HTML>
```

# Inputting Data Manually

Obviously, not all of your data will derive from HTML forms and sometimes you might want to manually set data within your script. If you created a script that printed a user's name in a greeting, you could establish a variable that contains the name separate from the rest of the greeting. That way you could easily change the name without having to change the greeting, the print statement, or the script itself. We will create a PHP script to demonstrate this process.

### To creating a PHP script that displays a greeting:

1. Create a new document within your text editor (**Script 3.5**).

   ```
   <HTML><HEAD><TITLE>Using Variables
   → </TITLE><BODY><?php
   /* This page may have numerous lines
   → of code containing the following
   → print statement. */
   ```

   I have put two comments into the script that are meant to represent the idea that the greeting line will mostly likely be part of a larger, more complicated page.

   ```
   print "<H2> <CENTER> <B> Hello,
   → $FirstName. </B> </CENTER> </H2>
   → <BR>\n";
   /* This page may have more code
   → after the print statement we are
   → focusing on. */
   ?></BODY></HTML>
   ```

2. Save the document as hello.php and upload it to your server.

   *continues on next page*

If you were to view this script now, it would only display "Hello, . " as the $FirstName variable has no value. There are two ways you can manually set this value, without using forms. The first is to use what you know about how the GET method passes data to a script.

### To use the GET method without an HTML form:

1. View the `hello.php` script in your Web browser by going to the appropriate URL (in this case, `http://www.DMCinsights.com/` → `php/hello.php` (**Figure 3.6**).

2. Append to the URL the text `?FirstName=Larry` (you can also use your own name, just ensure that there are no spaces in your entry).

   As you read earlier in this chapter (*Receiving Data from a Form in PHP*), when you send a variable to a script via a URL (i.e., by using the GET method in an HTML form), it uses the format of `www.url.com/script.php?variable=` → `value`.

3. Reload the page in your browser with the new URL (**Figure 3.7**).

   If you do not see the name printed in the browser, then you made a mistake. Check to make sure that you included the question mark, which separates the file location from the data itself. Then see that you used *FirstName*, as that is what `hello.php` is expecting as a variable (remember that *firstname* would constitute a different variable).

**Figure 3.6** Without the $FirstName variable being assigned a value, the browser prints out this awkward message.

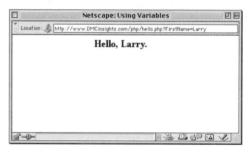

**Figure 3.7** By setting $FirstName equal to *Larry* or some other name, you've created a dynamic page that changes to address the specific user.

**Script 3.6** The $FirstName = "Jude"; line assigns the value "Jude" to the variable "FirstName" for the existence of this page.

```
                    script
1   <HTML>
2   <HEAD>
3   <TITLE>Using Variables</TITLE>
4   <BODY>
5   <?php
6   $FirstName = "Jude";
7   /* This page may have numerous lines of
    code containing the following print
    statement. */
8   print "<H2> <CENTER> <B> Hello, $FirstName.
    </B> </CENTER> </H2> <BR>\n";
9   /* This page may have more code after the
    print statement we are focusing on. */
10  ?>
11  </BODY>
12  </HTML>
```

**Figure 3.8** Setting the value of $FirstName to Jude, will have the same effect as changing the print line to read print "<H2> <CENTER> <B> Hello, Jude. </B> </CENTER> </H2> <BR>\n";, but it will be easier for us to change the value by using a variable instead.

**Figure 3.9** Since the page itself contains a line assigning the value "Jude" to $FirstName, no matter what you pass to the script via the URL, *Jude* will always be printed.

The second way you can preset a variable value is by directly assigning it within the script itself.

## To assign a value to a variable:

1. Open hello.php in your text editor.

2. On a line before the print statement, add $FirstName = "Jude"; (**Script 3.6**).

3. Save your page, upload it to your server, and view it in your Web browser (**Figure 3.8**).

4. Now view the same page using the appended version of the URL as you did in the last example (e.g., http://
→ www.DMCinsights.com/php/
→ hello.php?FirstName=Larry)
(**Figure 3.9**).

   This demonstrates an important point as to what happens when a variable is assigned a value multiple times: the last assigned value is what the variable becomes "worth" and, consequently in our case, what hello.php will print out. Be careful not to inadvertently override your variables in your programming!

The concept of pre-establishing variable values is especially useful as your program gets more complicated. Using an easily edited variable means that you never have to hunt through multiple lines of code to replace one value with another.

Likewise, by appending a variable to a URL, you can link one page to a dynamically generated second page (such as hello.php) simply by coding your Web page links to include variable values, where necessary. For example, one form on a Web site may take the user's first name, and pass that along to subsequent linked pages with the code <A HREF ="hello.php?
→ FirstName=Larry"> hello.php </A>.

*continues on next page*

## ✔ Tips

■ If you want to use the GET method to send data to your script, you can pass multiple values along by separating the `variable=value` pairs (e.g., `FirstName=` → `Larry`) with the ampersand (&). So an appended URL may be `hello.php?` → `FirstName=Larry&LastName=Ullman`.

■ Spaces within values that are passed as part of a URL should be replaced with a plus sign (+). In Chapter 5, *Using Strings*, I'll discuss how PHP can automatically prepare a string of text to be passed as part of a URL.

■ Although the example here—setting the value of a person's name—may not be very practical, creating an $email variable at the top of the script would allow you to later change that email address without looking through lines of code to find it. In fact, in Chapter 11, *Databases*, I'll make it a habit to establish the database access values through variables at the beginning of our scripts so they can be altered easily without changing every instance where those values are used.

# USING NUMBERS

In Chapter 2, *Variables*, I loosely discussed the different types of variables, how to assign values to them, and how they are generally used. In this chapter, you will work specifically with number variables—both integers (i.e., whole numbers) and floating-point (decimals). At the end of the section (see *Using Built-in Mathematical Functions*) I will demonstrate and introduce several more useful pre-existing functions available for manipulating numbers.

# Adding, Subtracting, Multiplying, and Dividing

Just as you learned in grade school, the most basic mathematics involve the principles of addition, subtraction, multiplication, and division. To demonstrate these principles, you'll create a PHP script that calculates the total cost for the sale of some widgets. This script could be the basis of a shopping cart application—a very practical Web page feature.

## To create your sales-cost calculator:

1. Open your text editor and create a new document (**Script 4.1**).

   ```
   <HTML><HEAD><TITLE>Using Numbers
   → </TITLE></HEAD><BODY><?php?>
   → </BODY></HTML>
   ```

2. Within the PHP tags, add
   `$Cost = 2000.00; $Tax = 0.06;`.

   You have manually set the cost of the widget at $2,000.00. Note that you do not use either a dollar sign or a comma within the value of the variable. You have also manually set the sales tax rate at 6%, "0.06" being the proper way to write a percentage as a decimal. Both of these are floating-point numbers.

   `$TotalCost = $Cost * $Quantity;`

   The asterisk (*) is used to indicate multiplication within PHP. The $Quantity value will be passed to the script as it would in a shopping cart application on a Web site. You can use the techniques demonstrated in Chapter 3, *HTML Forms and PHP* (see *Inputting Data Manually*), to make a form where the user enters a quantity, but here you'll just append that value to the URL.

**Script 4.1** While the calculations themselves are straightforward, you should feel free to add any other comments you feel necessary to illuminate the process here. If you want to improve your HTML skills, create a form that takes some information from the user (including Quantity and Discount) that gets passed to this script.

```
                        script
1    <HTML>
2    <HEAD>
3    <TITLE>Using Numbers</TITLE>
4    </HEAD>
5    <BODY>
6    <?php
7    /* $Quantity must be passed to this page
     from a form or via the URL. $Discount is
     optional. */
8    $Cost = 2000.00;
9    $Tax = 0.06;
10   $TotalCost = $Cost * $Quantity;
11   $Tax = $Tax + 1; // $Tax is now worth 1.06.
12   $TotalCost = $TotalCost - $Discount;
13   $TotalCost = $TotalCost * $Tax;
14   $Payments = $TotalCost / 12;
15   // Print the results.
16   print ("You requested to purchase $Quantity
     widget(s) at \$$Cost each.\n<P>");
17   print ("The total with tax, minus your
     \$$Discount, comes to \$$TotalCost.
     \n<P>");
18   print ("You may purchase the widget(s)in
     12 monthly installments`of \$$Payments
     each.\n<P>");
19   ?>
20   </BODY>
21   </HTML>
```

```
$Tax = $Tax + 1; // $Tax is now
→ worth 1.06.
```

Logically the plus sign (+) is used to perform addition. You can calculate how much something will cost with tax by adding 1 to the percent and then multiplying that new rate times the total. You've added a comment indicating as much for clarity sake (the comment can either be placed after the line, like I have here, on the next line, or omitted all together). One of the reasons I lumped together both types of numbers into one variable category is that, as you can see here, you can perform calculations on mixed variable types without any unfortunate consequences.

```
$TotalCost = $TotalCost - $Discount;
```

To demonstrate subtraction using the minus (-) symbol, you'll assume that a discount may be applied, which will also be appended to the URL (or entered in a form).

```
$TotalCost = $TotalCost * $Tax;
```

You can actually perform a calculation on a variable to determine its own value (in fact, it's quite common), but note that the original value of the variable is now gone. So on our line here, the original value of $TotalCost is replaced by the value of $TotalCost times $Tax.

```
$Payments = $TotalCost / 12;
```

As an example of division, let's assume that the widget can be paid for over the course of one year. Hence, you have divided the total, including taxes and any applicable discount by 12 to find your monthly payment.

*continues on next page*

ADDING, SUBTRACTING, MULTIPLYING, AND DIVIDING

```
// Print the results.
```

This comment differentiates where the calculations end and the output to the browser begins.

```
print ("You requested to purchase
→ $Quantity widget(s) at \$$Cost
→ each.\n<P>");
print ("The total with tax, minus
→ your \$$Discount, comes to
→ \$$TotalCost.\n<P>"); print ("You
→ may purchase the widget(s)in 12
→ monthly installments of
→ \$$Payments each.\n<P>");
```

**3.** Save your script as `numbers.php` and upload it to your server.

**4.** Test the script in your Web browser, insuring that you assign values to "Quantity" and "Discount" (**Figure 4.1**).

You can experiment with these values (even omitting the variables completely as in **Figure 4.2**) to see how effectively your calculator works.

**Figure 4.1** Your working calculator is illustrated here. Make sure you append values for "Quantity" and "Discount" to the URL or create a form to pass those values along or you'll see results like those in **Figure 4.2**.

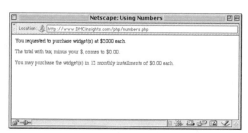

**Figure 4.2** Without receiving the necessary values, the script will still make its assigned calculations, resulting in errant data.

### ✔ Tips

■ As you will certainly notice, your calculator comes up with numbers that don't correspond well to real dollar values (see Figure 4.1). In the next section, *Formatting Numbers*, you'll learn how to adjust your numbers accordingly.

■ If you wanted to print out the value of the total, before tax and before the discount (or both), there are two ways to do this. One would be to insert the appropriate `print()` statements immediately after the proper value has been determined but before the $TotalCost variable has been changed. The second method would be to use new variables to contain the values of the subsequent calculations (e.g., $TotalWithTax and $TotalLessDiscount).

■ There are two methods you could have used to print a figure such as *$2000.00*. One is to escape the first dollar sign, as you did here; the other is to put a space between the dollar sign and the variable name, which would also create a space there in the browser. You cannot use *$$Variable* as the combination of two dollar signs together creates a type of variable too complex for the purposes of this book.

**Script 4.2** The `printf()` function will print the numbers formatted according to certain specifications, creating more logical numbers.

```
                    script
1    <HTML>
2    <HEAD>
3    <TITLE>Using Numbers</TITLE>
4    </HEAD>
5    <BODY>
6    <?php
7    /* $Quantity must be passed to this page
     from a form or via the URL. $Discount is
     optional. */
8    $Cost = 2000.00;
9    $Tax = 0.06;
10   $TotalCost = $Cost * $Quantity;
11   $Tax = $Tax + 1; // $Tax is now worth 1.06.
12   $TotalCost = $TotalCost - $Discount;
13   $TotalCost = $TotalCost * $Tax;
14   $Payments = $TotalCost / 12;
15   // Print the results.
16   print ("You requested to purchase $Quantity
     widget(s) at \$$Cost each.\n<P>");
17   print ("The total with tax, minus your
     \$$Discount, comes to $");
18   printf ("%01.2f", $TotalCost);
19   print (".\n<P>You may purchase the
     widget(s)in 12 monthly installments
     of $");
20   printf ("%01.2f", $Payments);
21   print (" each.\n<P>");
22   ?>
23   </BODY>
24   </HTML>
```

# Formatting Numbers

Although your calculator is on its way to being practical, you still have one legitimate problem: you cannot ask someone to make a monthly payment of $521.16666666667. In order to create a more usable number as your monthly payment, you will make your total cost an easily divisible number. To do this, you use the `printf()` function, which prints a formatted number according to your specifications.

To use `printf()`, you feed it a format and a string (or number). For example, to print out an amount variable in the form of a floating-point number with two digits to the right of the decimal (e.g., *1.02*), you would code:

`printf ("%01.2f", $Amount);`

The `"%01.2f"` segment tells PHP to print the $Amount using 0 to pad extra spaces, with at least one digit to the left of the decimal and with two digits to the right of the decimal. There are more complicated uses of `printf()`, but this will be more than sufficient for your need to make legitimate dollar amounts.

## To use printf():

1. Open `numbers.php` in your text editor.

2. Change line 17 to read (**Script 4.2**):
   ```
   print ("The total with tax, minus
   → your \$$Discount, comes to $");
   → printf ("%01.2f", $TotalCost);
   ```
   To use `printf()`, you'll want to separate the majority of the `print()` statements from the one that handles the formatting.

   *continues on next page*

**3.** Change line 18 to read:

```
print (".\n<P>You may purchase
→ the widget(s)in 12 monthly
→ installments of $");
printf ("%01.2f", $Payments);
print (" each.\n<P>");
```

You'll do the same thing to line 18 as you did to line 17. The original one line of code will become three but it will produce better results.

**4.** Save the file, upload it to your server, and test in your browser (**Figure 4.3**).

## ✔ Tip

■ A parallel to the printf() function is the sprintf() function. It works the same only printf() will actually send the results to the browser whereas sprintf() changes a variable without printing it.

```
$Amount = sprintf ("%01.2f",
→ $Amount);
```

**Figure 4.3** Your updated version of the script gives you better numbers for monthly payments (although at your expense) than it did before (see **Figure 4.1**) now that it incorporates the printf() function.

**Script 4.3** Your script is now marginally cleaner than it was before since you used the "++" incrementing method. The mathematical result will be the same regardless.

```
script
1   <HTML>
2   <HEAD>
3   <TITLE>Using Numbers</TITLE>
4   </HEAD>
5   <BODY>
6   <?php
7   /* $Quantity must be passed to this page
    from a form or via the URL. $Discount is
    optional. */
8   $Cost = 2000.00;
9   $Tax = 0.06;
10  $TotalCost = $Cost * $Quantity;
11  $Tax++; // $Tax is now worth 1.06.
12  $TotalCost = $TotalCost - $Discount;
13  $TotalCost = $TotalCost * $Tax;
14  $Payments = $TotalCost / 12;
15  // Print the results.
16  print ("You requested to purchase $Quantity
    widget(s) at \$$Cost each.\n<P>");
17  print ("The total with tax, minus your
    \$$Discount, comes to $");
18  printf ("%01.2f", $TotalCost);
19  print (".\n<P>You may purchase the
    widget(s)in 12 monthly installments
    of $");
20  printf ("%01.2f", $Payments);
21  print (" each.\n<P>");
22  ?>
23  </BODY>
24  </HTML>
```

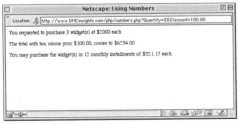

**Figure 4.4** It will not affect your calculations if you use the long or short version of incrementing a variable (compare **Scripts 4.2** and **4.3**).

# Incrementing and Decrementing a Number

PHP, like Perl and most other programming languages, includes some shortcuts so that you may avoid ugly constructs such as $Tax = $Tax + 1;. When you are in a situation where you need to increase the value of a variable by just one (called an "incremental" adjustment) or decrease the value of a variable by just one (a "decremental" adjustment) you can use "++" or "--" accordingly.

## To increment the value of a variable:

1. Open numbers.php in your text editor.

2. Change line 10 of **Script 4.3** to read $Tax++;

3. Save your script, upload it to the server, and test it in your browser (**Figure 4.4**).

## ✔ Tips

- Although functionally it will not matter whether you code $Tax = $Tax + 1; or the abbreviated $Tax++, the latter (using the increment operator) is the more professional and common method.

- In Chapter 6, *Conditional Statements and Loops*, you'll see how the increment operator is commonly used to count through a series of actions.

- To decrement a variable, you merely use the subtraction symbol (-) twice instead of the plus sign, like this:
  $Number--;

# Using Multiple Operators

Inevitably, after discussing the different sorts of mathematical operators, one comes to the discussion of *precedence*. Precedence refers to the order in which a series of calculations will be executed. For example, what will be the value of the following variable?

```
$Number = 10 - 4 / 2;
```

Will $Number be worth 3 (10 minus 4 equals 6 divided by 2 equals 3) or 8 (4 divided by 2 equals 2 subtracted from 10 equals 8)? The answer here is 8, because division takes precedence over subtraction. Appendix C: *PHP Resources* shows the complete list of operator precedence for PHP (including those we haven't covered yet).

However, instead of attempting to memorize a large table of peculiar characters, my recommendation would be to bypass the whole concept by using parentheses. Parentheses always take precedence over any other operator. Thus:

```
$Number = (10 - 4) / 2;
$Number = 10 - (4 / 2);
```

In the first example, $Number is now equal to 3, and in the second example, $Number is equal to 8. Using parentheses in your calculations will insure that you never obtain peculiar results from them because of precedence.

You can rewrite your script, combining multiple lines into one while still maintaining accuracy by using parentheses.

**Script 4.4** Instead of performing the calculations over several lines, you've trimmed it down to one, without affecting its mathematical basis. With parentheses, you do not need to concern yourself with precedence.

```
script
1   <HTML>
2   <HEAD>
3   <TITLE>Using Numbers</TITLE>
4   </HEAD>
5   <BODY>
6   <?php
7   /* $Quantity must be passed to this page
    from a form or via the URL. $Discount is
    optional. */
8   $Cost = 2000.00;
9   $Tax = 0.06;
10  $Tax++; // $Tax is now worth 1.06.
11  $TotalCost = (($Cost * $Quantity) -
    $Discount) * $Tax;
12  $Payments = $TotalCost / 12;
13  // Print the results.
14  print ("You requested to purchase $Quantity
    widget(s) at \$$Cost each.\n<P>");
15  print ("The total with tax, minus your
    \$$Discount, comes to $");
16  printf ("%01.2f", $TotalCost);
17  print (".\n<P>You may purchase the widget(s)
    in 12 monthly installments of $");
18  printf ("%01.2f", $Payments);
19  print (" each.\n<P>");
20  ?>
21  </BODY>
22  </HTML>
```

## To use parentheses to establish precedence:

1. Open numbers.php in your text editor (Script 4.3).

2. Change line 13 to read (**Script 4.4**):

   $TotalCost = (($Cost * $Quantity) -
   → $Discount) * $Tax;

   There is no reason not to make all of the calculations in one step, as long as you use parentheses to insure that the math works out properly. The other option is to memorize PHP's rules of precedence for multiple operators, but using parentheses is a lot easier.

3. Delete lines 10 and 12.

   Since all of the calculations are being made on one line, these other two lines are no longer necessary.

4. Save your script, upload it to the server, and test it in your browser (**Figure 4.5**).

## ✔ Tip

- Watch that you match your parentheses consistently as you create your formulas (every opening parentheses requires a closing parentheses).

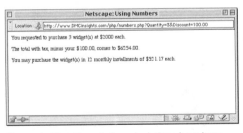

**Figure 4.5** Even though the calculations have been condensed, the math should still work out the same. If you see different results here or if you get an error message, double-check your parentheses.

# Using Built-in Mathematical Functions

PHP has a number of built-in functions for manipulating your mathematical data. I'll use a couple of them here to improve upon our numbers.php script and you can refer to the PHP manual, specifically the *Mathematical Functions* chapter, to learn about some of the others (see Appendix C, *PHP Resources*, regarding the PHP manual).

One built-in mathematical function, you can use in your calculator script is round(). As its name implies, round() takes whatever number and rounds it to the nearest integer, using standard conventions: anything .50 and above is rounded up, anything below .50 is rounded down. The assumption is that you will be rounding a decimal, but attempting to round an integer will cause no problems (it just won't do anything, since rounding 2 results in 2). Some examples are:

```
$Number = round(23.309); // $Number is
→ equal to 23.
$Number = round(23.51); // $Number is
→ equal to 24.
```

You can round a number to a particular decimal point by adding a second parameter to the equation.

```
$Number = round(23.51, 1); // $Number
→ is equal to 23.5.
```

PHP has broken round() down into two other functions. The first, ceil(), rounds every number to the next highest integer and the second, floor(), rounds every number to the next lowest integer.

Another function that our calculator page can make good use of is **abs()**, which returns the absolute value of a number. In case you do not remember your absolute values, it works like this:

```
$Number = abs(-23); // $Number is equal
→ to 23.
$Number = abs(23); // $Number is equal
→ to 23.
```

In laymen's terms, the absolute value of a number is always a positive number.

Two last functions which I'll introduce here are **srand()** and **rand()**. The latter is a random number generator and the first is a function which is used to seed **rand()**. You must use **srand()** before calling **rand()** in order to guarantee truly random numbers. The PHP manual recommends the following code:

```
srand ((double) microtime() * 1000000);
$RandomNumber = rand();
```

The manual itself is remarkably without explanation as to why you should use that exact line to seed the random number generator except to say that the creators of PHP 4 state that it guarantees the most random numbers.

The **rand()** function can also take a minimum and maximum parameter if you would prefer to limit the generated number to a specific range.

```
$RandomNumber = rand (0, 10);
```

Of the functions mentioned here, you'll incorporate **abs()** and **round()** into **numbers.php** to protect against invalid user input.

## To use built-in mathematical functions:

1. Open numbers.php in your text editor (Script 4.4).

2. After line 9, add (**Script 4.5**):

   $Quantity = abs($Quantity);
   $Discount = abs($Discount);

   If the user tries to enter in a negative quantity or discount, the page will automatically assume they meant a positive amount and will use **abs()** to adjust accordingly. You could also round the $Quantity value if you didn't want to sell some fraction of a widget. While you are rewriting this script, you could be extra careful and go one step further by applying the **abs()** function to $Payments too.

3. Change line 14, where the $Payments variable is calculated, to:

   $Payments = round ($TotalCost, 2)
   → / 12;

   In order to improve the accuracy of the calculator, the monthly payments will be based upon an actual dollar amount ($Totalcost rounded to two decimal points).

4. Save your script, upload it to the server, and test it in your browser, using a negative number for the quantity or discount (**Figure 4.6**).

**Script 4.5** Using the round() and abs() functions you are able to create logical payment amounts. In fact, any time that you need to insure whole numbers, use round(), and any time you need to guarantee positive numbers, use abs().

```
script
1   <HTML>
2   <HEAD>
3   <TITLE>Using Numbers</TITLE>
4   </HEAD>
5   <BODY>
6   <?php
7   /* $Quantity must be passed to this page
    from a form or via the URL. $Discount is
    optional. */
8   $Cost = 2000.00;
9   $Tax = 0.06;
10  $Quantity = abs($Quantity);
11  $Discount = abs($Discount);
12  $Tax++; // $Tax is now worth 1.06.
13  $TotalCost = (($Cost * $Quantity) -
    $Discount) * $Tax;
14  $Payments = round ($TotalCost, 2) / 12;
15  // Print the results.
16  print ("You requested to purchase $Quantity
    widget(s) at \$$Cost each.\n<P>");
17  print ("The total with tax, minus your
    \$$Discount, comes to $");
18  printf ("%01.2f", $TotalCost);
19  print (".\n<P>You may purchase the
    widget(s)in 12 monthly installments
    of $");
20  printf ("%01.2f", $Payments);
21  print (" each.\n<P>");
22  ?>
23  </BODY>
24  </HTML>
```

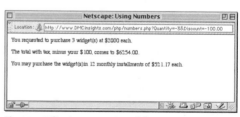

**Figure 4.6** The incorporation of the round() and abs() functions into your script makes it more professional by insuring consistent and meaningful results.

# USING STRINGS

As introduced in Chapter 2, *Variables*, the second category of variables is strings—a collection of characters enclosed within either single or double quotation marks. A string variable may consist of a single letter, a word, a sentence, a paragraph, or even a jumble of nonsensical letters, numbers, and symbols (which might represent a password). Strings may be the most common variable type used in PHP.

Passwords, names, e-mail addresses, comments and similar input from HTML forms all become strings in your PHP script as you witnessed when using your `form.html` and `HandleForm.php` pages in Chapter 3, *HTML Forms and PHP*.

In this chapter, we will cover the most basic built-in functions PHP has for manipulating your string data, whether the string originates from a form or not. Some common techniques will be introduced here—trimming strings, joining strings together, and extracting subsections of strings, although better uses for strings will be illustrated in the subsequent chapters.

# Trimming Strings

Either because a user entered information carelessly or because of sloppy HTML code, it's quite common for extra spaces to be added to a string variable. For purposes of clarity, data integrity, and Web design, it is worth your while to delete those spaces from the strings before using them. Extra spaces sent to the Web browser could make the page appear oddly and those sent to a database or cookie could have unfortunate consequences at a later date (e.g., if a password has a superfluous space it might not match when entered without the space).

The trim() function automatically strips away any extra spaces from both the front and the end of a string (but not within the middle). The format for using trim() is:

```
$String = " extra space before and
→ after text ";
$String = trim($String);
// $String is now equal to "extra space
→ before and after text".
```

You'll use the HandleForm.php script (Script 3.4) from Chapter 3, *HTML Forms and PHP*, and modify it with this in mind.

## To trim your strings:

1. Open HandleForm.php in your text editor (**Script 5.1**).

2. In Script 5.1, after line 6 (the comment), add the following lines (**Script 5.2**):

   ```
   $FirstName = trim($FirstName);
   ```

   By trimming the $FirstName variable you avoid sending a statement to the browser such as "Your first name is Larry." that contains extraneous spaces (**Figures 5.1** and **5.2**).

Script 5.1 The original HandleForm.php is quite simple and therefore lacks some extra measures for manipulating the received data.

```
1   <HTML>
2   <HEAD>
3   <TITLE>Form Results</TITLE>
4   <BODY>
5   <?php
6   /* This page receives and handles the
    data generated by "form.html". */
7   print "Your first name is
    $FirstName.<BR>\n";
8   print "Your last name is
    $LastName.<BR>\n";
9   print "Your E-mail address is
    $Email.<BR>\n";
10  print "This is what you had to say:<BR>\n
    $Comments<BR>\n";
11  ?>
12  </BODY>
13  </HTML>
```

Script 5.2 Besides trimming the extra white spaces from all the received data, I have also changed the title of our page, although it is not critical that you do so.

```
1   <HTML>
2   <HEAD>
3   <TITLE>Form Results/Using Strings</TITLE>
4   <BODY>
5   <?php
6   /* This page receives and handles the
    data generated by "form.html". */
7   $FirstName = trim($FirstName);
8   $LastName = trim($LastName);
9   $Email = trim($Email);
10  $Comments = trim($Comments);
11  print ("Your first name is
    $FirstName.<BR>\n");
12  print ("Your last name is
    $LastName.<BR>\n");
13  print ("Your E-mail address is
    $Email.<BR>\n");
14  print ("This is what you had to say:
    <BR>\n $Comments<BR>\n");
15  ?>
16  </BODY>
17  </HTML>
```

**Figure 5.1** The superfluous spaces here are subtle, but indicate a lack of foresight on the part of the Web developer. Figure 5.2, the HTML source of this image, is more revealing on this point.

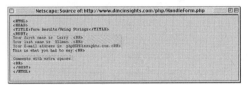

**Figure 5.2** By viewing the HTML source, you are better able to see the extraneous white spaces that have been passed on to the form. While not critical here, sometimes an unnecessary blank line can really destroy the HTML design of a page.

**Figure 5.3** For any number of reasons, it is pretty easy for the average user to add extra white spaces when entering values in a form. Preparing for this possibility is smart programming.

**Figure 5.4** Good programming frequently comes down to adjusting for the mistakes users may make, intentionally or not. Now your page has a slightly higher level of professionalism since you trimmed the user input.

**3.** `$LastName = trim($LastName);`

`$Email = trim($Email);`

Trimming the email address would be particularly useful, as added spaces could render the address unusable for sending emails, thus possibly defeating the purpose of requesting it.

**4.** `$Comments = trim($Comments);`

Regardless of whether the string is drawn from a short piece of text (like the $FirstName or $Email variable) derived from an HTML text box, or a paragraph of writing from a text area, `trim()` will work the same.

**5.** Save your script (still as HandleForm.php), upload it to your server, then test in your Web browser (**Figures 5.3**, **5.4**, and **5.5**).

## ✔ Tip

■ If you need to trim off excess spaces from the beginning or the end of a string, but not both, PHP has broken the `trim()` function down into two more specific ones: `rtrim()`will remove those spaces found at the end of a string variable and `ltrim()` will handle those at the beginning. They are both used just like `trim()`:

`$String = rtrim($String);`

`$String = ltrim($String);`

**Figure 5.5** Compare the HTML source of Figure 5.3 here to that of Figure 5.2 and you'll easily see the differences that the `trim()` function made.

# Connecting Strings (Concatenation)

It's an unwieldy term, but a useful concept—
*concatenation*. It refers to the process of
linking items together. Specifically in programming, you concatenate strings. The
period (.) is the operator for performing this
action, and it's used like so:

```
$NewString = $aString . $bString;
```

You can link as many strings as you want in
this way. You can even join numbers to strings:

```
$NewString = $aString . $bString .
→ $cNumber;
```

This works because PHP is weakly typed,
meaning that its variables are not locked in
to one particular format. Here, the $cNumber
variable will be turned into a string and
appended to the value of the $NewString
variable.

Your HandleForm.php script contains strings
that could logically be concatenated. It's
quite common and even recommended to
take a user's first and last name as separate
inputs, as you did with your form. On the
other hand, it would be advantageous to be
able to refer to the two together as one name.
You'll modify your script with this in mind.

## To use concatenation in your script:

**1.** Open HandleForm.php in your text editor
(Script 5.2).

**2.** Change line 11 to read:
```
$Name = $FirstName . " " .
→ $LastName; (Script 5.3).
```
Since you'll be joining the two names into
one, you'll no longer need separate print
statements (lines 11 and 12 of Script 5.2),
so you'll replace this line and then modify
the next. You have also made sure that
the concatenation takes place after the

**Script 5.3** Concatenation is one of the most common manipulations of a string variable. Think of it as addition for strings.

```
script
1   <HTML>
2   <HEAD>
3   <TITLE>Form Results/Using Strings</TITLE>
4   <BODY>
5   <?php
6   /* This page receives and handles the
    data generated by "form.html". */
7   $FirstName = trim($FirstName);
8   $LastName = trim($LastName);
9   $Email = trim($Email);
10  $Comments = trim($Comments);
11  $Name = $FirstName . " " . $LastName;
12  print ("Your name is $Name.<BR>\n");
13  print ("Your E-mail address is
    $Email.<BR>\n");
14  print ("This is what you had to
    say:<BR>\n $Comments<BR>\n");
15  ?>
16  </BODY>
17  </HTML>
```

**Figure 5.6** Although the HTML form itself won't change, the HandleForm.php script will be able to create the user's full name out of the separate values entered here (see **Figure 5.7**).

**Figure 5.7** Via a simple concatenation of the two name variables, you are able to derive a more useful variable—the user's full name.

trim() statements, because you cannot delete extra spaces from within a string using trim() once you've concatenated the two names together. Last, you have inserted a space between the two names so that they do not run together.

**3.** Change line 12 to:

```
print ("Your name is $Name.<BR>\n");
```

**4.** Save your script, upload it to your server, and test in your Web browser (**Figures 5.6** and **5.7**).

### ✔ Tips

■ Due to the nature of how PHP deals with variables, the same effect could be accomplished using $Name = "$FirstName → $LastName";. This is because variables used within double quotation marks are replaced with their value when handled by PHP. However, the formal method of using the period to concatenate strings— as you did here—is more commonly used and I therefore recommend doing it that way (it will be more obvious what is occurring in your code).

■ You could also have written $FirstName = → $FirstName . " " . $LastName; but there are two reasons why you shouldn't. First, doing so would have overwritten the original value of the $FirstName variable. Second, "FirstName" would no longer be an appropriate description of the variable's value. You should always try to maintain valid variable names as you program.

**CONNECTING STRINGS (CONCATENATION)**

# Encoding and Decoding Strings

At the end of Chapter 3 (see *Inputting Data Manually*), I demonstrated how to use the thinking behind the GET method to send data to a page by appending it to the URL. At that time, I only used this technique to send a variable with a numeric or single word value. We used the same process in Chapter 4, *Using Numbers*, in much the same way. But what if you want to pass several words as one variable value?

For these instances you have the `urlencode()` function. As its name implies, this function takes a string and encodes it (changes its form) so that it can properly be passed as part of a URL. It replaces spaces with plus signs (+) and translates special characters (for example, the apostrophe) into a less problematic version. The syntax for this function is:

`$String = urlencode($String);`

To demonstrate one use of this function, you'll pass your newly created $Name variable to a page which will then greet the user by their full name.

## To use urlencode():

1. Open `HandleForm.php` in your text editor (Script 5.3).

2. After line 14, add the following (**Script 5.4**):

   ```
   $Name = urlencode($Name);
   print ("<P>Click <A HREF=\
    → "welcome.php?Name=$Name\">
    → here</A> to see your personalized
    → greeting!\n");
   ```

3. Create a new document entitled `welcome.php`. You can either write your own, using the information you've learned so far, or you can duplicate the code from **Script 5.5.**

**Script 5.4** Two things to note: first, the HREF tag is another HTML element that requires use of double quotation marks which you must escape within the `print()` statement and, second, PHP will replace the $Name variable with its value when sent to the browser (see **Figure 5.10**).

```
script
1   <HTML>
2   <HEAD>
3   <TITLE>Form Results/Using Strings</TITLE>
4   <BODY>
5   <?php
6   /* This page receives and handles the
       data generated by "form.html". */
7   $FirstName = trim($FirstName);
8   $LastName = trim($LastName);
9   $Email = trim($Email);
10  $Comments = trim($Comments);
11  $Name = $FirstName . " " . $LastName;
12  print ("Your name is $Name.<BR>\n");
13  print ("Your E-mail address is
        $Email.<BR>\n");
14  print ("This is what you had to say:
        <BR>\n $Comments<BR>\n");
15  $Name = urlencode($Name);
16  print ("<P>Click <A HREF=\"welcome.php?
        Name=$Name\"> here</A> to see your
        personalized greeting!\n");
17  ?>
18  </BODY>
19  </HTML>
```

**Script 5.5** Much like the first "Hello, world!" script from Chapter 1, *Getting Started with PHP*, the `welcome.php` page creates a simple, slightly decorated greeting in the Web browser (see **Figure 5.11**). This greeting is personalized, though.

```
script
1   <HTML>
2   <HEAD>
3   <TITLE>Welcome!</TITLE>
4   <BODY>
5   <?php
6   print ("<B><CENTER>Hello, $Name.</CENTER>
        </B>\n");
7   ?>
8   </BODY>
9   </HTML>
```

**Figure 5.8** If you fail to escape your HREF double quotation marks, this last, added line may not appear correctly.

This new page will receive the $Name value passed to it by the HandleForm.php script. I will use it to help demonstrate how you can pass a value from one page to another to another (from form.html to HandleForm.php to welcome.php).

4. Save both scripts, upload them to your server, and test in your Web browser (**Figures 5.8, 5.9, 5.10, 5.11, 5.12, 5.13** and **5.14**).

**Figure 5.9** This is the HTML source of your PHP generated page. Notice how the encoded name appears appended to the link. If you failed to use the urlencode() function, the result would be like that in Figure 5.12.

**Figure 5.12** It will not be obvious until you arrive at the welcome.php page (Figure 5.13), but the space between "Larry" and "Ullman" will result in the last name being dropped in transition from the one page to the other, which is why you need to URL encode variables to be passed on like this.

**Figure 5.10** This latest, dynamic PHP generated page receives a variable not from a form but from another PHP script—a common and useful technique.

**Figure 5.13** If a receiving PHP page is only ever printing out the first word from a string, it is because that string was not passed in an encoded format.

**Figure 5.11** Merely by looking at the page itself, you cannot tell whether or not the name value has been encoded properly or not. However the HTML source code (Figure 5.12) and the welcome.php page itself (Figure 5.13) will reveal any problems.

**Figure 5.14** One of the special characters that the urlencode() function addresses is the apostrophe, translated here into its ASCII equivalent, %27.

## ✔ Tips

- The `urldecode()` function does just the opposite of the `urlencode()`—it takes an encoded URL and turns it back into a standard form.

- Remember that values sent directly from a form are automatically URL-encoded prior to being sent and decoded upon arrival at the receiving script. It is only when you need to manually encode data that the `urlencode()` function is needed (as in the example).

- In Chapter 11, *Databases*, we'll use functions similar to `urlencode()`— `addslashes()` and `stripslashes()`. The former prepares data for entry into a database by escaping problematic characters (single quotation marks, double quotation marks, and the backslash). The later removes the escapes from these same characters. The syntax is exactly as you would expect:

  ```
  $Data = addslashes($Data);
  $Data = stripslashes($Data);
  ```

  Just as with the `urlencode()` function, data received from a form is automatically escaped for proper database entry.

# Encrypting and Decrypting Strings

For security reasons, encryption and decryption are a necessary aspect of most Web sites, especially those that deal with e-commerce. Frequently, in order to protect data, programmers will encrypt it—alter its state by transforming it to a form that's more difficult, if not virtually impossible, to discern. Passwords are an example of a variable you might want to encrypt. Depending upon the level of security you want to establish, usernames, e-mail addresses, and phone numbers are likely candidates for encryption, too.

Note, however, that merely encrypting data does not guarantee the security of your Web site. First, with enough effort, encrypted data can be broken into. Second, since PHP is a server-side technology, it can only introduce a level of security once the information has been received by the PHP module on the server. While in transit from the user's computer to the server, data must be secured using other methods (like a secure socket connection), if security is so desired. See Appendix B, *Security*, for more information and resources on this topic.

I'll introduce three functions for encrypting and decrypting your strings and you'll incorporate one into your script for demonstration purposes.

*continues on next page*

The first function—`crypt()`—can be used to encrypt data, but be aware that there is no decryption option available. So a password may be encrypted using it, then stored, but the decrypted value of the password can never be determined. Using this in a Web application, you might have a user's password encrypted upon registration and then when the user logs in, the password they enter at that time will also be encrypted and the two protected versions of the password will be compared. The syntax for using `crypt()` is:

`$Data = crypt($Data);`

A second encryption function is `encrypt()`, which can be decrypted, using the appropriately named `decrypt()` function (note that `crypt()` and `encrypt()` are two different functions). Unfortunately, to be able to use these two functions, the crypt extension must be installed with the PHP module. You will need to check with your ISP to see if this is the case. Do not be surprised if these two functions are not available and you are therefore limited to just `crypt()` encryption without the possibility of decryption. (In fact, you should get used to the idea of your ISP not supporting any number of features, as they have to make choices, which translates to limits in what you can do. It is the resourceful programmer who learns how to work around the inevitable obstacles.)

## To encrypt data using crypt():

**1.** Open `HandleForm.php` in your text editor (Script 5.4).

**2.** Replace lines 15 and 16 (where you used `urlencode()` to pass the user's name to the `welcome.php` page) with (**Script 5.6**):

`$CryptName = crypt($Name);`

`print ("<P>This is the crypt()`
`→ version of your name:`
`→ $CryptName\n");`

**Script 5.6** I've added the `crypt()` lines just to demonstrate how it functions. Although this would not be a productive use of the technology in reality, it quickly reveals how encryption works with strings.

```
1   <HTML>
2   <HEAD>
3   <TITLE>Form Results/Using Strings</TITLE>
4   <BODY>
5   <?php
6   /* This page receives and handles the
      data generated by "form.html". */
7   $FirstName = trim($FirstName);
8   $LastName = trim($LastName);
9   $Email = trim($Email);
10  $Comments = trim($Comments);
11  $Name = $FirstName . " " . $LastName;
12  print ("Your name is $Name.<BR>\n");
13  print ("Your E-mail address is
      $Email.<BR>\n");
14  print ("This is what you had to say:
      <BR>\n $Comments<BR>\n");
15  $CryptName = crypt($Name);
16  print ("<P>This is the crypt() version
      of your name: $CryptName\n");
17  ?>
18  </BODY>
19  </HTML>
```

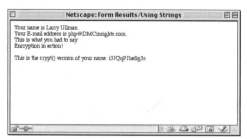

**Figure 5.15** The crypt() function returns a unique, 12-character long version of whatever it encrypts.

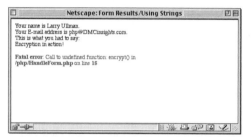

**Figure 5.16** I added a call to the encrypt() function to the HandleForm.php page, resulting in this error message, indicating that the server does not support that function.

There's no reason to encrypt a URL-encoded version of your name, so you've replaced that part of the script.

**3.** Save your script, upload it to your server, and test it in your Web browser (**Figure 5.15**).

## ✔ Tips

- There is a similar encryption function to crypt() called md5(), which you'll use later in this chapter. To learn more about its use, as well as the syntax for encrypt() and decrypt(), see Appendix C, *PHP Resources*.

- A direct way to know if a function is not supported by the PHP installation on the server is if you see an error message like the one in **Figure 5.16**, derived by calling the encrypt() function on a server that doesn't support it. As a precaution, before assuming that something is not supported, double-check your spelling and syntax. (In the figure, if I called an encrpyt() function, it would generate a similar error message.)

- Be careful not to confuse encrypting a string and encoding it. Encryption is used for security purposes and changes the entire text. Encoding only replaces certain characters with equivalents that can be used within a URL.

# Pulling Out Parts from a String

Earlier in this chapter you learned how to join strings together using concatenation. Besides making larger strings out of smaller pieces, you can also extract subsections of a string. There are a number of built-in functions that can do this in different ways, and I'll cover two here. The trick to using any method to pull out a subsection of a string is that you must know something about the string itself in order to do so effectively.

The strtok() function creates a sub-string, referred to as a *token*, from a larger string based upon a predetermined separator (a comma or a space, perhaps). For example, if you have users enter their full name in one field (presumably with their first and last names separated by a space), you could ascertain their first name with the code:

```
$FirstName = strtok($Name, " ");
```

where $Name is the name of the variable received from the form which contains the user's full name. This line of programming tells PHP to pull out everything from $Name up until it finds a blank space. If you had the user enter their full name in the format of "LastName, FirstName", you could find their surname by writing:

```
$LastName = strtok($Name, ",");
```

Since you have wisely kept the two names distinct in your form, you will not need to use this function at this time.

A second way to pull out sections of a string is by referring to the *indexed position* of the characters within the string. When I refer to the index of a string, I mean the numerical location of a character, counting from the beginning. However, PHP—like most programming languages—begins all indexes with the number 0. So to index the string "Larry," you would begin with the "L" at position 0, "a" at 1, "r" at 2, the second "r" at 3, and the "y" at 4. Even though the string length of "Larry" is 5, its index goes from 0 to 4. With this in mind, you can utilize the `substr()` function to create a sub-string based upon the index position of the sub-string's characters, like this:

```
$SubString = substr($String,0,10);
```

First, you must enter in the master string from which your sub-string will be derived (here, $String). Second, you indicate where the sub-string begins, as its indexed position (0—so you want to start with the first character). Third, you determine how many characters, from that starting point, the sub-string is composed of (10). If, in this case, $String is not 10 characters long, the resulting $SubString will end with the end of $String.

Frequently you'll use the `strlen()` function to help determine the ending point of the string. This function calculates how long a string is (i.e., how many characters is contains) and is very easy to use:

```
$StringLength = strlen($String);
```

You'll use the notion of `substr()`, along with `strlen()`, and `md5()`, to write a nifty password generation program.

Passwords you use are more secure the more random they are. In fact, passwords which have no special meaning, are not based upon common words, and use a variety of upper- and lowercase letters and numbers are the most secure of all. This script will create a new, random password each time you reload the page.

## To create a password generator in PHP:

**1.** Start by creating a new PHP document in your text editor with the lines (**Script 5.7**):

```
<HTML><HEAD><TITLE>Password
→ Generator</TITLE><BODY><?php
$String = "This is the text which
→ will be encrypted so that we may
→ create random and more secure
→ passwords!";
```

You can put any string here that you want, the specific text will not make a difference for our purposes. This text will be encrypted to create a more random string from which the password will be taken.

```
$Length = 8;
```

By establishing your password length as a variable, you can simply change this one value to get different sized passwords. There is a limit of a password that is 32 characters long, which is the length of an encrypted string using md5().$String = md5($String);

md5() is similar in use to crypt() but it will generate a string 32 characters long as opposed to crypt() which creates a string 12 characters long. . See the PHP manual or the PHP home page for more information on md5().

```
$StringLength = strlen($String);
```

In order to extract a sub-string, you'll need to know the length of the encrypted string, so we use the strlen() function which returns how many characters are in the given string. Although you do know for a fact, that by using md5() the string length will always be 32, it's better to be safe, which is why you'll use the strlen() function. This way, should you change your methods at later date (using encrypt() instead of md5() for example), this line will still work properly.

**Script 5.7** It may seem like you took a couple of major jumps to get to this point, but the passwords.php script is just a useful conglomeration of what you've learned up until this point. And all in 16 lines!

```
1   <HTML>
2   <HEAD>
3   <TITLE>Password Generator</TITLE>
4   <BODY>
5   <?php
6   $String = "This is the text which will be
    encrypted so that we may create random
    and secure passwords!";
7   $Length = 8; // Change this value to
    indicate how long your passwords should
    be. 32 character limit.
8   $String = md5($String);
9   $StringLength = strlen($String);
10  srand ((double) microtime() * 1000000);
11  $Begin = rand(0,($StringLength-$Length-1));
    // Pick an arbitrary starting point.
12  $Password = substr($String, $Begin,
    $Length);
13  print ("Your recommended password
    is:<P><BIG>$Password</BIG>\n");
14  ?>
15  </BODY>
16  </HTML>
```

**Figure 5.17** The passwords.php page takes the work out of creating your own secure passwords.

**Figure 5.18** Every time you reload the page, a new and different password will be delivered for the most part. (In actuality, due to the fact that md5() creates a 32-character string, there is a finite limit to the number of unique passwords this script will generate but it will create dozens of different passwords.)

```
srand ((double) microtime() *
→ 1000000);
$Begin = rand(0,($StringLength -
→ $Length - 1));
```

You need to determine the beginning point for your substr() function. The rand() function creates a random number between (and including) a minimum (here it is 0) and a maximum. (Remember to use the srand() line first or else you may not get truly random results from rand().) You have set your maximum to be the length of the string minus the length of the password minus one. Here's the reason why: if your encrypted string is 30 characters long and you require your passwords to be 8 characters long then the latest you can begin your substr() and still have an 8-character password is 21 (which refers to the 22nd character in the string, due to how indexing behaves). We put the calculation within parentheses for clarity sake, but rand() does not require it.

```
$Password = substr($String, $Begin,
→ $Length);
```

The final step is to make a substr() call with your determined values. You are stating that the $Password variable is equal to a sub-string derived from the $String variable, beginning with indexed position $Begin, and continuing for $Length characters.

```
print ("Your recommended password is:
→ <P><BIG>$Password </BIG>\n");
```

Now print the results (emphatically).

2. Close your PHP and HTML code with:
   ?></BODY></HTML>

3. Save your script as passwords.php, upload it to your server, and test in your Web browser (**Figures 5.17** and **5.18**).

## ✔ Tips

■ Instead of setting the $Length variable at the onset of our page, you could use the URL/GET trick to send the page a length value by appending `?Length=8` to the URL (if you do so, then be sure to remove line 7).

■ Databases have a date format which stores calendar dates as YYYY-MM-DD (or something similar to this). Since you would know the exact format of the string retrieved from the database, the sub-strings—year, month, and day— could be calculated using `substr()`:

```
$Year = substr($Date,0,4);
$Month = substr($Date,5,2);
$Day = substr($Date,8,2);
```

■ Using `strlen()` is definitely a situation where you absolutely do not want to write `$Password = strlen($Password);`, in which case you would replace the actual password value with a number indicating how many characters were once, but are no longer, in the variable!

# CONTROL STRUCTURES

Now that I've covered the basics of the variable types (aside from arrays, which will be covered in Chapter 7, *Using Arrays*), I can get into the real meat of programming—control structures (i.e., conditionals and loops). In the process, I'll finish the discussion of the various operators PHP uses. (I've already covered arithmetic and assignment in the variable chapters.)

Conditional structures are a staple of programming languages. They allow you to establish a parameter and then perform an action based upon the results of that parameter. This gives you the ability to make your Web sites even more dynamic. For example, if the time of day is before noon, you can greet the user with a "Good Morning!" If it is after noon, you'll print "Good Afternoon!" There are two general conditionals—*if* and *switch*—in PHP that you'll begin using in this chapter.

While I am discussing *if* conditionals, I'll introduce two last categories of operators—comparison and logical. You'll commonly use these in your conditionals along with the PHP concepts of TRUE and FALSE.

Finally, you'll begin programming with loops, which allow you to repeat an action for a specified number of iterations. Loops can save you programming time and help you get the most functionality out of arrays, as you'll see in the next chapter. PHP supports two major loop constructs—*while* (and its counterpart *do...while*) and *for*.

# The If Conditional

The basic programming conditional is the standard *if* (what used to be called an *if-then* conditional—the *then* is now implied). The syntax for this kind of conditional is very simple:

```
if (condition) {
    statement(s);
}
```

The condition must go within parentheses and then you begin the statements area after a curly brace. The statements section of the conditional is where executable commands are placed (for example, printing a string, adding two numbers together, and so forth). Each separate statement (or command) must have its own semicolon indicating the end of the command line, but there is no limit to how many statements you write as the result of a conditional. You then close the statements section with another curly brace. Commonly programmers put these statements indented from the initial *if* line to indicate that they are the result of a conditional but that is not syntactically required. Failure to use a semicolon after each statement, forgetting an opening or closing parentheses or curly brace, or using a semicolon after either of the braces will all cause errors to occur.

PHP uses the concepts of TRUE/FALSE when determining whether or not to execute the statements. If the condition is TRUE, the statements will be executed; if FALSE, they will not be. The next section, *More Operators*, goes into TRUE/FALSE in more detail.

To begin working with the *if* conditional, you'll rewrite the calculator page from Chapter 4, *Using Numbers*, so it works only if the necessary quantity has been submitted. This will prevent calculations from being made without all the requisite data, which could cause illogical and erroneous Web page results.

**Script 6.1** In the original `numbers.php` script, the calculations were made and the results printed based upon the assumption that the $Quantity and $Discount values were received, which is not a good programming practice.

```
script
1   <HTML>
2   <HEAD>
3   <TITLE>Using Numbers</TITLE>
4   </HEAD>
5   <BODY>
6   <?php
7   /* $Quantity must be passed to this page
    from a form or via the URL. $Discount is
    optional. */
8   $Cost = 2000.00;
9   $Tax = 0.06;
10  $Quantity = abs($Quantity);
11  $Discount = abs($Discount);
12  $Tax++; // $Tax is now worth 1.06.
13  $TotalCost = (($Cost * $Quantity) -
    $Discount) * $Tax;
14  $Payments = round ($TotalCost, 2) / 12;
15  // Print the results.
16  print ("You requested to purchase
    $Quantity widget(s) at \$$Cost
    each.\n<P>");
17  print ("The total with tax, minus your
    \$$Discount, comes to $");
18  printf ("%01.2f", $TotalCost);
19  print (".\n<P>You may purchase the
    widget(s)in 12 monthly installments of $");
20  printf ("%01.2f", $Payments);
21  print (" each.\n<P>");
22  ?>
23  </BODY>
24  </HTML>
```

**Script 6.2** Frequent use of *if* conditionals makes your programming more professional by establishing particular parameters before going through corresponding processes. Here you'll insure that a $Quantity was received before proceeding with the calculations.

```
                        script
1    <HTML>
2    <HEAD>
3    <TITLE>Conditionals</TITLE>
4    </HEAD>
5    <BODY>
6    <?php
7    /* $Quantity must be passed to this page
     from a form or via the URL. $Discount is
     optional. */
8    $Cost = 2000.00;
9    $Tax = 0.06;
10   if ($Quantity) {
11       $Quantity = abs($Quantity);
12       $Discount = abs($Discount);
13       $Tax++; // $Tax is now worth 1.06.
14       $TotalCost = (($Cost * $Quantity) -
         $Discount) * $Tax;
15       $Payments = round ($TotalCost, 2) / 12;
16       // Print the results.
17       print ("You requested to purchase
         $Quantity widget(s) at \$$Cost each.
         \n<P>");
18       print ("The total with tax, minus
         your \$$Discount, comes to $");
19       printf ("%01.2f", $TotalCost);
20       print (".\n<P>You may purchase the
         widget(s)in 12 monthly installments
         of $");
21       printf ("%01.2f", $Payments);
22       print (" each.\n<P>");
23   }
24   ?>
25   </BODY>
26   </HTML>
```

## To create an *if* conditional:

1. Open numbers.php (**Script 6.1**) in your text editor.

2. Change the title (line 3) to <TITLE>
   → Conditionals</TITLE> (**Script 6.2**).

3. Change lines 10–23 to be the result of an *if* conditional.

   ```
   if ($Quantity) {
       $Quantity = abs($Quantity);
       $Discount = abs($Discount);
       $Tax++; // $Tax is now worth
       → 1.06.
       $TotalCost = (($Cost *
       → $Quantity) - $Discount) * $Tax;
       $Payments = round ($TotalCost, 2)
       → / 12;
       // Print the results.
       print ("You requested to purchase
       → $Quantity widget(s) at \$$Cost
       → each.\n<P>");
       print ("The total with tax,
       → minus your \$$Discount, comes
       → to $");
       printf ("%01.2f", $TotalCost);
       print (".\n<P>You may purchase
       → the widget(s) in 12 monthly
       → installments of $");
       printf ("%01.2f", $Payments);
       print (" each.\n<P>");
   }
   ```

In PHP, simply using a variable name as your condition (as you have here with $Quantity) is the same as saying, "If the variable $Quantity exists (i.e., has a value other than zero)." Here you are telling the PHP to execute the following lines only if $Quantity has a value that's not zero. In other words, the calculations will only be made if there is a quantity to use.

*continues on next page*

**4.** Save your script, upload it to the server, and test the page in your Web browser both with and without the requisite $Quantity information (**Figures 6.1** and **6.2**).

## ✔ Tips

■ If the statement area of your conditional is only one line long, you technically do not need the curly braces. If that is the case, you can actually place the whole conditional on one line like so:

```
if (condition) statement;
```

I mention this fact here as you may run across code in this format. However, I would suggest that you always use the multi-line format (as demonstrated in the syntax introduction above) to improve consistency and minimize errors.

■ You can nest *if* conditionals—placing a second *if* as the result of a prior condition—without a problem in PHP as long as you remember to close your conditionals appropriately.

■ Later in the chapter (see *Using* Else), you'll learn how to execute commands if a condition isn't met. Then, if a necessary value isn't received, you could program the script to specifically request it in order to proceed.

■ You can also use the `isset()` function to determine if a variable exists. Unlike simply referring to a variable by name as you have done here, `isset()` will return TRUE if the variable is equal to zero. For example:

```
$Quantity = 0;
    if ($Quantity) { ... // FALSE
    if (isset($Quantity)) { ... // TRUE
```

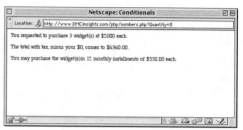

**Figure 6.1** As long as the page receives a value for the $Quantity variable, it will proceed as it had prior to adding the *if* conditional.

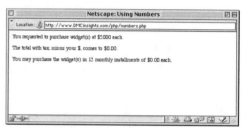

**Figure 6.2** Thanks to the *if* conditional, your Web site will never produce ugly results like this again.

# More Operators

I discussed most of PHP's operators in the previous chapters along with the variables that use them. These operators include arithmetic for numbers: addition (+), subtraction (-), multiplication (*), and division (/), along with the incremental (++) and decremental (--) shortcuts for increasing or decreasing the value of a number by 1. Then there is the assignment operator (=) which is used to set the value of a variable, regardless of type. I also introduced concatenation (.), for appending one string to another.

These are all handy for establishing the value of a variable but they are not of much use when it comes to conditionals. Now you will explore comparison and logical operators for working with conditionals.

## Comparison

When I first introduced the assignment operator (the equal sign), in Chapter 2, *Variables*, I was careful to explain that its meaning is not exactly what you would conventionally think it would be. In the line $Variable = 5; you are not stating that $Variable "is equal to" *5* but that it "is set to the value of" *5*.

When writing conditionals, you will often want to see if a variable is equal to a specific value (to match user names or passwords, perhaps), which you cannot do with the equal sign alone (since that is for assigning a value not equating values). For this purpose you have the equal operator (==), created by using two equal signs together.

```
$Variable = 5;
$Variable == 5;
```

*continues on next page*

Using these two lines of code together first establishes the value of $Variable as 5, then makes a TRUE statement when seeing if $Variable is equal to 5. This demonstrates the significant difference one more equal sign makes in your PHP code and why you will want to distinguish carefully between the assignment and comparison operators.

Not equal to, in PHP, is represented by an exclamation mark coupled with an equals sign (!=). In fact, the exclamation point, in general, means "not." So as **$Variable** means "$Variable exists and has a value (other than zero)", **!$Variable** is the way of saying "$Variable does not exist and has no value (or a value of zero)."

The remaining comparison operators are identical to their mathematical counterparts: less than (<), greater than (>), less than or equal to (<=), and greater than or equal to (>=).

In order to add functionality to your widget calculator, you'll rewrite the numbers.php script so that it only applies a discount for a sale of greater than $50.

## To use comparison operators:

1. Open numbers.php (Script 6.2) in your text editor.

2. Change the cost of the widget to a much smaller number so that a $50 limit is less easily reached (**Script 6.3**, line 8).

   $Cost = 20.00;

3. After the $Tax++; line (line 13), change the $TotalCost equation to read:

   $TotalCost = ($Cost * $Quantity);

   Since the discount is only going to apply if the total is over $50, you should first calculate the total separately.

**Script 6.3** The comparative operators like the *less than or equal to* (<=) here allow you to specify better numeric conditions in your code.

```
                          script
1    <HTML>
2    <HEAD>
3    <TITLE>Conditionals</TITLE>
4    </HEAD>
5    <BODY>
6    <?php
7    /* $Quantity must be passed to this page
     from a form or via the URL. $Discount is
     optional. */
8    $Cost = 20.00;
9    $Tax = 0.06;
10   if ($Quantity) {
11       $Quantity = abs($Quantity);
12       $Discount = abs($Discount);
13       $Tax++; // $Tax is now worth 1.06.
14       $TotalCost = ($Cost * $Quantity);
15           if ($TotalCost >= 50) {
16               $TotalCost = $TotalCost -
                 $Discount;
17           }
18       $TotalCost = $TotalCost * $Tax;
19       $Payments = round ($TotalCost, 2) / 12;
20       // Print the results.
21       print ("You requested to purchase
         $Quantity widget(s) at \$$Cost
         each.\n<P>");
22       print ("The total with tax, minus
         your \$$Discount, comes to $");
23       printf ("%01.2f", $TotalCost);
24       print (".\n<P>You may purchase the
         widget(s)in 12 monthly installments
         of $");
25       printf ("%01.2f", $Payments);
26       print (" each.\n<P>");
27   }
28   ?>
29   </BODY>
30   </HTML>
```

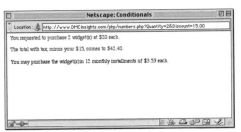

**Figure 6.3** If you do the math you'll see that the discount is not applied because the total was less than $50. Compare this with the math in Figure 6.4.

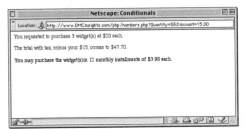

**Figure 6.4** Now that the user has ordered enough widgets to push the total over $50, the discount has been applied.

**4.** Create an *if* conditional checking to see if the value of the sale is over $50.

```
if ($TotalCost >= 50) {
    $TotalCost = $TotalCost -
    → $Discount;
}
```

Using comparative operators within the condition of the *if* conditional, you can specify that the discount will only be applied if the $TotalCost value is greater than or equal to $50 (don't write the dollar sign in your condition). The subtraction of $Discount is the statement that is executed if the condition is TRUE. If the condition is FALSE, no discount will be subtracted.

**5.** Now apply the tax to the total cost.

```
$TotalCost = $TotalCost * $Tax;
```

**6.** The rest of this script is unchanged from before, including the determination of the monthly payments and printing all of the results.

**7.** Save your script, upload it to the server, and test in your Web browser using different $Quantity values (**Figures 6.3** and **6.4**).

## ✔ Tip

■ In an *if* conditional, if you make the mistake of writing $Variable = 5 as opposed to $Variable == 5, you'll see that the corresponding conditional statements will always be executed. This is because, while the condition $Variable == 5 may or may not be TRUE, the condition $Variable = 5 will always be TRUE.

## Logical

Logical operators help you create reasonable constructs—statements that have a value of either TRUE or FALSE. In PHP, a condition is TRUE if it is simply a variable name and that variable has a value that is not zero (as you've seen already), such as:

```
$Variable = 5;
if ($Variable) { ...
```

A condition is also TRUE if it makes logical sense, like:

```
if (5 >= 3) { ...
```

Your condition will be FALSE if it refers to a variable and that variable has no value or if you have created an illogical construct. The following conditional will always be false:

```
if (5 <= 3) { ...
```

To go beyond simple one-part conditions, PHP supports six types of logical operators: two versions of *and* (AND or &&); two versions of *or* (OR or ||—a character called the pipe put together twice); *not* (NOT); and *or not* (XOR). When you have two options for one operator (as with *and* and *or*), they differ only in precedence. See Appendix C, *PHP Resources*, to view the table of operator precedence.

Using parentheses and logical operators, you can create even more in-depth conditionals for your *if* conditionals. For an AND conditional, every conjoined part must be TRUE. With OR, one subsection must be TRUE to render the whole condition TRUE. These conditionals are TRUE:

```
if ( (5 <= 3) OR (5 >= 3) ) { ...
if ( (5 > 3) AND (5 < 10) ) { ...
```

These conditionals are FALSE:

```
if ( (5 != 5) AND (5 > 3) ) { ...
if ( (5 != 5) OR (5 < 3) ) { ...
```

**Script 6.4** In this script the logical operator AND establishes a specific condition under which the message will be printed. The AND requires that both sub-conditions are TRUE in order for the whole condition to be TRUE.

```
script

1   <HTML>
2   <HEAD>
3   <TITLE>Conditionals</TITLE>
4   </HEAD>
5   <BODY>
6   <?php
7   /* $Quantity must be passed to this page
    from a form or via the URL. $Discount is
    optional. */
8   $Cost = 20.00;
9   $Tax = 0.06;
10  if ($Quantity) {
11      $Quantity = abs($Quantity);
12      $Discount = abs($Discount);
13      $Tax++; // $Tax is now worth 1.06.
14      $TotalCost = ($Cost * $Quantity);
15      if ( ($TotalCost < 50) AND
        ($Discount) ) {
16          print ("Your \$$Discount discount
            will not apply because the total
            value of the sale is under
            $50!\n<P>");
17      }
18      if ($TotalCost >= 50) {
19          $TotalCost = $TotalCost -
            $Discount;
20      }
21      $TotalCost = $TotalCost * $Tax;
22      $Payments = round ($TotalCost, 2) / 12;
23      // Print the results.
24      print ("You requested to purchase
        $Quantity widget(s) at \$$Cost
        each.\n<P>");
25      print ("The total with tax, minus
        your \$$Discount, comes to $");
26      printf ("%01.2f", $TotalCost);
27      print (".\n<P>You may purchase the
        widget(s)in 12 monthly installments
        of $");
28      printf ("%01.2f", $Payments);
29      print (" each.\n<P>");
30  }
31  ?>
32  </BODY>
33  </HTML>
```

As you construct your conditionals, remember two important things: first, in order for the statements which are the result of a conditional to be executed, the conditional has to have a TRUE value; second, by using parentheses, you can ignore rules of precedence and insure that your operators are addressed in the order of your choosing.

To demonstrate logical operators, you should add another conditional to the numbers.php page letting the user know if their discount does not apply.

## To use logical operators:

1. Open numbers.php (Script 6.3) in your text editor.

2. After the $TotalCost value is first calculated (Script 6.3, line 14) but before the if ($TotalCost >= 50) conditional, add (**Script 6.4**):

```
if ( ($TotalCost < 50) AND
→ ($Discount) ) {
    print ("Your \$$Discount
    → discount will not apply
    → because the total value
    → of the sale is under
    → $50!\n<P>");
}
```

This conditional will check for two things. First it will see if $TotalCost is less than $50. Second, it will determine if a non-zero $Discount value exists. If both of these are TRUE, the message will be printed. If at least one of these conditions is FALSE, the whole condition will also be FALSE (because the larger conditional is ruled by the logical AND operator) and therefore the message will not be printed.

*continues on next page*

**3.** Since those are the only changes to the script, you can now save your script, upload it to the server, and test in your Web browser (**Figures 6.5** and **6.6**).

## ✔ Tips

■ It is another common programming convention—which I've maintained in this book—to write the terms TRUE and FALSE in all capitals.

■ It is very easy in long, complicated conditionals to forget an opening or closing parentheses, which will either produce error messages or unexpected results. Find some system (like spacing out your conditionals as I have done) to help clarify your code.

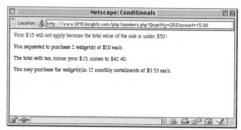

**Figure 6.5** The widget calculator is slightly more professional now that it lets the user know that their discount will not apply to the sale.

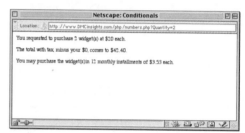

**Figure 6.6** Even though the total sale value is less than $50, no message is printed to the user since $Discount does not have a value.

**Script 6.5** You'll normally find that it makes sense to write *if-else* conditionals instead of just standard *if* conditionals (as you've done here) since you'll likely want to perform some action if a condition you were expecting isn't met.

```
1   <HTML>
2   <HEAD>
3   <TITLE>Conditionals</TITLE>
4   </HEAD>
5   <BODY>
6   <?php
7   /* $Quantity must be passed to this page
    from a form or via the URL. $Discount is
    optional. */
8   $Cost = 20.00;
9   $Tax = 0.06;
10  if ($Quantity) {
11      $Quantity = abs($Quantity);
12      $Discount = abs($Discount);
13      $Tax++; // $Tax is now worth 1.06.
14      $TotalCost = ($Cost * $Quantity);
15      if ( ($TotalCost < 50) AND
        ($Discount) ) {
16          print ("Your \$$Discount will not
            apply because the total value of
            the sale is under $50!\n<P>");
17      }
18      if ($TotalCost >= 50) {
19          $TotalCost = $TotalCost -
            $Discount;
20      }
21      $TotalCost = $TotalCost * $Tax;
22      $Payments = round ($TotalCost, 2) / 12;
23      // Print the results.
24      print ("You requested to purchase
        $Quantity widget(s) at \$$Cost each.
        \n<P>");
25      print ("The total with tax, minus
        your \$$Discount, comes to $");
26      printf ("%01.2f", $TotalCost);
27      print (".\n<P>You may purchase the
        widget(s)in 12 monthly installments
        of $");
28      printf ("%01.2f", $Payments);
29      print (" each.\n<P>");
30  } else {
31      print ("Please make sure that you
        have entered both a quantity and an
        applicable discount and then
        resubmit.\n"); }
32  ?>
33  </BODY>
34  </HTML>
```

# Using Else

The next logical formation after an *if* conditional is the *if-else* (sometimes called the *if-then-else*) conditional. This allows you to establish a condition as to why one statement would be executed and then another statement which would be executed if that condition is not met.

```
if (condition) {
    statement(s);
} else {
    statement(s)2;
}
```

The important thing to remember when using this construct is that unless the condition is explicitly met, the *else* statement will be executed. In other words, the statements after the *else* constitute the default action while the statements after the *if* condition are the exception to the rule. You can now rewrite the numbers.php page incorporating *else* into the *if* statement.

### To use *else*:

1.  Open numbers.php in your text editor (Script 6.4).

2.  Immediately after the closing curly brace of your *if* conditional (line 30), type (**Script 6.5**):

    ```
    else { print ("Please make sure that
    → you have entered both a quantity
    → and an applicable discount and
    → then resubmit.\n"); }
    ```

    Rather than just display a blank screen if the page does not receive a quantity, it will now print an appropriate error message.

    *continues on next page*

**3.** Save your script, upload it to your server, and test in your Web browser (**Figure 6.7**).

### ✔ Tip

- You could also, at this time, add an *if-else* conditional to `numbers.php` so that a message is printed if the discount does apply. Or, if you want to be very particular, you could use an *if-else* conditional to print the singular "widget" if only one widget is ordered but the plural "widgets" otherwise (as opposed to "widget(s)" as I've been writing).

**Figure 6.7** Now you've achieved a far more professional Web site that reacts according to what the user or system does—in this case, omitting the quantity. Conditionals help you prepare against assumptions which may or may not come true.

**Script 6.6** You have nested one *if-elseif-else* within another *if-else* conditional which is perfectly acceptable as long as you maintain your syntax (continuing to indent subsequent lines helps).

```
script
1   <HTML>
2   <HEAD>
3   <TITLE>If-elseif Conditionals</TITLE>
4   <BODY>
5   <?php
6   if ($Username) {
7       print ("Good ");
8       if (date("A") == "AM") {
9           print ("morning, ");
10      } elseif ( ( date("H") >= 12 ) and
        ( date("H") < 18 ) ) {
11          print ("afternoon, ");
12      } else {
13          print ("evening, ");
14      } // Close the date if.
15      print ("$Username");
16      print ("!\n");
17  } else {
18      print ("Please log in.\n");
19  } // Close the username if.
20  ?>
21  </BODY>
22  </HTML>
```

# Using Elseif

Similar to the *if-else* conditional is the *if-elseif* (or *if-elseif-else*). It acts like a running *if* statement and can be expanded to whatever length you require.

```
if (conditional) {
    statement(s);
} elseif (conditional2) {
    statement(s)2;
}
```

Here's another example:

```
if (conditional) {
    statement(s);
} elseif (conditional2) {
    statement(s)2;
} else {
    statement(s)3;
}
```

You'll create a new hello.php page similar to the one from Chapter 3, *HTML Forms and PHP*, which utilizes an *if-elseif* conditional and the date() function to write a customized greeting to the user.

### To use *elseif*:

1. Create a new PHP document in your text editor.

2. Write the standard HTML header and open the PHP section of the page (**Script 6.6**).

   ```
   <HTML><HEAD><TITLE>If-elseif
   → Conditionals</TITLE><BODY>
   <?php
   ```

3. Create the main *if* conditional.

   ```
   if ($Username) {
   ```

   As a matter of good form, you'll only print this greeting if you have the username.

*continues on next page*

**4.** `print ("Good ");`

You'll set up the code to print the first part of the greeting separately, rather than along with each of the three following specific salutations. This way, if you want to later change the specific wording, you only need to make alterations in one place.

**5.** `if (date("A") == "AM") {`

The **date()** function is used to determine any date specific information—day of the week, month, etc.—based upon the parameter it is fed. Here, **date("A")** will return either "AM" or "PM". The **date()** function will be covered in more detail in Chapter 13, *Creating Web Applications*.

**6.** `print ("morning, ");`
`} elseif ( ( date("H") >= 12 ) and`
`→ ( date("H") < 18 ) ) {`

Date("H") returns the hour of the day in military format. So if it is between noon and 6 p.m., you'll say "Good afternoon."

**7.** `print ("afternoon, ");`
`} else {`
`print ("evening, ");`

If it is not the morning or the afternoon, it must be the evening, so you'll use *else* as a catch-all.

**8.** `} // Close the date if.`
`print ("$Username");`
`print ("!\n");`
`} else {`
`print ("Please log in.\n");`

If you do not have a username, you'll request that the user log in before proceeding.

**9.** `} // Close the username if.`

The comments help you keep track of complicated and nested *if* conditionals, helping to insure that you close your *if* conditionals properly.

**Figure 6.8** The page greets you like so if it has the $Username value and the time on the server is between 6 p.m. midnight.

**Figure 6.9** This is the greeting the page gives you assuming it receives the $Username and it is between noon and 6 p.m.

**10.** Save your script as `hello.php`, upload it to the server, and test it in your Web browser (**Figures 6.8** and **6.9**).

### ✔ Tips

■ You should always put the *else* as the last part of a conditional since it will be executed unless one of the conditions to that point has been met.

■ You can continue to use *elseif*s as many times as you want as part of one *if* conditional.

■ PHP also allows you to write *elseif* as two words if you would prefer to do so:

```
if (condition) {
    statement(s);
} else if (condition2) {
    statement(s)2;
}
```

■ The `date()` function is very useful but it only reflects the time on the server, not the time where the user is. (In fact, if the time on the server is incorrect, the `date()` function will reflect the incorrect time and date.)

# The Switch Conditional

Once you get to the point where you have very elaborate *if-elseif-else* conditionals, you may find that it saves you time and clarifies your programming to use a *switch* conditional instead. The *switch* conditional takes only one possible condition and that is the value of a variable.

```
switch ($Variable) {
    case "value1":
        statement(s)1;
        break;
    case "value2":
        statement(s)2;
        break;
    default:
        statement(s)3;
        break;
}
```

It is critical that you comprehend how a *switch* conditional works. Starting at the beginning, once PHP finds the case that matches the value of the set variable, it will continue to execute statements until it either comes to the end of the *switch* conditional (the closing curly brace) or hits a **break** statement, at which point it will exit the *switch* construct. Thus, it is imperative that you close every case (and even the default case, for consistency sake) with a **break**.

This above *switch* conditional is somewhat like a rewrite of this:

```
if ($Variable == "value1") {
    statement(s)1;
} elseif ($Variable=="value2") {
    statement(s)2;
} else {
    statement(s)3;
}
```

**Script 6.7** This HTML form uses a pull-down menu to give the user a list of options (created by the SELECT input type).

```
                    script
1    <HTML>
2    <HEAD>
3    <TITLE>HTML Contact Form</TITLE>
4    </HEAD>
5    <BODY>
6    <FORM ACTION="HandleContact.php"
     METHOD=POST>
7    First Name <INPUT TYPE=TEXT
     NAME="FirstName" SIZE=20><BR>
8    Last Name <INPUT TYPE=TEXT
     NAME="LastName" SIZE=20><BR>
9    How would you prefer to be contacted:
     <SELECT NAME="ContactHow">
10   <OPTION VALUE="">Select One:</OPTION>
11   <OPTION VALUE="Telephone">
     Telephone</OPTION>
12   <OPTION VALUE="Mail">Mail</OPTION>
13   <OPTION VALUE="E-Mail">E-Mail</OPTION>
14   <OPTION VALUE="Fax">Fax</OPTION>
15   </SELECT><BR>
16   Comments <TEXTAREA NAME="Comments"
     ROWS=5 COLS=40></TEXTAREA><BR>
17   <INPUT TYPE=SUBMIT NAME="SUBMIT"
     VALUE="Submit!">
18   </FORM>
19   </BODY>
20   </HTML>
```

I'll explain: because the *switch* conditional uses the value of $Variable as its condition, it will first check to see if $Variable is equal to **value1** and, if so, will execute **statement(s)1**. If not, it will check to see if $Variable is equal to **value2**, and, if so, will execute **statement(s)2**. If neither condition is met, the default action of the *switch* condition is to execute **statement(s)3**.

In the next section, *The While Loop*, you'll use *switch* in connection with a loop to create an HTML form that tells you how many days are in a month but to demonstrate *switch*'s capabilities here, you'll write a simple script that prints a message based upon what choice the user selects in an HTML form.

## To use a switch conditional:

1. Create a new HTML document in your text editor.

2. Begin with the standard HTML header (**Script 6.7**):

   ```
   <HTML><HEAD><TITLE>HTML
   → Contact Form</TITLE></HEAD><BODY>
   ```

3. Make a form that takes some information from the user and gives them the option of how they want to be contacted.

   ```
   <FORM ACTION="HandleContact.php"
   → METHOD=POST>
   First Name <INPUT TYPE=TEXT NAME=
   → "FirstName" SIZE=20><BR>
   Last Name <INPUT TYPE=TEXT NAME=
   → "LastName" SIZE=20><BR>
   How would you prefer to be contacted:
   → <SELECT NAME="ContactHow">
   → <OPTION VALUE="">Select One:
   → </OPTION>
   <OPTION VALUE="Telephone">
   → Telephone</OPTION>
   <OPTION VALUE="Mail">Mail</OPTION>
   <OPTION VALUE="E-Mail">E-Mail
   → </OPTION>
   <OPTION VALUE="Fax">Fax</OPTION>
   </SELECT><BR>
   ```

*continues on next page*

THE SWITCH CONDITIONAL

**83**

I envision this as part of a feedback system for a larger Web application. This particular document and its handling page will constitute a couple of steps in the feedback process. Here the user will enter their name then choose how they want to be contacted.

**4.** Complete the form with a comments box, then close the form, and the HTML document.

```
Comments <TEXTAREA NAME="Comments"
→ ROWS=5 COLS=40></TEXTAREA><BR>
<INPUT TYPE=SUBMIT NAME="SUBMIT"
→ VALUE="Submit!">
</FORM></BODY></HTML>
```

**5.** Save your form as `contact.html` and upload it to your server.

**6.** Now you'll need to create the page which will process one part of the `contact.html` page.

**7.** Create a new PHP document in your text editor.

**8.** Code the standard HTML header (**Script 6.8**).

```
<HTML><HEAD><TITLE>Contact
→ Information Request</TITLE><BODY>
```

**9.** Create an HTML form and then open the PHP section.

```
<FORM ACTION="HandleContact2.php"
→ METHOD=POST><?php
```

In order to retrieve more information from the user and to gather more, you'll use another form.

**10.** Store the values retrieved from `contact.html` in HIDDEN form elements.

```
print ("<INPUT TYPE=HIDDEN
→ NAME=\"FirstName\"
→ VALUE=\"$FirstName\">\n");
print ("<INPUT TYPE=HIDDEN
→ NAME=\"LastName\"
```

**Script 6.8** The *switch* conditional in this script uses the value of $ContactHow to determine what to request from the user: telephone number, fax number, E-mail address, or mailing address. HIDDEN input types are also utilized to pass along other existing values.

```
1   <HTML>
2   <HEAD>
3   <TITLE>Contact Information Request</TITLE>
4   <BODY>
5   <FORM ACTION="HandleContact2.php"
    METHOD=POST>
6   <?php
7   // Pass on the received values using
    HIDDEN INPUT types.
8   print ("<INPUT TYPE=HIDDEN
    NAME=\"FirstName\"
    VALUE=\"$FirstName\">\n");
9   print ("<INPUT TYPE=HIDDEN
    NAME=\"LastName\"
    VALUE=\"$LastName\">\n");
10  print ("<INPUT TYPE=HIDDEN
    NAME=\"Comments\"
    VALUE=\"$Comments\">\n");
11  print ("<INPUT TYPE=HIDDEN
    NAME=\"ContactHow\"
    VALUE=\"$ContactHow\">\n");
12
13  switch ($ContactHow) {
14      case "Telephone":
15          print("<B>Please enter a daytime
            phone number where you can be
            reached:</B><BR>\n");
16          print ("<INPUT TYPE=TEXT NAME=
            \"Telephone\" SIZE=10><BR>v");
17          print ("<INPUT TYPE=SUBMIT NAME=
            SUBMIT VALUE=\"Continue\">\n");
18          break;
19      case "Mail":
20          print("<B>Please enter your
            complete mailing address:
            </B><BR>\n");
21          print ("<TEXTAREA
            NAME=\"MailAddress\" ROWS=5
            COLS=40></TEXTAREA><BR>\n");
22          print ("<INPUT TYPE=SUBMIT NAME=
            SUBMIT VALUE=\"Continue\">\n");
23          break;
24      case "E-Mail":
```

*Code continues on next page*

**Script 6.8** *continued*

```
                        script
25      print("<B>Please enter your
        E-Mail address:</B><BR>\n");

26      print ("<INPUT TYPE=TEXT NAME=
        \"E-Mail\" SIZE=40><BR>\n");

27      print ("<INPUT TYPE=SUBMIT NAME=
        SUBMIT VALUE=\"Continue\">\n");

28      break;

29  case "Fax":

30      print("<B>Please enter your Fax
        number:</B><BR>\n");

31      print ("<INPUT TYPE=TEXT NAME=
        \"Fax\" SIZE=10><BR>\n");

32      print ("<INPUT TYPE=SUBMIT NAME=
        SUBMIT VALUE=\"Continue\">\n");

33      break;

34  default:

35      print("<B>Please go back and
        select how you would prefer to
        be contacted!</B><BR>\n");

36      break;

37  }

38  ?>

39  </FORM>

40  </BODY>

41  </HTML>
```

```
→ VALUE=\"$LastName\">\n");
print ("<INPUT TYPE=HIDDEN
→ NAME=\"Comments\"
→ VALUE=\"$Comments\">\n");
print ("<INPUT TYPE=HIDDEN
→ NAME=\"ContactHow\"
→ VALUE=\"$ContactHow\">\n");
```

I mentioned in Chapter 3, *HTML Forms and PHP*, that you could pass along variable information using the HIDDEN INPUT type. Here the PHP will place all of the data collected from contact.html into hidden elements so that the data continues to be passed along to the next page—HandleContact2.php.

**11.** Create a switch conditional that reacts differently based upon which contact option the user selected in contact.html.

```
switch ($ContactHow) {
case "Telephone":
print("<B>Please enter a daytime
→ phone number where you can be
→ reached:</B><BR>\n");
print ("<INPUT TYPE=TEXT NAME=
→ \"Telephone\" SIZE=10><BR>");
print ("<INPUT TYPE=SUBMIT NAME=
→ SUBMIT VALUE=\"Continue\">\n");
break;
case "Mail":
print("<B>Please enter your complete
→ mailing address:</B><BR>\n");
print ("<TEXTAREA NAME=
→ \"MailAddress\" ROWS=5 COLS=40>
→ </TEXTAREA><BR>\n");
print ("<INPUT TYPE=SUBMIT NAME=
→ SUBMIT VALUE=\"Continue\">\n");
break;
case "E-Mail":
print("<B>Please enter your E-Mail
→ address:</B><BR>\n");
print ("<INPUT TYPE=TEXT NAME=
→ \"E-Mail\" SIZE=40><BR>\n");
```

*continues on next page*

```
print ("<INPUT TYPE=SUBMIT NAME=
→ SUBMIT VALUE=\"Continue\">\n");
break;
case "Fax":
print("<B>Please enter your Fax
→ number:</B><BR>\n");
print ("<INPUT TYPE=TEXT NAME=
→ \"Fax\" SIZE=10><BR>\n");
print ("<INPUT TYPE=SUBMIT NAME=
→ SUBMIT VALUE=\"Continue\">\n");
break;
default:
print("<B>Please go back and select
→ how you would prefer to be
→ contacted!</B><BR>\n");
break;
}
```

This switch conditional is set up to print out different things depending upon the value of $ContactHow. In short, if they want to be telephoned, the page will request a phone number, if they prefer E-mail, an e-mail address is requested, and so forth. If $ContactHow has no value, the default case will be triggered and a message requesting they return to the `contact.html` page to select a contact method is printed.

12. Close the PHP section, then the form, and the HTML page.

    `?></FORM></BODY></HTML>`

13. Save your script as `HandleContact.php`, upload it to your server (in the same directory as `contact.html`) and test both pages in your Web browser (**Figures 6.10**, **6.11**, **6.12**, **6.13**, and **6.14**).

**Figure 6.10** Here is the HTML form created by `contact.html`. It constitutes step one of a feedback system.

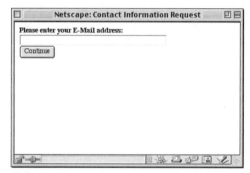

**Figure 6.11** Because I requested that I be contacted via E-mail (see Figure 6.10), `HandleContact.php` will now request an E-mail address and display a TEXT input type where I can enter that information.

**Figure 6.12** This is the source of what you see in Figure 6.11. Notice that the HIDDEN fields are storing the information already gathered so that too will be passed on to `HandleContact2.php`.

THE SWITCH CONDITIONAL

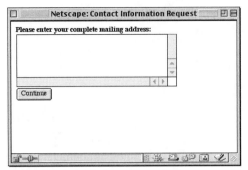

**Figure 6.13** If I decided that I wanted to be contacted by standard mail, HandleContact.php would request a mailing address and this time provide a large TEXTAREA where I can enter that information.

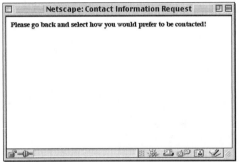

**Figure 6.14** If the user does not select a preference for how they want to be contacted, they will see this message and not be allowed to continue on.

## ✔ Tips

■ I have not created a HandleContact2.php page which handles the results of this HandleContact.php page (as I mentioned, I was only going to develop a couple of steps in a larger process). If you want to make sure that HandleContact.php works as it should, write a simple PHP script that prints out all the array values.

■ A default case is not required in your *switch* conditional (you could set it up so that if the value is not explicitly met by one of the cases, nothing happens), but if used, it must be listed as the last case.

■ If you are using a string in your *switch* conditional, keep in mind that it is case-sensitive, meaning that "Value" will not match a string "value".

# The While Loop

As I suggested earlier in this chapter, loops are used to execute a section of code repeatedly. You may want to create a pull-down menu consisting of the days of the month (print the numbers 1 through 31). You might want to print out each value of an array. For either of these cases, and for many more, you'll want to use a loop (I'll demonstrate the latter example in the next chapter).

The first of the two types of loops that exist in PHP—the *while* loop—is designed to continue working as long as the condition you establish is TRUE. It will check the value of the condition before each iteration. Once the condition becomes FALSE, the *while* loop is exited.

```
while (condition) {
    statement(s);
}
```

To demonstrate the *while* loop, you'll create a script that dynamically generates a date pull-down menu (month, day, year) for an HTML form. While the form itself won't do anything as is, you'll be able to see how you can use PHP to improve upon and expedite the creation of a standard HTML form element.

## To use *while*:

1. Create a new PHP document in your text editor. Type (**Script 6.9**):

   ```
   <HTML><HEAD><TITLE>Select Menu
   → </TITLE><BODY><?php
   ```

2. Establish the current year using the date() function.

   ```
   $Year = date ("Y");
   ```

   By feeding the date() function the value "Y", it will return the current year. You'll use the value to print out this year, plus the next ten, in the select menu. This way, the form will not need to be changed from year to year.

**Script 6.9** The two *while* loops will quickly print out all the requisite HTML to generate two of the pull-down menus (see **Figure 6.16**). By using the date() function to base the year loop on the current year, this script will never be outdated.

```
script
1   <HTML>
2   <HEAD>
3   <TITLE>Select Menu</TITLE>
4   <BODY>
5   <?php
6   $Year = date ("Y");
7   // Create the form.
8   print ("<FORM ACTION=\"$PHP_SELF\"
    METHOD=POST>\n");
9   // Create the month pull-down menu.
10  print ("Select a month:<BR>\n");
11  print ("<SELECT NAME=Month><OPTION>
    Choose One</OPTION>\n");
12  print ("<OPTION VALUE=January>January
    </OPTION>\n");
13  print ("<OPTION VALUE=February>February
    </OPTION>\n");
14  print ("<OPTION VALUE=March>March
    </OPTION>\n");
15  print ("<OPTION VALUE=April>April
    </OPTION>\n");
16  print ("<OPTION VALUE=May>May
    </OPTION>\n");
17  print ("<OPTION VALUE=June>June
    </OPTION>\n");
18  print ("<OPTION VALUE=July>July
    /OPTION>\n");
19  print ("<OPTION VALUE=August>August
    </OPTION>\n");
20  print ("<OPTION VALUE=September>September
    </OPTION>\n");
21  print ("<OPTION VALUE=October>October
    </OPTION>\n");
22  print ("<OPTION VALUE=November>November
    </OPTION>\n");
23  print ("<OPTION VALUE=December>December
    </OPTION>\n");
24  print ("</SELECT>\n");
25  // Create the day pull-down menu.
26  print ("<P>Select a day:<BR>\n");
27  print ("<SELECT NAME=Day><OPTION>Choose
    One</OPTION>\n");
28  $Day = 1;
```

*Code continues on next page*

THE WHILE LOOP

**Script 6.9** *continued*

```
            script
29  while ($Day <= 31) {
30      print ("<OPTION VALUE=$Day>$Day
        </OPTION>\n");
31      $Day++;
32  }
33  print ("</SELECT>\n");
34  // Create the year pull-down menu.
35  print ("<P>Select a year:<BR>\n");
36  print ("<SELECT NAME=Year><OPTION>
        Choose One</OPTION>\n");
37  $EndYear = $Year + 10;
38  while ($Year <= $EndYear ) {
39      print ("<OPTION VALUE=$Year>$Year
        </OPTION>\n");
40      $Year++;
41  }
42  print ("</SELECT>\n");
43  print ("<P><INPUT TYPE=SUBMIT NAME=
        SUBMIT VALUE=\"Go!\"></FORM>\n");
44  ?>
45  </BODY>
46  </HTML>
```

**3.** Create an HTML form that includes a pull-down menu for every month.

```
print ("<FORM ACTION=\"$PHP_SELF\"
→ METHOD=POST>\n");
print ("Select a month:<BR>\n");
print ("<SELECT NAME=Month>
→ <OPTION>Choose One</OPTION>\n");
print ("<OPTION VALUE=January>
→ January</OPTION>\n");
print ("<OPTION VALUE=February>
→ February</OPTION>\n");
print ("<OPTION VALUE=March>March
→ </OPTION>\n");
print ("<OPTION VALUE=April>April
→ </OPTION>\n");
print ("<OPTION VALUE=May>May
→ </OPTION>\n");
print ("<OPTION VALUE=June>June
→ </OPTION>\n");
print ("<OPTION VALUE=July>July
→ </OPTION>\n");
print ("<OPTION VALUE=August>August
→ </OPTION>\n");
print ("<OPTION VALUE=September>
→ September</OPTION>\n");
print ("<OPTION VALUE=October>
→ October</OPTION>\n");
print ("<OPTION VALUE=November>
→ November</OPTION>\n");
print ("<OPTION VALUE=December>
→ December</OPTION>\n");
print ("</SELECT>\n");
```

**4.** Use a while loop to create the pull-down menu for the days.

```
print ("<P>Select a day:<BR>\n");
print ("<SELECT NAME=Day><OPTION>
→ Choose One</OPTION>\n");
$Day = 1;
while ($Day <= 31) {
    print ("<OPTION VALUE=$Day>$Day
    → </OPTION>\n");
    $Day++;
}
print ("</SELECT>\n");
```

*continues on next page*

The first step taken is to set the value of $Day to 1. This must be done before the loop is called. The loop itself will then see if $Day is less than or equal to 31. If it is, it will print the value of $Day as an option in the select menu and then increase the value of $Day by 1. This process will continue until $Day is equal to 32, at which point PHP will stop the loop and continue through the script. Using a loop to generate the requisite HTML is much easier than printing out 31 lines of code one at a time.

**5.** Use another while loop to create the year pull-down menu.

```
print ("<P>Select a year:<BR>\n");
print ("<SELECT NAME=Year><OPTION>
→ Choose One</OPTION>\n");
$EndYear = $Year + 10;
while ($Year <= $EndYear ) {
    print ("<OPTION VALUE=$Year>
    → $Year</OPTION>\n");
    $Year++;
}
print ("</SELECT>\n");
```

The listed years in the pull-down menu will be generated based upon the current year, plus the next ten. The current year was assigned earlier to the $Year variable. The last year then, $EndYear, is equal to $Year plus 10 (this value could easily be changed to print out 5 or 15 years). The loop states that as long as the $Year value is less than or equal to the $EndYear value, it should print out the $Year value and then increment the value by one.

**6.** Create a submit button, close the form, the PHP, and the HTML.

```
print ("<P><INPUT TYPE=SUBMIT NAME=
→ SUBMIT VALUE=\"Go!\"></FORM>\n");
?></BODY></HTML>
```

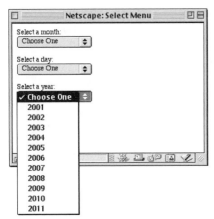

**Figure 6.15** The select.php page generates three pull-down menus allowing the user to choose a month, day, and year. The code could easily be pasted within a larger HTML form any time these menus are needed.

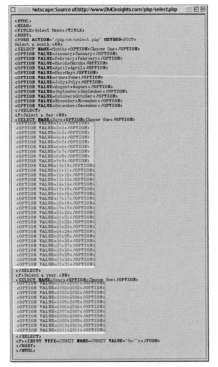

**Figure 6.16** This is the source code for the form pictured in **Figure 6.15**. Notice how a dozen lines from **Script 6.9** (containing two *while* loops) generated 40-50 lines of HTML (the Day and Year select menus).

Although this page is designed to be part of a larger HTML form and therefore doesn't do anything in its own right, it's best to be consistent so I've added the submit button regardless.

**7.** Save your page as `select.php`, upload it to the server, and test it in your Web browser (**Figures 6.15** and **6.16**).

## ✔ Tips

■ You also have the option of using the *do...while* loop which will guarantee that the statements are executed at least once, which is not necessarily true of the *while* loop.

```
do {
    statement(s);
} while (condition);
```

■ Be sure to think twice about what elements need to be included within a loop and which ought to be excluded. Failure to increase the value of $Day or $Year within a loop would create an endless loop (as, for example, $Day would always be less than or equal to 31). Similarly, inclusion of the <SELECT> tags within the loop will create multiple pull-down menus.

■ Just as the *if* conditional can be written on one line if you only have one statement, the same can be done with the *while* loop, although, again, I would recommend against it.

# The For Loop

The *for* loop is designed to perform the specific statements for a determined number of iterations (unlike *while*, which runs until the condition is FALSE—similar, but significantly different, concepts). You normally use a dummy variable in the loop for this purpose. The *for* loop's syntax is more complicated than the *while* loop and although the uses of these loops can easily overlap, you'll find one more suited to some tasks than the other.

```
for (initial expression; condition;
→ closing expression) {
    statement(s);
}
```

The initial expression will be executed once, the very first time the loop is called. Then the condition is used to determine whether or not to execute the statements. Finally, the closing expression will be executed after each time that the condition is found to be TRUE, but only after the statements are executed. Thus, to print out each value in an array, you would code:

```
for ($n = 0; $n < count($Array); $n++) {
    print ("$Array[$n]<BR>\n");
}
```

It may help your comprehension of the *for* loop syntax if I were to rewrite the $Day *while* loop from Script 6.9 as a *for* loop. The original code was:

```
$Day = 1;
while ($Day <= 31) {
    print ("<OPTION VALUE=$Day>$Day
    → </OPTION>\n");
    $Day++;
}
```

**Script 6.10** This short script is a simple use of the *for* loop, reiterating through a process 1000 times.

```
1   <HTML>
2   <HEAD>
3   <TITLE>Prime Numbers</TITLE>
4   <BODY>
5   <?php
6   // Change this value if you want to print
    more primes.
7   for ($n = 1; $n <= 1000; $n++) {
8       if ( ($n == 1) OR ($n == 2) OR
        ($n == 3) OR ($n == 5)) {
9           print("$n<BR>\n");
10      } elseif (($n % 2 != 0) AND
        ($n % 3 != 0) AND ($n % 5 != 0)) {
11          print("$n<BR>\n");
12      } // Close the IF.
13  } // Close the FOR.
14  ?>
15  </BODY>
16  </HTML>
```

First the value of $Day was set, then the *while* loop stated the conditional ($Day <= 31). Finally, if TRUE, the print() statement was executed and $Day was incremented. As a *for* loop, that same code would look like this:

```
for ($Day = 1; $Day <= 31; $Day++) {
    print ("<OPTION
VALUE=$Day>$Day</OPTION>\n");
}
```

You'll use the *for* loop to print out all the prime numbers between 1 and 1000, a common programming example.

## To write a *for* loop:

1. Create a new PHP document in your text editor. Type (**Script 6.10**):

   ```
   <HTML><HEAD><TITLE>Prime Numbers
   → </TITLE><BODY><?php
   ```

2. Begin the *for* loop.

   ```
   for ($n = 1; $n <= 1000; $n++) {
   ```

   Using the syntax of the *for* loop, $n is established as a dummy variable. It is immediately set to 1, then the loop will check to see if $n is less than or equal to 1000. In other words, this loop will be executed 1000 times. Finally, if the condition of the loop ($n <= 1000) is TRUE, the *statement(s)* will be executed, $n will be incremented, and the process will start again.

3. Write the contents (i.e., the *statement(s)* section) for the loop.

   ```
   if ( ($n == 1) OR ($n == 2) OR
   → ($n == 3) OR ($n == 5)) {
       print("$n<BR>\n");
   } elseif (($n % 2 != 0) AND ($n
   → % 3 != 0) AND ($n % 5 != 0)) {
       print("$n<BR>\n");
   }
   ```

   *continues on next page*

A number is prime, if it is not cleanly divisible by any numbers other than itself and 1. In other words, if you divide the number by any other number than the number itself and 1, and you always get a remainder, then the number is prime. For example, 4 can be divided cleanly by 2 so it is not prime whereas 7 cannot be cleanly divided by 2, 3, or 5, which are the basis for establishing prime. Offhand, you know that 1, 2, 3, and 5 are primes, so if $n is equal to any of these, it will be printed automatically. Notice that I used the logical OR operator because if any of those conditions are TRUE, you'll want to print out $n.

If $n is not equal to 1, 2, 3, or 5, you'll have to check it for prime. To do so, you see if the division of $n by 2, 3, or 5 leaves a remainder, calculated using the modulus operator (%). Modulus simply returns the remainder of a division and while it's not the most useful operator, it's invaluable here. So 4 modulus 2 is 0 and 7 modulus 5 is .4 (four-tenths). If a non-zero remainder is returned when dividing $n by 2, 3, and 5, the number is a prime and should be printed. Notice that I used the logical AND operator because if any of those conditions are FALSE, the number is not prime.

4. Close the for loop, the PHP, and the HTML.
```
}
?>
</BODY>
</HTML>
```

5. Save the script as `primes.php`, upload it to your server, and test in your Web browser (**Figure 6.17**).

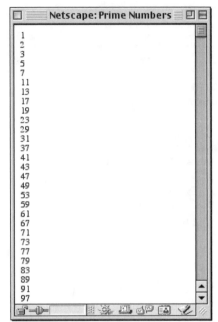

**Figure 6.17** This is only the listing of the primes through 100, automatically calculated and spit out using the *for* loop. Here the 16 lines of Script 6.10 created a total of approximately 300 lines in the HTML window.

## ✔ Tip

■ Although there is a fair amount of overlap as to when the two major loop constructs, *while* and *for*, can be used, you will discover as you program that sometimes one is more logical than the other. The *while* loop is frequently used in the retrieval of data from a database (see Chapter 11, *Databases*) and the *for* loop is a standard for working with arrays (as you'll discover in Chapter 7, *Using Arrays*).

# USING ARRAYS

The last type of variable I will discuss in this text is arrays. (Objects are beyond the scope this book, although once you are comfortable with PHP, you'll likely want to learn how to use them.)

Arrays constitute a complicated but very useful notion: they are a collection of multiple values assembled into one overriding variable. An array can consist of numbers and/or strings (and/or other arrays), which allows this one variable to hold exponentially more information than a simple string or number ever could. For example, if you wanted to create a grocery list using strings, your code would look something like:

```
$Item1 = "apples";
$Item2 = "bananas";
$Item3 = "oranges";
```

For each added item, you would need to create a new string. This is cumbersome and it makes it difficult to refer back to the entire list or any specific value later in your code. You can greatly simplify matters by placing your entire list into one array (say, $Items), which contains everything you need to put on that list. As an array, your list can be augmented, sorted, searched, and so forth. With this context in mind, let's look into the syntax of arrays.

The other variable types you've dealt with—numbers and strings—have a variable name and a corresponding value (e.g., $FirstName which could be equal to "Larry"). Arrays also have a name, derived using the same conventions (the dollar sign followed by a letter or underscore, followed by any combination of letters, numbers, and the underscore), but arrays differ in that they contain what I will refer to as multiple elements. Each element has its own index or key (the two words can be used interchangeably), which is used to access that element's value. The terms index and key refer to a number or word which is used as a reference point to the values. An array can have either a number or a string as its key, depending upon how you set it up.

You may find it easiest to think of an array like a two-column table. The first column would be the index (acting like a row number or name) and the second column would be the value for that row. Using the index, you can determine the value stored at a particularly point in the table (**Figures 7.1** and **7.2**).

Generally, the format for an array looks the same as that of any other variable, except that it will include a key in square brackets ([]) when referring to particular elements. So $Array refers to the array as a whole but $Array[0] points to the first element in the array. (Characters within a string are indexed beginning at zero, as explained in Chapter 5, *Using Strings*. The same is true when indexing the elements of an array.)

In this chapter, I'll discuss the fundamentals of handling arrays. I'll introduce a few of the key concepts and you'll learn how to incorporate them into your existing scripts.

| Index or Key | Value |
|---|---|
| 1 | Getting Started with PHP |
| 2 | Variables |
| 3 | HTML Forms and PHP |
| 4 | Using Numbers |
| 5 | Using Strings |
| 6 | Control Structures |
| 7 | Using Arrays |

**Figure 7.1** A spreadsheet table is a good metaphor for what an array is. Here the array which stores chapter titles uses numbers as its index (or key).

| Index or Key | Value |
|---|---|
| Chapter_1 | Getting Started with PHP |
| Chapter_2 | Variables |
| Chapter_3 | HTML Forms and PHP |
| Chapter_4 | Using Numbers |
| Chapter_5 | Using Strings |
| Chapter_6 | Control Structures |
| Chapter_7 | Using Arrays |

**Figure 7.2** In this table version of the array, the index (or key) are words, not numbers.

**Script 7.1** This is another example where adding white space to the page in order to clarify your programming (when initializing the array) won't have any adverse affects and is therefore recommended.

```
                      script
1   <HTML>
2   <HEAD>
3   <TITLE>Using Arrays</TITLE>
4   <BODY>
5   <?php
6   $Soups = array(
7   "Monday"=>"Clam Chowder", "Tuesday"=>
    "White Chicken Chili",
8   "Wednesday"=>"Vegetarian"
9   );
10  print ("$Soups<P>\n");
11  ?>
12  </BODY>
13  </HTML>
```

# Creating an Array

The formal method of creating an array is to use `array()`, the syntax of which is:

```
$List = array ("apples", "bananas",
→ "oranges");
```

In this example—where you have not specified an index for the elements—the first item, *apples*, will automatically be indexed at 0, the second at 1, and the third at 2. You can assign the index when using `array()` as follows:

```
$List = array (1=>"apples",
→ 2=>"bananas", 3=>"oranges");
```

The index value you specify does not have to be a number, you could use words as well. This technique of indexing is very practical for making more meaningful lists. As an example, you could create an array which records the soup of the day for each day of the week.

### To create an array:

1. Create a new PHP document in your text editor.

2. Write the standard HTML header (**Script 7.1**).
   ```
   <HTML><HEAD><TITLE>Using Arrays
   → </TITLE><BODY>
   ```

3. Begin the PHP section of the script and use the `array()` function to create an array.
   ```
   <?php
   $Soups = array(
   "Monday"=>"Clam Chowder",
   "Tuesday"=>"White Chicken Chili",
   "Wednesday"=>"Vegetarian"
   );
   ```
   This is the proper format for initializing (creating and assigning a value to) an array in PHP, using strings as the indices.

*continues on next page*

**4.** Print the array to the Web browser.

```
print ("$Soups<P>\n");
```

**5.** Close the PHP and the HTML.

```
?></BODY></HTML>
```

**6.** Save your document as `soups.php`, upload it to your server, and test in your Web browser (**Figure 7.3**).

### ✔ Tip

- The practice of beginning any index at zero is standard in PHP and most other programming languages. As unnatural as it may seem, it's here to stay, so you have two possible coping techniques. First, manually start all of your arrays indexed at the position *1*. Second, unlearn a life-time of counting from one. You can decide which is easier but most programmers just get used to this odd construct.

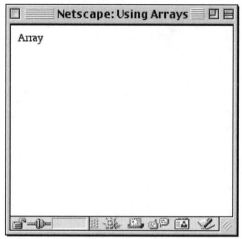

**Figure 7.3** Because an array is structured differently than other variable types, a request to print an array will result in the word *array* being printed. While printing that is not as useful as printing out the individual values of the array (as you'll learn to do), it does confirm for you that the array was successfully created.

CREATING AN ARRAY

# Adding Items to an Array

In PHP, once an array exists, you can add extra elements to your array by directly assigning them with the assignment operator (the equal sign), similar to how you assign a value to a string or a number. When doing so, you can either specify the key of the added element or not, but in either case, you must refer to the array with the square brackets. To add two items to the $List list, you would write:

```
$List[] = "pears";
$List[] = "tomatoes";
```

If you do not specify the key, each element will be appended to the existing array, indexed with the next logical number. Assuming that this is the same array from the previous section, where it was indexed at *1*, *2*, and *3*, *pears* is now located at *4* and *tomatoes* at *5*.

If you do specify the index, the value will be assigned at that location and any existing value already indexed at that point will be overwritten, like so:

```
$List[3] = "pears";
$List[4] = "tomatoes";
```

Now, the value of the element in the fourth position of the array is *tomatoes* and no element of $List is equal to *oranges*. With this in mind, I would caution that unless you intend to overwrite any existing data, you'll be better off not including a specific key when adding values to your arrays. (However, if the array uses strings for indices, you'll want to specify keys so that values do not get lost.)

To test this process, you'll rewrite `soups.php` to add more elements to the array. In order to see the difference adding more elements makes, you'll print out how many elements were in the array before and after the new additions.

*continues on next page*

ADDING ITEMS TO AN ARRAY

Just as you can find the length of a string—how many characters it contains—using `strlen()`, you can also determine the number of elements in an array, using `count()`.

```
$HowMany = count($Array);
```

## To add elements to an array:

1. Open `soups.php` in your text editor, if it is not already.

2. After the array is initialized, using `array()`, add (**Script 7.2**):

   ```
   $HowMany = count($Soups);
   print ("The array contains $HowMany
    → elements.<P>\n");
   ```

   The `count()` function will determine how many elements are in $Soups. By assigning that value to a variable, you'll be able to easily print it out.

3. Add three more elements to the array.

   ```
   $Soups["Thursday"] = "Chicken Noodle";
   $Soups["Friday"] = "Tomato";
   $Soups["Saturday"] = "Cream of
    → Broccoli";
   ```

4. Recount how many elements are in the array and print this value.

   ```
   $HowManyNow = count($Soups);
   print ("The array now contains
    → $HowManyNow elements.<P>\n");
   ```

5. Save your script, upload it to your server, and test in your Web browser (**Figure 7.4**).

New to PHP 4.0 is a function that allows you to append one array onto another. Think of it as concatenation for arrays. The function, `array_merge()`, works like so:

```
$NewArray = array_merge ($OneArray,
 → $TwoArray);
```

You can rewrite the `soups.php` page using this new function if you are working with a server that has PHP 4.0.

**Script 7.2** You can directly add elements to an array one at a time by assigning each element a value with the assignment operator. The count() function will help you keep track of how many elements the array contains.

```
script
1   <HTML>
2   <HEAD>
3   <TITLE>Using Arrays</TITLE>
4   <BODY>
5   <?php
6   $Soups = array(
7   "Monday"=>"Clam Chowder", "Tuesday"=>
    "White Chicken Chili",
8   "Wednesday"=>"Vegetarian"
9   );
10  $HowMany = count($Soups);
11  print ("The array contains $HowMany
    elements.<P>\n");
12  $Soups["Thursday"] = "Chicken Noodle";
13  $Soups["Friday"] = "Tomato";
14  $Soups["Saturday"] = "Cream of Broccoli";
15  $HowManyNow = count($Soups);
16  print ("The array now contains
    $HowManyNow elements.<P>\n");
17  ?>
18  </BODY>
19  </HTML>
```

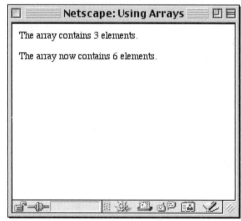

**Figure 7.4** A direct way to insure that the new elements were successfully added to the array is to count the number of elements before and after the additions were made.

**Script 7.3** The `array_merge()` function is new to PHP 4. It's just one of several new array functions designed to save the programmer time.

```
                      script
1    <HTML>
2    <HEAD>
3    <TITLE>Using Arrays</TITLE>
4    <BODY>
5    <?php
6    $Soups = array(
7    "Monday"=>"Clam Chowder", "Tuesday"=>
     "White Chicken Chili",
8    "Wednesday"=>"Vegetarian"
9    );
10   $HowMany = count($Soups);
11   print ("The \$Soups array contains
     $HowMany elements.<P>\n");
12   $Soups2 = array(
13   "Thursday"=>"Chicken Noodle",
14   "Friday"=>"Tomato",
15   "Saturday"=>"Cream of Broccoli"
16   );
17   $HowMany2 = count($Soups2);
18   print ("The \$Soups2 array contains
     $HowMany2 elements.<P>\n");
19   $TheSoups = array_merge ($Soups, $Soups2);
20   $HowMany3 = count($TheSoups);
21   print ("The \$TheSoups array contains
     $HowMany3 elements.<P>\n");
22   ?>
23   </BODY>
24   </HTML>
```

## To merge two arrays:

1. Open `soups.php` in your text editor, if it is not already.

2. After the $Soups array is initialized, count and print the number of elements it contains (**Script 7.3**):

   ```
   $HowMany = count($Soups);
   print ("The \$Soups array contains
   → $HowMany elements.<P>\n");
   ```

3. Create a second array, then count and print the number of elements it contains.

   ```
   $Soups2 = array(
   → "Thursday"=>"Chicken Noodle",
   → "Friday"=>"Tomato",
   → "Saturday"=>"Cream of Broccoli"
   );
   $HowMany2 = count($Soups2);
   print ("The \$Soups2 array contains
   → $HowMany2 elements.<P>\n");
   ```

4. Merge the two arrays into one new array.

   ```
   $TheSoups = array_merge ($Soups,
   → $Soups2);
   ```

   Make sure you put the arrays in this order ($Soups then $Soups2) so that the Thursday through Saturday elements will be appended to the Monday through Wednesday elements and not the other way around.

   *continues on next page*

**101**

5. Count and print the number of elements in the newly created array.

```
$HowMany3 = count($TheSoups);
print ("The \$TheSoups array contains
→ $HowMany3 elements.<P>\n");
?>
```

6. Close the PHP and the HTML document.

7. Save the file, upload it to your server, and test in your Web browser (**Figure 7.5**).

## ✔ Tips

■ Be very careful when directly adding elements to an array. There's a correct way to do it (`$Array[] = "Add This";` or `$Array[1] = "Add This";`) and an incorrect way (`$Array = "Add This";`). Forgetting to use the brackets will result in the added value replacing the entire existing array and you will be left with a simple string or number.

■ PHP 4 includes a slew of new functions for handling arrays not all of which are covered here. The PHP manual, available through the PHP home page, discusses them all. Be careful not to use a PHP 4 specific function if your server is running PHP 3.

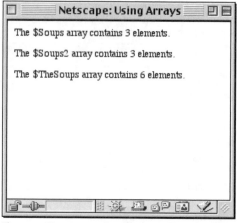

**Figure 7.5** The count() function is used here to insure that all of the elements of both arrays are present in the newly created array.

# Accessing Array Elements

Regardless of how you establish your array, there is only one way to retrieve a specific element (or value) from it, and that is to refer to its index. One option for handling arrays is to assign a specific element's value to a separate variable using the assignment operator:

```
$Total = $Array[1];
```

By doing this you can preserve the original value within the array and still manipulate it separately as a variable.

However, you can also refer to a specific element's value directly and use it as you would a string in most circumstances:

```
print ("The total of your order comes
→ to $Array[Total]");
```

When printing from an array, you must omit the double quotation marks that you would normally use around the index as they conflict with the print() statement itself. This line will cause you problems:

```
print ("The total of your order comes
→ to $Array["Total"]");
```

Here's an example where using quotation marks will not be problematic:

```
$Array["Name"] = trim($Array["Name"]);
```

Ironically, the feature which makes arrays so useful—being able to store multiple values within one variable—also gives it a limitation that the other variable types do not have, namely, that you must know the keys of the array in order to access its elements. If the array was set using strings, such as the $Soups array, referring to $Soups[1] will point to nothing. For that matter, since variables are case-sensitive, $Soups["monday"] will be worthless as you indexed Clam Chowder at $Soups["Monday"].

*continues on next page*

Fortunately, the fastest and easiest way to access all the values of an array is to use a loop, in conjunction with the each() function. This function creates an array of the index and values of the array. Within a *for* loop, each() can be repeated as many times as there are array elements until every value has been returned.

```
for ($n = 0; $n < count($Array); $n++) {
    $Line = each ($Array);
    print ("Key is equal to
$Line[key].<BR>Value is equal to
→ $Line[value].");
}
```

In this example the each() function will create an array called $Line that contains the key and value for the $Array at its current position. You can think of the array as having an internal pointer. Upon first using the each() function, the pointer is at $Array's first element. The each() function will retrieve those values and assign them to $Line[key] (as well as $Line[0]) and $Line[value] (also $Line[1]), then move the pointer ahead one element. The second time each() is called it will retrieve the second set of values and the process will be repeated until there are no more elements in the array and the loop is exited.

You can now rewrite the soups.php script to use this knowledge. Instead of merely being able to print out how many elements are in an array (as you've done to this point), you will now be able to access the actual values.

## To print the values of any array:

**1.** Create a new PHP document in your text editor.

**2.** Write the standard HTML header (**Script 7.4**).

```
<HTML><HEAD><TITLE>Using Arrays
→ </TITLE><BODY>
```

**Script 7.4** A loop is the most common way to access every element in an array. In this script, the each() function is used to determine the array's keys and values, which are then printed to the Web browser.

```
1   <HTML>
2   <HEAD>
3   <TITLE>Using Arrays</TITLE>
4   <BODY>
5   <?php
6   $Soups = array(
7       "Monday"=>"Clam Chowder",
8       "Tuesday"=>"White Chicken Chili",
9       "Wednesday"=>"Vegetarian",
10      "Thursday"=>"Chicken Noodle",
11      "Friday"=>"Tomato",
12      "Saturday"=>"Cream of Broccoli"
13  );
14  for ($n = 0; $n < count($Soups); $n++) {
15      $Line = each ($Soups);
16      print ("$Line[key]'s soup is
        $Line[value].<P>\n");
17  }
18  ?>
19  </BODY>
20  </HTML>
```

**Figure 7.6** The execution of the loop for every element in the array generates this page. The each() function allows the PHP to access each key and value without prior knowledge of what they were.

**3.** Start the PHP section of the page and initialize the $Soups array.

```php
<?php
$Soups = array(
"Monday"=>"Clam Chowder",
"Tuesday"=>"White Chicken Chili",
"Wednesday"=>"Vegetarian",
"Thursday"=>"Chicken Noodle",
"Friday"=>"Tomato",
"Saturday"=>"Cream of Broccoli"
);
```

**4.** Begin a *for* loop to access every element in the array.

```php
for ($n = 0; $n < count($Soups);
→ $n++) {
```

This *for* loop assigns 0 to the dummy variable $n. It will then check to see if $n is less than the number of items in the array. If so it will execute the loop then increment the $n variable.

**5.** Use the each() function to retrieve the keys and values, then print them out.

```php
$Line = each ($Soups);
print ("$Line[key]'s soup is
→ $Line[value].<P>\n");
```

The loop will assign the keys and values of the array to the $Line array via the each() function. It will then print out the key and the value.

**6.** Close the loop, the PHP and the HTML page.

```php
}?></BODY></HTML>
```

**7.** Save the page as soups.php, upload to your server, and test in your Web browser (**Figure 7.6**).

## ✔ Tip

■ An alternative is to set a variable to the value of count($Array) and use that in your loop. This way, the PHP does not have to recount the array on each iteration.

# Sorting Arrays

PHP supports a variety of ways to sort an array (when I say sort, I am referring to an alphabetical sort if it is a string, and a numerical sort if it is a number). When sorting an array, you must keep in mind that an array consists of several pairs of keys and values. Thus, an array can be sorted based upon the values or the keys. Also, you can sort the values and keep the corresponding keys matched up or sort the values and have them receive new keys.

To sort the values, without regard to the keys, you use **sort()**. To sort these values (again without regard to the keys), in reverse order, you use **rsort()**. The syntax for every sorting function is like this:

```
function($Array);
```
So, **sort()** and **rsort()** are simply:
```
sort($Array);
rsort($Array);
```

To sort the values, while maintaining the correlation between the value and its key, you use **asort()**. To sort them in reverse, while maintaining the key correlation, you use **arsort()**.

To sort by the keys, while still maintaining the correlation between the key and its value, you use **ksort()**. Conversely, **krsort()** will sort the keys in reverse.

Last, **shuffle()** randomly reorganizes the order of an array.

As an example of sorting arrays, you'll create a list of students and the grades they received on a test, then sort this list first by grade then by name.

## To sort an array:

1. Open your text editor and create a new PHP document.

2. Begin with the standard HTML and PHP document code (**Script 7.5**):

   ```
   <HTML><HEAD><TITLE>Sorting Arrays
   → </TITLE><BODY><?php
   ```

**Script 7.5** There are a number of different functions available in PHP for sorting arrays, including `arsort()` and `ksort()` which are used here.

```
1    <HTML>
2    <HEAD>
3    <TITLE>Sorting Arrays</TITLE>
4    <BODY>
5    <?php
6    $Grades = array(
7        "Richard"=>"95",
8        "Sherwood"=>"82",
9        "Toni"=>"98",
10       "Franz"=>"87",
11       "Melissa"=>"75",
12       "Roddy"=>"85"
13   );
14   print ("Originally, the array looks like
         this:<BR>");
15   for ($n = 0; $n < count($Grades); $n++) {
16       $Line = each ($Grades);
17       print ("$Line[key]'s grade is
             $Line[value].<BR>\n");
18   }
19   arsort($Grades);
20   reset($Grades);
21   print ("<P>After sorting the array by
         value using arsort(), the array looks
         like this:<BR>");
22   for ($n = 0; $n < count($Grades); $n++) {
23       $Line = each ($Grades);
24       print ("$Line[key]'s grade is
             $Line[value].<BR>\n");
25   }
26   ksort($Grades);
27   reset($Grades);
28   print ("<P>After sorting the array by
         key using ksort(), the array looks
         like this:<BR>");
29   for ($n = 0; $n < count($Grades); $n++) {
30       $Line = each ($Grades);
31       print ("$Line[key]'s grade is
             $Line[value].<BR>\n");
32   }
33   ?>
34   </BODY>
35   </HTML>
```

**3.** Create the array:

```
$Grades = array(
"Richard"=>"95",
"Sherwood"=>"82",
"Toni"=>"98",
"Franz"=>"87",
"Melissa"=>"75",
"Roddy"=>"85"
);
```

**4.** Print a caption and then print each element of the array using a loop.

```
print ("Originally, the array looks
→ like this:<BR>");
for ($n = 0; $n < count($Grades);
→ $n++) {
    $Line = each ($Grades);
    print ("$Line[key]'s grade is
    → $Line[value].<BR>\n");
}
```

**5.** Sort the array in reverse order by values to determine who had the highest grade.

```
arsort($Grades);
```

Because you are determining who has the highest grade, you need to use **arsort()** instead of **asort()**. The latter, which sorts the array by numeric order, would order them *75, 82, 85,* etc. and not the desired *98, 95, 87,* etc.

You also must use **arsort()** and not just **rsort()** in order to maintain the key-value relationship (which **rsort()** would eradicate).

**6.** Reset the array's pointer using the **reset()** function.

```
reset($Grades);
```

Just to make sure that the loop begins with the first element of the $Grade array, you use the **reset()** function which returns the pointer to the first element in the array. This has to be done because the previous loop moved the pointer to the end of the array.

*continues on next page*

**7.** Print the array again (with a caption), using another loop.

```
print ("<P>After sorting the array
→ by value using arsort(), the
array → looks like this:<BR>");
for ($n = 0; $n < count($Grades);
→ $n++) {
    $Line = each ($Grades);
    print ("$Line[key]'s grade is
    → $Line[value].<BR>\n");
}
```

**8.** Now sort the array by key to put the array in alphabetical order by student name and reset the array again.

```
ksort($Grades);
```

```
reset($Grades);
```

The ksort() function will organize the array by key (in this case, alphabetically) while maintaining the key-value correlation.

**9.** Print a caption and the array one last time.

```
print ("<P>After sorting the array
→ by key using ksort(), the array
→ looks like this:<BR>");
for ($n = 0; $n < count($Grades);
→ $n++) {
    $Line = each ($Grades);
    print ("$Line[key]'s grade is
    → $Line[value].<BR>\n");
}
```

**10.** Close the script with the standard PHP and HTML tags:

```
?></BODY></HTML>
```

**11.** Save your script as **sort.php**, upload it to the server, and test in your Web browser (**Figure 7.7**).

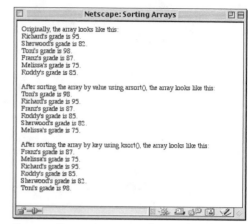

Originally, the array looks like this:
Richard's grade is 95.
Sherwood's grade is 82.
Toni's grade is 98.
Franz's grade is 87.
Melissa's grade is 75.
Roddy's grade is 85.

After sorting the array by value using arsort(), the array looks like this:
Toni's grade is 98.
Richard's grade is 95.
Franz's grade is 87.
Roddy's grade is 85.
Sherwood's grade is 82.
Melissa's grade is 75.

After sorting the array by key using ksort(), the array looks like this:
Franz's grade is 87.
Melissa's grade is 75.
Richard's grade is 95.
Roddy's grade is 85.
Sherwood's grade is 82.
Toni's grade is 98.

**Figure 7.7** You can sort an array in a number of ways with varied results. Pay close attention to whether or not you want to maintain your key-value association when choosing a sort function.

# Transforming Between Strings and Arrays

Now that you understand both strings and arrays, I'll introduce two functions for switching between the two formats. One, `implode()`, turns an array into a string. The second, `explode()`, does just the opposite. Here are a some reasons to use these functions:

◆ You might want to turn an array into a string in order to pass that value appended to a URL (which you cannot do as easily with an array).

◆ You might want to turn an array into a string in order to store that information in a database.

◆ You might want to turn a string into an array to convert a comma-delimited text field (say a keyword search area of a form) into its separate parts.

The syntax for using `explode()` is:
```
$Array = explode ($Separator, $String);
```

The separator refers to whatever character(s) define where one array element ends and another begins. Commonly this would be either a comma or a blank space. Thus your code would be:
```
$Array = explode(",", $String);
```

Or:
```
$Array = explode(" ", $String);
```

To go from an array to a string, you need to define what the separator (a.k.a., the glue) is going to be and PHP does the rest.

```
$String = implode($Glue, $Array);
$String = implode(",", $Array);
```

Or:
```
$String = implode(" ", $Array);
```

*continues on next page*

To demonstrate how to use explode() and implode(), you'll create an HTML form that takes a comma delimited string of names from the user. The PHP will then turn the string into an array so that it can sort the list. Finally the code will create and return the alphabetized string.

## To convert between strings and arrays:

1. Create a new HTML document in your text editor.

2. Write the standard HTML header (**Script 7.6**):

   ```
   <HTML><HEAD><TITLE>HTML Form
   → </TITLE></HEAD><BODY>
   ```

3. Create an HTML form with a TEXT input.

   ```
   <FORM ACTION="HandleList.php"
   → METHOD=POST>
   Enter the words you want alphabetized
   → with each individual word separated
   → by a space:<BR>
   <INPUT TYPE=TEXT NAME="List"
   → SIZE=80><BR>
   ```

   It's important in cases like this to instruct the user. For example, if they enter a comma delimited list, you won't be able to handle the string properly (after completing both scripts, try using commas in lieu of spaces and see what results).

4. Create a submit button, then close the form and the HTML page.

   ```
   <INPUT TYPE=SUBMIT NAME="SUBMIT"
   → VALUE="Submit!">
   </FORM></BODY></HTML>
   ```

5. Save your script as list.html and upload it to your server.

   Now you'll write the HandleList.php page to process the data generated by list.html.

**Script 7.6** This is just a simple HTML form where a user can submit a list of words. Including detailed instructions for the user is a prudent Web design policy.

```
1   <HTML>
2   <HEAD>
3   <TITLE>HTML Form</TITLE>
4   </HEAD>
5   <BODY>
6   <FORM ACTION="HandleList.php" METHOD=POST>
7   Enter the words you want alphabetized
    with each individual word separated by a
    space:<BR>
8   <INPUT TYPE=TEXT NAME="List" SIZE=80><BR>
9   <INPUT TYPE=SUBMIT NAME="SUBMIT"
    VALUE="Submit!">
10  </FORM>
11  </BODY>
12  </HTML>
```

**Script 7.7** Because the explode() and implode() functions are so simple and powerful, you can quickly and easily sort a submitted list of words (of practically any length) in just a couple of lines.

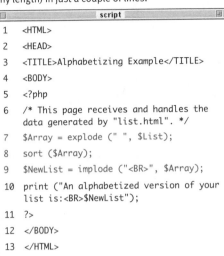

```
1   <HTML>
2   <HEAD>
3   <TITLE>Alphabetizing Example</TITLE>
4   <BODY>
5   <?php
6   /* This page receives and handles the
    data generated by "list.html". */
7   $Array = explode (" ", $List);
8   sort ($Array);
9   $NewList = implode ("<BR>", $Array);
10  print ("An alphabetized version of your
    list is:<BR>$NewList");
11  ?>
12  </BODY>
13  </HTML>
```

6. Create a new HTML document in your text editor.

7. Write the standard HTML header and then open the PHP section of the page (**Script 7.7**):

   <HTML><HEAD><TITLE>Alphabetizing
   → Example</TITLE><BODY><?php

8. Turn the incoming string, $List, into an array.

   $Array = explode (" ", $List);

   This line of code creates a new array, $Array, out of the string $List. Each space between the words in $List indicates to set the next word as a new array element. Hence the first word becomes $Array[0], then there is a space in $List, then the second word becomes $Array[1], and so forth until the end of $List.

9. Sort the array alphabetically.

   sort ($Array);

   Because you do not need to maintain key-value associations in the $Array, you can use **sort()** instead of **asort()** which you used before.

10. Create a new string out of the sorted array.

    $NewList = implode ("<BR>", $Array);

    You'll print out the new list and since arrays do not print as easily as strings, you'll turn $Array into a string called $NewList first. The resulting string will start with the value of $Array[0], followed by the HTML <BR> tag, followed by the value of $Array[1], etc. Using <BR> instead of a space or comma will give the list a more readable format when printed to the browser.

    *continues on next page*

**11.** Print the new string to the browser.

```
print ("An alphabetized version of
→ your list is:<BR>$NewList");
```

**12.** Close your PHP section and the HTML page.

```
?></BODY></HTML>
```

**13.** Save your page as HandleList.php, upload it to the server (in the same directory as list.html), and test both scripts in your Web browser (**Figures 7.8** and **7.9**).

### ✔ Tip

■ You'll also run across code written using the join() function, which is identical to implode().

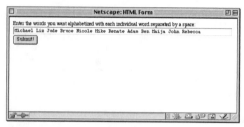

**Figure 7.8** The HTML form here takes a list of words which will then be alphabetized in the HandleList.php script (**Figure 7.9**).

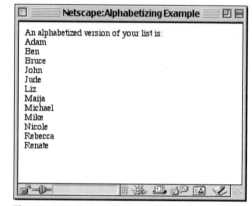

**Figure 7.9** Here's the same list, alphabetized for the user. It's a quick and easy process to code but impossible without the existence of arrays.

**Script 7.8** This is the HTML form with an array for INPUT names. You don't even have to specify keys for each field, you could label every field Array[] in which case HandleForm.php would hold the first name data in Array[0], the last name in Array[1], the email address in Array[2], and the comments in Array[3].

```
script

1    <HTML>
2    <HEAD>
3    <TITLE>HTML Form</TITLE>
4    </HEAD>
5    <BODY>
6    <FORM ACTION="HandleForm.php"
     METHOD=POST>
7    First Name <INPUT TYPE=TEXT NAME=
     "Array[FirstName]" SIZE=20><BR>
8    Last Name <INPUT TYPE=TEXT NAME=
     "Array[LastName]" SIZE=40><BR>
9    E-mail Address <INPUT TYPE=TEXT NAME=
     "Array[Email]" SIZE=60><BR>
10   Comments <TEXTAREA NAME="Array[Comments]"
     ROWS=5 COLS=40></TEXTAREA><BR>
11   <INPUT TYPE=SUBMIT NAME="SUBMIT"
     VALUE="Submit!">
12   </FORM>
13   </BODY>
14   </HTML>
```

# Creating an Array from a Form

Throughout this chapter we have established arrays entirely from within a PHP page. You can, however, send an array of data to a PHP script via an HTML form. The coding is only slightly trickier than you've witnessed so far. You can rewrite the feedback page from Chapter 3, *HTML Forms and PHP*, so that it generates an array instead of individual variables.

## To create an array with an HTML form:

1. Create a new HTML document in your text editor.

2. Create the standard HTML header (**Script 7.8**).

   ```
   <HTML><HEAD><TITLE>HTML Form
   → </TITLE></HEAD><BODY>
   ```

3. Begin the HTML form.

   ```
   <FORM ACTION="HandleForm.php"
   → METHOD=POST>
   ```

4. Create three TEXT input boxes with arrays for the NAME attributes.

   ```
   First Name <INPUT TYPE=TEXT NAME=
   → "Array[FirstName]" SIZE=20><BR>
   Last Name <INPUT TYPE=TEXT NAME=
   → "Array[LastName]" SIZE=40><BR>
   E-mail Address <INPUT TYPE=TEXT NAME=
   → "Array[Email]" SIZE=60><BR>
   ```

   When you created your form before, the HandleForm.php script received variables such as $FirstName and $LastName. Now it will receive $Array[FirstName], $Array[LastName], etc., which will automatically create the array, indexed accordingly. I've omitted the quotation marks around array's key (e.g., Array["LastName"]) which is perfectly acceptable and helps to avoid syntactical errors in this situation.

*continues on next page*

**5.** Create a TEXTAREA that is also part of the array.

```
Comments <TEXTAREA NAME=
→ "Array[Comments]" ROWS=5
→ COLS=40></TEXTAREA><BR>
```

**6.** Save your script as `form.html` and upload it to your server.

You'll also need to write a new `HandleForm.php` page to reflect your changes to `form.html`.

**7.** Create a new PHP document in your text editor.

**8.** Begin with the standard HTML header, followed by the initial PHP tag (**Script 7.9**).

```
<HTML><HEAD><TITLE>Form Results/
→ Using Arrays</TITLE><BODY><?php
```

**9.** Take the two name elements of the array and join them together to form a new array element.

```
$Array["Name"] =
→ $Array["FirstName"] . " " .
→ $Array["LastName"];
```

Now you've added another piece of information to the array but you can still handle all the data with just the one variable.

**10.** Print the submitted complete name to the Web browser to confirm successful receipt of the form data.

```
print ("Your full name is
→ $Array[Name].<BR>\n");
```

**11.** Save the page as `HandleForm.php`, upload it to your server (in the same directory as `form.html`), and test both pages in your Web browser (**Figures 7.10**, **7.11** and **7.12**).

### ✔ Tip

■ Another great time to use arrays in HTML forms is when using multiple checkboxes or a pull-down menu where several options can be selected.

**Script 7.9** It doesn't matter to the PHP whether it receives a number of strings from an HTML form or just one array as it does here. However, using an array leaves you with fewer variables to manage.

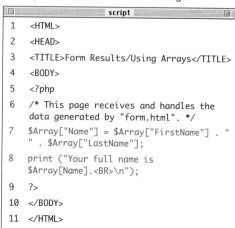

```
1    <HTML>
2    <HEAD>
3    <TITLE>Form Results/Using Arrays</TITLE>
4    <BODY>
5    <?php
6    /* This page receives and handles the
     data generated by "form.html". */
7    $Array["Name"] = $Array["FirstName"] . "
     " . $Array["LastName"];
8    print ("Your full name is
     $Array[Name].<BR>\n");
9    ?>
10   </BODY>
11   </HTML>
```

**Figure 7.10** This is the source of the `form.html` page, now that it uses an array for the input names.

**Figure 7.11** It will make no difference to the user what names you use in your form as a user normally only sees this view. With this in mind, choose names that will make your programming job easier.

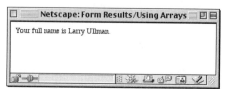

**Figure 7.12** To confirm that the data from the form (Figure 7.11) successfully made it to the `HandleForm.php` page, a simple message is printed.

# Creating Multidimensional Arrays

Multidimensional arrays—the PHP equivalent of a Perl hash—are both simple and complicated at the same time. This is another topic you may want to delve into once your overall comfort level has improved.

The theory behind a multidimensional array is that you can create an array with even more information than a standard array can by incorporating other arrays for values instead of just strings and numbers. For example:

```
$Array1 = array("apples", "bananas",
→ "oranges");
$Array2 = array("steaks", "hamburgers",
→ "pork chops");
$List = array("fruits"=>$Array1,
→ "meats"=>$Array2,
"other"=>"peanuts",
"cash" => 30.00);
```

This array, $List, now consists of one string (*peanuts*), one floating-point number (*30.00*), and two arrays (*fruits* and *meats*).

Pointing to an element within an array within an array is tricky. The key (pardon the pun) is to continue adding indices as necessary. So in our example, *bananas* is at `$List["fruits"][1]`.

First, you point to the element (in this case, an array) in the $List array, by using `["fruits"]`. Then, you point to the element within that array based upon its position—the second item so you use the index `[1]`.

*continues on next page*

CREATING MULTIDIMENSIONAL ARRAYS

## ✔ Tips

- You can create a multidimensional array in one statement by using a series of nested **array()** calls (instead of through several steps as in this example), but I wouldn't recommend it because it is all too easy to make syntactical errors as a statement becomes more and more nested. Once you do have the interest and necessity to use multidimensional arrays, start by assigning each individual array, as you have here, and then putting them into another array rather than trying to program with nested **array()** statements.

- Attempting to print a value from a multidimensional array can be complicated as well. Versions of PHP prior to 4 will not let you print such an element directly. In PHP 4, you can use curly braces to print from multidimensional arrays within a string: `print ("The value I want to` → `print is {$Array[index1]` → `[index2]}.");`. But `print ("The` → `value I want to print is $Array` → `[index1][index2].");` will not work in any version of PHP.

# REGULAR EXPRESSIONS

If there were just two things you should understand about regular expressions, they would be, one, that regular expressions are supremely useful in advanced programming, and, two, they are easy to comprehend but taxing to write. However, once you understand the rules for writing regular expressions, that extra knowledge will pay off in spades as regular expressions can vastly improve the quality of your programming and save you time in the long run.

In this chapter, I'll identify what regular expressions are, discuss constructing them in great detail, and provide some useful examples demonstrating their capabilities.

# What are Regular Expressions?

One chapter on regular expressions can cover only the tip of the iceberg, yet it should be enough to get you on your way. Should you take to regular expressions and desire to learn more, Appendix C, *PHP Resources*, will lead you to deeper waters.

Think of regular expressions as an elaborate system of matching patterns. You first write the pattern, then use one of PHP's built-in functions to apply the pattern to a text string (regular expressions are specifically for use with strings). PHP has essentially two functions for using regular expressions to match patterns (one case sensitive and one not) and two for matching patterns and replacing matched text with other text (again, one case sensitive and one not).

I'll begin with how to define and match a simple pattern, then I'll delve into more complex patterns and I'll finish with how to match and replace patterns.

## ✔ Tips

- Some text editors, such as BBEdit for Macintosh, TextPad for Windows and emacs for Unix, allow you to use regular expressions to match and replace patterns within and throughout several documents (**Figure 8.1**). This may be another good reason to learn regular expressions and is perhaps something to consider when choosing your text editor.

- The PHP manual examines the differences between how PHP and Perl treat regular expressions (see *Perl-compatible Regular Expression Functions* under section four, *Function Reference*). For those of you who are coming to PHP from the latter, you may want to read the manual pages first.

**Figure 8.1** Within BBEdit's standard Find dialog box, you have the option of using regular expressions (even across several files or folders) by checking the Use Grep box. BBEdit can also store regular expression patterns for you and has some built-in.

# Defining a Simple Pattern

Before you can use one of PHP's built-in regular expression functions, you have to be able to define a pattern that the function will use for matching purposes. PHP has a number of rules for creating a pattern, many of which are similar to those you'll use with Perl, C, and Java. You can use these rules separately or in combination, making your pattern either quite simple or very complex.

In order to explain how patterns are created, I'll start by introducing the symbols used, then discuss how to group characters together, and finish with classes. The combination of symbols, groupings, and classes define your pattern. As a formatting, rule, I'll define my patterns within quotes ("") and will indicate what the pattern matches in *italics*.

## Literals

The first type of character you will use for defining patterns is a literal. A literal is a value that is written exactly as it is interpreted. For example, the pattern "a" will only match the letter *a*, "ab" will only match *ab*, and so forth.

Literals allow us to match exact combinations, but regular expressions would be fairly useless if you could only match literals (in which case some of the string functions would suffice, see *Chapter 5, Using Strings*). You can also use specific symbols which have their own meaning, to create less rigid patterns. I'll discuss these next.

# Metacharacters

Just one step beyond literals in terms of complexity are metacharacters. These are special symbols that have a meaning beyond their literal value. While "a" simply means *a*, the first metacharacter, the period (.), will match any single character ("." matches *a*, *b*, *c*, etc.). This is pretty straightforward, although I should note that if you want to refer to a metacharacter literally, you will need to escape it, much like you escape a quotation mark to print it. Hence "\." will match the period.

Next, there are three metacharacters that allow for multiple occurrences: "a*" will match zero or more a's (*a*, *aa*, *aaa*, etc.); "a+" matches one or more a's (*a*, *aa*, *aaa*, etc., but there must be at least one); and, "a?" will match up to one a (*a* or no a's match).

To match a certain quantity of a letter, put the quantity between curly braces ({}), stating either a specific number, a minimum, or a minimum and a maximum. Thus, "a{3}" will only match *aaa*; "a{3,}" will match *aaa*, *aaaa*, etc. (three or more a's); and "a{3,5}" matches just *aaa*, *aaaa*, and *aaaaa* (between three and five).

Lastly there is the caret (^)—pronounced like the vegetable and sometimes referred to as the hat—which will match a string that begins with the letter following the caret. There is also the dollar sign ($), for anything that ends with the preceding letter. Accordingly, "^a." will match any two-character string beginning with an *a*, followed by whatever, while ".a$" will correspond to any two-character string ending with an *a*. Therefore, "^a$" will only match *a*, making it the equivalent of just "a".

## Special Characters for Regular Expression

| CHARACTER | MATCHES |
|-----------|---------|
| . | any character |
| ^a | begins with a |
| a$ | ends with a |
| a+ | at least one a |
| a? | zero or one a |
| \n | new line |
| \t | tab |
| \ | escape |
| (ab) | ab grouped |
| a\|b | a or b |
| a{2} | aa |
| a{1,} | a, aa, aaa, etc. |
| a{1,3} | a, aa, aaa |
| [a-z] | any lowercase letter |
| [A-Z] | any uppercase letter |
| [0-9] | any digit |

**Table 8.1** This is a fairly complete list of special characters used to define your regular expression patterns (including metacharacters but not literals— *a*, *b*, *c*, etc.).

Regular expressions also make use of the pipe (|) as the equivalent of *or*. Therefore, "a|b" will match the strings *a* or *b* and "gre|ay" matches both potential spellings of the color. (Using the pipe within patterns is called *alternation*).

Practically, of course, there's little use to matching repetitions of a letter in a string, but these examples are good ways to demonstrate how a symbol works. You should begin by focusing on understanding what the various symbols mean and how they are used. I'll build on this knowledge over the course of this chapter.

### ✔ Tips

■ When using curly braces to specify a number of characters, you must always include the minimum number while the maximum is optional—"a{3}" and "a{3,}" are acceptable but "a{,3}" is not.

■ To include special characters (^.[]$()|*?{}\) in a pattern, they need to be escaped (a backslash put before them). This is true for the metacharacters and the grouping symbols (parenthesis and brackets). You can also use the backslash to match new lines ("\n") and tabs ("\t"), essentially creating a metacharacter out of a literal.

■ **Table 8.1** lists all these symbols and combinations for your reference (along with those being described hereafter).

# Matching Patterns

There are two functions built in to PHP expressly for the purpose of matching a pattern within a string: `ereg()` and `eregi()`. The only difference between the two is that `ereg()` treats patterns as case-sensitive whereas `eregi()` is case-insensitive, making it less particular. The latter is generally recommend for common use, unless you need to be more explicit (perhaps for security purposes, as with passwords). Both functions will be evaluated to TRUE if the pattern is matched, FALSE if it is not. Here are two different ways to use these functions:

```
ereg("pattern", "string");
```

Or:

```
$Pattern = "pattern";
$String = "string";
eregi($Pattern, $String);
```

Throughout the rest of the chapter, I will assign the pattern to a variable, as in the second example above, to draw more attention to the pattern itself—the heart of any regular expression.

To demonstrate matching a pattern, you'll create a new `HandleForm.php` that works in conjunction with `form.html` from Chapter 7, *Using Arrays* (**Script 8.1**). The `HandleForm.php` script will validate the submitted email address.

**Script 8.1** The original `form.html` was designed to accept an e-mail address and user comments, as well as the user's first and last names.

```
1    <HTML>
2    <HEAD>
3    <TITLE>HTML Form</TITLE>
4    </HEAD>
5    <BODY>
6    <FORM ACTION="HandleForm.php" METHOD=POST>
7    First Name <INPUT TYPE=TEXT NAME=
     "Array[FirstName]" SIZE=20><BR>
8    Last Name <INPUT TYPE=TEXT NAME=
     "Array[LastName]" SIZE=40><BR>
9    E-mail Address <INPUT TYPE=TEXT NAME=
     "Array[Email]" SIZE=60><BR>
10   Comments <TEXTAREA NAME="Array[Comments]"
     ROWS=5 COLS=40></TEXTAREA><BR>
11   <INPUT TYPE=SUBMIT NAME="SUBMIT"
     VALUE="Submit!">
12   </FORM>
13   </BODY>
14   </HTML>
```

**Script 8.2** This script makes a very practical use of regular expressions to validate that the user not only entered an email address in the HTML form, but actually submitted a valid one.

```
                       script
1   <HTML>
2   <HEAD>
3   <TITLE>Using Regular Expressions</TITLE>
4   <BODY>
5   <?php
6   /* This page receives and handles the
    data generated by "form.html". */
7   if (($Array["FirstName"]) AND
    ($Array["LastName"])) {
8       $Array["Name"] = $Array["FirstName"] .
    " " . $Array["LastName"];
9   } else {
10      print ("Please enter your first and
    last names.<BR>\n");
11  }
12  $Pattern = ".+@.+\..+";
13  if (eregi($Pattern, $Array["Email"])) {
14      print ("Your information has been
    received!<BR>\n");
15  } else {
16      print ("Please enter a valid email
    address!\n");
17  }
18  ?>
19  </BODY>
20  </HTML>
```

## To match a pattern using eregi:

1. Create a new HandleForm.php script in your text editor.

2. Begin with the standard HTML and PHP header (**Script 8.2**):
   ```
   <HTML>
   <HEAD>
   <TITLE>Using Regular Expressions
   → </TITLE>
   <BODY>
   <?php
   /* This page receives and handles the
   → data generated by "form.html". */
   ```

3. Create the necessary conditionals.
   ```
   if (($Array["FirstName"]) AND
   → ($Array["LastName"])) {
       $Array["Name"] =
   → $Array["FirstName"] . " " .
   → $Array["LastName"];
   } else {
       print ("Please enter your first
   → and last names.<BR>\n");
   }
   ```
   You could use a regular expression to make sure that they have entered a valid first name, consisting only of alphabetic characters, but ensuring that the variable has a value is sufficient. Then, if the user entered a value for both the first and last names, the names will be merged into one element and assigned to the array. But, if either is omitted, a request will be printed.

4. Next, you'll establish the pattern for matching an email address:
   ```
   $Pattern = ".+@.+\..+";
   ```
   This will be the pattern to match a valid email address. Although it is quite simple, it will work just fine (a more elaborate one will be developed later in the chapter though for comparison).

*continues on next page*

**MATCHING PATTERNS**

**123**

The first step in the pattern says that an email address must begin with at least one character (.+). Second, there is the *at* symbol (@), which is required in any email address. Third, the pattern insists upon at least one more character. Fourth, an email address must include a period. Finally, there must be at least one more character concluding the string (it cannot end with a period).

5. Use the pattern to check for a match with the submitted email address.

```
if (eregi($Pattern,
$Array["Email"])) {
print ("Your information has been
→ received!<BR>\n");
} else {
    print ("Please enter a valid
    → email address!\n");
}
```

In order to use the matching function, **eregi()**, you will feed it the pattern as defined above and the $Array["Email"] variable which comes from **form.html**. If PHP finds the pattern within the variable, the condition will be TRUE and the proper message will be printed. If it does not find the pattern within the variable, a request will be made to enter a valid email address. As email addresses are case-insensitive, you will use **eregi()** and not **ereg()**.

6. Save your script, upload it to your server, and test it in your Web browser (**Figures 8.2**, **8.3 and 8.4**).

**Figure 8.2** The form.html page takes the user input and sends it on to be checked using regular expressions in the HandleForm.php page (Figure 8.3).

**Figure 8.3** Using eregi(), if the user enters an email address that matches the defined pattern, the HandleForm.php script will create this message. Compare this to Figure 8.4.

**Figure 8.4** Here I supplied *php@DMCinsights*, which is not a valid email address, resulting in the error message displayed.

## ✔ Tips

■ Although it demonstrates dedication to programming to learn how to write and execute your own regular expressions, numerous working examples (including variants of the email matching pattern) are available already from the various PHP Web sites, referenced in Appendix C, *PHP Resources*.

■ For demonstration purposes, I have assigned a pattern to a variable and then referred to the variable in the `eregi()` function. You could, however, place your pattern directly within the function, if you wanted, like so:

```
if (eregi(".+@.+\..+", $Array
→ ["Email"])) {...
```

■ Form validation, similar to what you have just coded above, can also be achieved as a client-side process using JavaScript and regular expressions. Depending upon your circumstances, you may use regular expressions in one language or the other or both.

**MATCHING PATTERNS**

# Defining More Complicated Patterns

Once you understand how to use literals and metacharacters to create a pattern, you can learn about groupings and classes, which will allow you to define more complex patterns.

## Groupings

Using the basic symbols established so far, you can begin to incorporate parentheses to group characters into more involved patterns. Grouping works as you might expect: "(abc)" will only match *abc*, "(trout)" will only match *trout*. These examples are moot points, though, as "abc" will also only match *abc*. It is when you begin to use metacharacters with parentheses that you will see how groupings affect your patterns.

Essentially, think of parentheses as being used to establish a new literal. Logically, whereas "a" is a literal that matches only *a*, "(abc)" is a literal that matches only *abc*. From this notion, quantifiers, instead of applying solely to the immediately preceding literal, will apply to the whole group. Hence, "a{3}" matches *aaa*, but "(abc){3}" matches *abcabcabc*. As a better example, "bon+" will only match a string beginning with *bon* followed by one or more n's (say, *bonnet*), but "(bon)+" will match a string beginning with bon, followed by zero or more bon's (*bonbon*). The parentheses restrict and control our pattern.

Similarly, while "yes|no" matches either *yeso* or *yeno* (*ye* plus either *s* or *n* plus *o*), "(Yes)|(No)", accepts either of those two words in their entirety, which is certainly what you would rather look for.

**Predefined Classes for Regular Expression**

| CLASS | MATCHES |
|---|---|
| [[:alpha:]] | any letter |
| [[:digit:]] | any digit |
| [[:alnum:]] | any letter or digit |
| [[:space:]] | any white space |
| [[:upper:]] | any uppercase letter |
| [[:lower:]] | any lowercase letter |
| [[:punct:]] | any punctuation mark |

**Table 8.2** These are the most common predefined classes built-in to PHP, which will save you a lot of time in lieu of defining your own classes.

## Classes

Regardless of how you combine your letters into various groups, they will only ever be useful for matching specific words. But what if you wanted to match any four-letter lowercase word or any number sequence? For this, you define and utilize classes (more formally referred to as character classes).

Classes are created by placing characters within square brackets ([]). For example, you can match any one vowel with "[aeiou]". Or you can use the hyphen to indicate a range of characters: "[a-z]" is any single lowercase letter and "[A-Z]" is any uppercase, "[A-Za-z]" is any letter in general, and "[0-9]" matches any digit. You should note that these patterns will only ever match one character, but, "[a-z]{3}" would match *abc*, *def*, etc.

Within the square brackets, the caret symbol, which is normally used to indicate an accepted beginning of a string, is used to exclude a character. So "[^a]" will match any single character that isn't *a*.

PHP has already defined some classes which will be most useful to you in your programming. There is "[[:alpha:]]" for matching any letter (the equivalent of "[A-Za-z]"), "[[:digit:]]" for any number (or "[0-9]"), and "[[:alnum:]]" for any letter or number (otherwise written as "[A-Za-z0-9]").

By defining your own classes and using those built-in to PHP (see **Table 8.2**), you can make better patterns for regular expressions.

## Examples of patterns

Using the information introduced above, you can now create some useful patterns, and I'll give some detailed explanations of how I arrived there.

"^([0-9]{5})(-[0-9]{4})?$"

The pattern above is a pattern for matching a zip code, which begins with precisely five numbers, possibly followed by a dash and four more digits. In the first parenthetical, it is stated that you need precisely five digits (the class followed by the curly braces), and you use the caret to indicate that this must be the beginning of the string. Then you make a second parenthetical which starts with a dash, followed by precisely four numbers. You utilize the question mark to state that this section is optional (i.e., there can be zero or one of these) but you use the dollar sign as well to mandate that if it does exist, it must be the very end of the string.

Here is a more involved pattern for matching an email. address: "^([0-9a-z]+)([ 0-9a-z\.-_]+)@([0-9a-z\.-_]+)\.([0-9a-z]+) "

Since you will use **eregi()** for matching, you need not concern yourself with alphabetic case so the character classes only include "a-z" and not "A-Z" as well.

The first step in the pattern says that an email address must begin with at least one letter or number, followed by any quantity of letters, numbers, underscores, periods, and dashes.

Second, there is the *at* symbol, which is required in any email address.

Third, the pattern insists upon at least one letter, number, dash, period, or underscore.

Fourth, an email address must include a period.

**Script 8.3** The more complex email validation pattern has been inserted into the HandleForm.php script to provide a more specific level of matching.

```
script

1   <HTML>
2   <HEAD>
3   <TITLE>Using Regular Expressions</TITLE>
4   <BODY>
5   <?php
6   /* This page receives and handles the
    data generated by "form.html". */
7   if (($Array["FirstName"]) AND
    ($Array["LastName"])) {
8       $Array["Name"] = $Array["FirstName"] .
        " " . $Array["LastName"];
9   } else {
10      print ("Please enter your first and
        last names.<BR>\n");
11  }
12
13  $Pattern = "^([0-9a-z]+)([ 0-9a-z\.-_]+)
    @([0-9a-z\.-_]+)\.([0-9a-z]+) ";
14  if (eregi($Pattern, $Array["Email"])) {
15      print ("Your information has been
        received!<BR>\n");
16  } else {
17      print ("Please enter a valid email
        address!\n");
18  }
19  ?>
20  </BODY>
21  </HTML>
```

Lastly, there must be at least one letter or number concluding the string (it cannot end with a period).

The space, a literal character, will mark the end of the string (so that, if the email address is found within other text, the words following the email address will not be included in the pattern). **Script 8.3** is a modification of HandleForm.php using this more specific pattern.

# Back Referencing

Finally, there is one more concept to discuss with regards to establishing patterns: back referencing. You'll learn more about this process when you are matching and replacing text later in the chapter.

In the zip code matching pattern, "^([0-9]{5}) (-[0-9]{4})?$", notice that there are two groupings within parentheses—"^([0-9]{5})" and "(-[0-9]{4})". Within a regular expression pattern, PHP will automatically number parenthetical groupings beginning at 1. Back referencing allows you to refer to each individual section by using a double backslash (\\) in front of the corresponding number. For example, if you match the zip code *94710-0001* with this pattern, referring back to \\1 will give you "94710". You'll see an example of this in action in the next section.

# Matching and Replacing Patterns

While the `ereg()` and `eregi()` functions are great for validating a string, you can take your programming one step further by matching a pattern and then replacing it with a slightly different pattern or with specific text. The syntax for using the two functions is:

```
ereg_replace("pattern", "replace",
→ "string");
```

Or:

```
$Pattern = "pattern";
$Replace = "replace";
$String = "string";
eregi_replace($Pattern, $Replace,
→ $String);
```

One reason you might want to use this would be to turn a user-entered Web site address (a URL) into a clickable HTML link, by encapsulating it in the `<A HREF="URL"></A>` tags. I'll modify the `form.html` (Script 8.1) and `HandleForm.php` (Script 8.3) scripts to do just that.

## To use eregi_replace to match and replace a pattern:

**1.** Open `form.html` in your text editor. You'll slightly alter the `form.html` page to accept a URL and a description.

**2.** Change line 9 (**Script 8.4**) (which takes the email address) to:
```
URL <INPUT TYPE=TEXT NAME=
→ "Array[URL]" SIZE=60><BR>
```

**3.** Change line 10, the comments, to:
```
Description <TEXTAREA NAME=
→ "Array[Description]" ROWS=5
→ COLS=40></TEXTAREA><BR>
```

**Script 8.4** I have slightly modified the `form.html` page in order to have it accept URL submissions and descriptions instead of email addresses and comments.

| | script |
|---|---|
| 1 | `<HTML>` |
| 2 | `<HEAD>` |
| 3 | `<TITLE>HTML Form</TITLE>` |
| 4 | `</HEAD>` |
| 5 | `<BODY>` |
| 6 | `<FORM ACTION="HandleForm.php" METHOD=POST>` |
| 7 | `First Name <INPUT TYPE=TEXT NAME="Array[FirstName]" SIZE=20><BR>` |
| 8 | `Last Name <INPUT TYPE=TEXT NAME="Array[LastName]" SIZE=40><BR>` |
| 9 | `URL <INPUT TYPE=TEXT NAME="Array[URL]" SIZE=60><BR>` |
| 10 | `Description <TEXTAREA NAME="Array[Description]" ROWS=5 COLS=40></TEXTAREA><BR>` |
| 11 | `<INPUT TYPE=SUBMIT NAME="SUBMIT" VALUE="Submit!">` |
| 12 | `</FORM>` |
| 13 | `</BODY>` |

**Script 8.5** The `eregi_replace()` function will turn the user-submitted URL into a hot clickable link automatically. This is possible largely due to back referencing.

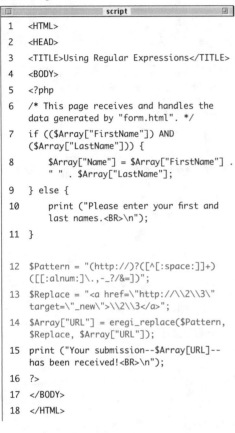

```
1   <HTML>
2   <HEAD>
3   <TITLE>Using Regular Expressions</TITLE>
4   <BODY>
5   <?php
6   /* This page receives and handles the
    data generated by "form.html". */
7   if (($Array["FirstName"]) AND
    ($Array["LastName"])) {
8       $Array["Name"] = $Array["FirstName"] .
        " " . $Array["LastName"];
9   } else {
10      print ("Please enter your first and
        last names.<BR>\n");
11  }

12  $Pattern = "(http://)?([^[:space:]]+)
    ([[:alnum:]\.,-_?/&=])";
13  $Replace = "<a href=\"http://\\2\\3\"
    target=\"_new\">\\2\\3</a>";
14  $Array["URL"] = eregi_replace($Pattern,
    $Replace, $Array["URL"]);
15  print ("Your submission--$Array[URL]--
    has been received!<BR>\n");
16  ?>
17  </BODY>
18  </HTML>
```

**4.** Save your script and upload it to the server. Now you'll rework the `HandleForm.php` page.

**5.** Open `HandleForm.php` in your text editor (Script 8.3).

**6.** Replace line 12 with the following code (**Script 8.5**):

`$Pattern = "(http://)?([^[:space:]]+)` → `([[:alnum:]]\.,-_?/&=])";`

Here is a liberal pattern set to recognize a URL. In fact, this pattern is more adept for matching and replacing purposes than validating entered data, as it is not very restrictive.

The pattern contains three groupings: the `http://`, the bulk of the URL, and the trailing part of the URL. A URL may begin with a *http://* or not. To check this, you start with the `http` followed by the colon and two slashes, and use the question mark to indicate that the entire section is optional.

After that, a URL contains characters that aren't spaces (the second, and very liberal, grouping)—letters, numbers, dashes, underscores, periods, etc. Finally, allow for more alpha-numeric characters, as well as the slash, question mark, ampersand, and equals sign. This final parenthetical would match the end of a URL such as *.com/php/*.

*continues on next page*

**MATCHING AND REPLACING PATTERNS**

**8.** $Replace = "<a href=\"http://
→ \\2\\3\" target=\"_new\">
→ \\2\\3</a>";

Here you've defined the replacement text. Using the back referencing technique, you can grab a sub-section of a string and place it within another string. Since the http:// section is optional, the easiest way to insure consistency is to drop it during replacement (notice there is no \\1 reference) and then manually insert the http:// so that all URLs will display with the same formatting. After making this adjustment, and adding the <a href= tag, the remaining part of the URL is inserted, followed by the closing HTML tag (</a>).

**9.** $Array["URL"] = eregi_replace
→ ($Pattern, $Replace,
→ $Array["URL"]);

You reset the value of the URL to the new, replaced string. Now, whenever the URL is sent to the browser (as in the next line), it will appear as a clickable link. This altered form could also be stored in a database or file for later use.

**10.** print ("Your submission–$Array[URL]–
→ has been received!<BR>\n");

Lastly, you conclude the if statement.

Save your script, upload it to the server, and test it in your Web browser (**Figures 8.5, 8.6,** and **8.7**). If the script works as intended, it will take a user-submitted URL, check it for validity, and then turn it into a clickable link. This is a process that you will most likely be able to use in any number of Web applications.

**Figure 8.5** The form.html page now requires a URL and description which will be checked using regular expressions (**Figure 8.6**).

**Figure 8.6** With the eregi_replace() function, you are able to turn a submitted URL, with or without the http://prefix, into a clickable link.

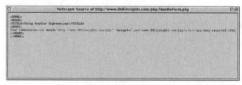

**Figure 8.7** The source of the page reveals the <A HREF> tags which have been added to the user entered URL.

# CREATING FUNCTIONS

On the same level of usefulness as regular expressions, but far easier to understand and implement, are functions. The functions I am referring to in this chapter are not exactly the same as those you have encountered up until this point, such as phpinfo(), count(), and eregi_replace(). Whereas those functions have already been defined by PHP, now you will be creating your own. However, once created, functions you have written and built-in PHP functions are handled in the very same manner.

Creating functions can save you oodles of time over the course of your programming life. In fact, they constitute a strong step towards creating Web applications and building a solid library of PHP code to use in future projects.

In this chapter, you will see how to write your own functions that perform specific tasks. After that, you'll learn how to pass information to the function, have your function return a value, and learn how functions and variables work together.

# Creating and Using Simple Functions

As you program, you'll discover that there are certain sections of code you frequently use, either within a single script or in several. Placing these routines into a self-defined function can save you time and make your programming easier, especially as your Web sites become larger. Once you create a function, the actions of that function take place each time the function is called, just as `print()` will send text to the browser with each use.

The syntax to create a user-defined function is:

```
function FunctionName () {
    statement(s);
}
```

You can use roughly the same naming conventions for the function name as you do for variables, just without the initial dollar sign. The most important rule is to remain consistent. Second to that is the suggestion of creating meaningful function names, just as you ought to write representative variable names (*CreateHeader* would be a better function name than *Function1*). Remember not to use spaces, though, as that would constitute two separate words for the function name, which will result in error messages (the underscore is a logical replacement for the space, for example *Create_Header* is a valid function name).

Any valid PHP code can go within the statement(s) area of the function, including calls to other functions. There is also no limit to the number of statements a function has, but make sure each statement ends with a semi-colon.

The formatting of a function is not important as long as the requisite elements are there. These elements include the word *function*, the function's name, the opening and closing parentheses, the opening and closing braces,

**Script 9.1** This is the original passwords script that doesn't use functions. You'll create your first function using the code at the heart of this page.

```
script
1   <HTML>
2   <HEAD>
3   <TITLE>Password Generator</TITLE>
4   <BODY>
5   <?php
6   $String = "This is the text which will be
    encrypted so that we may create random
    and secure passwords!";
7   $Length = 8; // Change this value to
    indicate how long your passwords should
    be. 32 character limit.
8   $String = md5($String);
9   $StringLength = strlen($String);
10  srand ((double) microtime() * 1000000);
11  $Begin = rand(0,($StringLength-$Length-
    1)); // Pick an arbitrary starting point.
12  $Password = substr($String, $Begin,
    $Length);
13  print ("Your recommended password is:
    <P><BIG>$Password</BIG>\n");
14  ?>
15  </BODY>
16  </HTML>
```

and the statement(s). It is conventional to indent a function's statement(s) from the previous line (as I have done), for clarity's sake. In any case, select a format style that you like (which is both syntactically correct and logically sound) and stick to it.

You call (or enact) the function by referring to it just as you do any built-in function. The line of code `FunctionName();` will cause the `statement(s);` part of the predefined function above to be executed.

Let's begin by rewriting the password-generating script from Chapter 5, *Using Strings*, as its own function.

## To create and call a basic function:

1. Open `passwords.php` in your text editor (**Script 9.1**).

2. Make the first line of the page <?php, as opposed to the standard beginning of the HTML header (**Script 9.2**, next page).

   To insure that the function is created before it is called (which is required in PHP 3), I'll write the function as the very first part of the script, even before any HTML code.

3. `function CreatePassword () {`

   The name of the function will be *CreatePassword* which is representative of what the function does and will consequently be easy to remember.

   *continues on next page*

**4.** Now place the PHP code (lines 6–13) from `passwords.php` into the function. As indicated in **Script 9.2**, I would recommend placing these lines indented from the function name to indicate they belong to the function.

```
$String = "This is the text which will
→ be encrypted so that we may create
→ random and secure passwords!";
$Length = 8;  $String = md5($String);
$StringLength = strlen($String);
srand ((double) microtime() *
→ 1000000);
$Begin = rand(0,($StringLength-
→ $Length-1)); $Password = substr
→ ($String, $Begin, $Length);
print ("Your recommended password is:
→ <P><BIG>$Password</BIG><P>\n");
```

**5.** Close the function on the next line with a curly brace: }.

Omitting the opening or closing brace is another common cause of errors so be sure to follow the syntax carefully.

**6.** Close the PHP code with ?>.

Since you are now going to write the basic HTML part of the page, you need to close the PHP section. You could also keep the PHP section open and then use `print()` to send the HTML to the browser, if you so desire, in which case you would skip this step.

**7.** Write the common HTML heading code, `<HTML><HEAD><TITLE>Password Generator` → `within a Function</TITLE><BODY>`.

**8.** Begin a new PHP section of the page with `<?php`.

You can actually open and close several sections of PHP code within an HTML document. It is common for programmers to do so.

**Script 9.2** Placing the function at the very beginning of the script is a good way to separate it out. Likewise, indenting the function's statements help to indicate their relationship to the function. Then, in the main body of your script, one-line of code executes the function's many statements.

```
1   <?php
2   function CreatePassword () {
3       $String = "This is the text which
        will be encrypted so that we may
        create random and secure passwords!";
4       $Length = 8; // Change this value to
        indicate how long your passwords
        should be. 32 character limit.
5       $String = md5($String);
6       $StringLength = strlen($String);
7       srand ((double) microtime() * 1000000);
8       $Begin = rand(0,($StringLength-
        $Length-1)); // Pick an arbitrary
        starting point.
9       $Password = substr($String, $Begin,
        $Length);
10      print ("Your recommended password is:
        <P><BIG>$Password</BIG><P> \n");
11  } // End of the CreatePassword function.
12  ?>
13  <HTML>
14  <HEAD>
15  <TITLE>Password Generator within a
    Function</TITLE>
16  <BODY>
17  <?php
18  CreatePassword(); // Call the function.
19  ?>
20  </BODY>
21  </HTML>
```

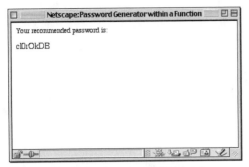

**Figure 9.1** By placing the several PHP lines of password.php into one function, you've begun to modularize your code. This is the first step towards making dynamic Web sites even if the obvious visual result is the same as it was before you created the function.

**9.** CreatePassword();

Once you've created your function, you simply have to call it by name (being careful to use the exact spelling) to make the function work. Be sure to include the parentheses as well.

**10.** ?></BODY></HTML>

Close the second PHP part and finish the HTML.

**11.** Save your script, upload it to the server, and test it in your Web browser (**Figure 9.1**).

## ✔ Tips

■ If the server you are working on is running PHP 3, you must define the function before calling it. Although this is not true in PHP 4, I would recommend that you habitually set your functions at the beginning of a script, insuring they will always be created before being called.

■ Function names for the functions you create are case-insensitive, just as existing PHP functions are case-insensitive. Therefore it won't matter in your code if you use *createpassword* instead of the more proper *CreatePassword*.

# Creating and Calling Functions that Take Arguments

Although being able to create a simple function is useful, writing one that takes input and does something with that input is even better. The input a function takes is called an *argument* and there are no limits to how many arguments a function can take. Functions that take arguments is a concept you've seen before: the print() function takes a string as an argument which it then sends to the browser.

The syntax for writing functions that take arguments is as follows:

```
function FunctionName ($Argument1,
→ $Argument2, etc.) {
    statement(s);
}
```

These arguments will be in the form of variables which get assigned the value sent to the function when you call it. Functions that take input are called much like those which do not, you just need to remember to pass along the necessary values. You can do this either by passing variables:

```
FunctionName ($Variable1, $Variable2,
→ etc.);
```

or by placing values within quotes, as in

```
FunctionName ("Value1", "Value2", etc.);
```

or some combination thereof:

```
FunctionName ($Variable1, "Value2",
→ etc.);
```

The important thing to note is that arguments are passed quite literally in that the first value in the function will be equal to the first value in the call line, the second function value matches the second call value, and so forth. Functions are not smart enough to intuitively understand how you meant the

**Script 9.3** The existing hello.php page creates a customized greeting over several lines of code within the rest of the page.

```
1   <HTML>
2   <HEAD>
3   <TITLE>If-elseif Conditionals</TITLE>
4   <BODY>
5   <?php
6   if ($Username) {
7       print ("Good ");
8       if (date("A") == "AM") {
9           print ("morning, ");
10      } elseif ( ( date("H") >= 12 ) and
            ( date("H") < 18 ) ) {
11          print ("afternoon, ");
12      } else {
13          print ("evening, ");
14      } // Close the date if.
15      print ("$Username");
16      print ("!\n");
17  } else {
18      print ("Please log in.\n");
19  } // Close the username if.
20  ?>
21  </BODY>
22  </HTML>
```

**Script 9.4** Here is a function that takes one argument which must be passed to it when the function is called. To insure that the function works properly, it is only called if $Username has a value.

```
1    <?php
2    function GreetUser ($TheUser) {
3        print ("Good ");
4        if (date("A") == "AM") {
5            print ("morning, ");
6        } elseif ((date("H")>12) and
         (date("H")<18)) {
7            print ("afternoon, ");
8        } else {
9            print ("evening, ");
10       } // Close our date if.
11       print ("$TheUser");
12       print ("!\n");
13   } // End of the GreetUser function.
14   ?>
15   <HTML>
16   <HEAD>
17   <TITLE>The GreetUser Function</TITLE>
18   <BODY>
19   <?php
20   if ($Username) {
21       GreetUser ($Username); // Call the
         function.
22   } else {
23       print ("Please log in.\n");
24   } // Close our username if.
25   ?>
26   </BODY>
27   </HTML>
```

values to be associated. This is also true if you fail to pass a value, in which case the function will assume that value is null (*null* is not the mathematical 0, which is actually a value, but closer to the idea of the word *nothing*). The same thing applies if a function takes four arguments and you pass three—the fourth will be null.

To demonstrate functions that take arguments, you'll rewrite the hello.php page from Chapter 6, *Control Structures*. You'll place the greeting code into a simple function that takes an argument—the user's name.

## To create and call a function that takes an argument:

1. Open hello.php in your text editor (**Script 9.3**).

2. Begin with the opening PHP tag, <?php, then take lines 7-16 from the original script (Script 9.3) and place them within a function at the beginning of the page (**Script 9.4**).

```
function GreetUser ($TheUser) {
print ("Good ");
    if (date("A") == "AM") {
        print ("morning, ");
    } elseif ((date("H")>12) and
  → (date("H")<18)) {
print ("afternoon, ");
    } else {
        print ("evening, ");
    } // Close our date if.
    print ("$TheUser");
    print ("!\n");
} // End of GreetUser function.
```

After you give the function an appropriate name, the function itself consists of the same lines used before. The $TheUser variable will receive the value of $Username sent to the function once it is called (see line 21 of Script 9.4).

*continues on next page*

FUNCTIONS THAT TAKE ARGUMENTS

3. Close the initial PHP section and create the HTML header.

```
?><HTML><HEAD><TITLE>The GreetUser
→ Function</TITLE><BODY>
```

4. Reopen a PHP section and place the *if-else* conditional there, including a call to the new function.

```
<?php
if ($Username) {
    GreetUser ($Username); // Call
    → the function.
} else {
    print ("Please log in.\n");
} // Close our username if.
```

You should keep the if ($Username) conditional here so that the function is only called if the $Username exists.

5. Close the PHP and HTML.

```
?></BODY></HTML>
```

6. Save your script, upload it to the server, and test it in your Web browser (**Figure 9.2**). Remember to send the script a Username value—by appending it to the URL or via an HTML form—or else you'll get a result like that in **Figure 9.3**.

### ✔ Tips

■ In Chapter 13, *Creating Web Applications*, you'll see how to place certain information into external files which can be used in several pages. An external file will often be the best place to put your own functions, such as GreetUser, so they will be universally accessible throughout the entire Web site.

■ Technically, if you pass a number as an argument in a function, it does not need to be within quotation marks, but there is no harm in using them anyway to remain consistent as to how arguments are passed.

**Figure 9.2** Now that you've created a function for making a time-specific welcome, even though it may appear similar to our original hello.php page, this greeting can quickly be generated multiple times without rewriting any code.

**Figure 9.3** As you learn more and more advanced things about PHP programming, do not forget the simple facts. Here the omission of sending hello.php a Username value (compare with the URL in **Figure 9.2**) generates this message, as you prudently programmed it to do.

**Script 9.5** This is the most recent version of numbers.php, last modified in Chapter 6, *Control Structures*. You'll modularize the processes in this script by creating two functions.

```
1    <HTML>
2    <HEAD>
3    <TITLE>Conditionals</TITLE>
4    </HEAD>
5    <BODY>
6    <?php
7    /* $Quantity must be passed to this page
     from a form or via the URL. $Discount is
     optional. */
8    $Cost = 20.00;
9    $Tax = 0.06;
10   if ($Quantity) {
11       $Quantity = abs($Quantity);
12       $Discount = abs($Discount);
13       $Tax++; // $Tax is now worth 1.06.
14       $TotalCost = ($Cost * $Quantity);
15       if ( ($TotalCost < 50) AND
         ($Discount) ) {
16           print ("Your \$$Discount will not
             apply because the total value of
             the sale is under $50!\n<P>");
17       }
18       if ($TotalCost >= 50) {
19           $TotalCost = $TotalCost -
             $Discount;
20       }
21       $TotalCost = $TotalCost * $Tax;
22       $Payments = round ($TotalCost, 2) / 12;
23       // Print the results.
24       print ("You requested to purchase
         $Quantity widget(s) at \$$Cost
         each.\n<P>");
25       print ("The total with tax, minus
         your \$$Discount, comes to $");
26       printf ("%01.2f", $TotalCost);
27       print (".\n<P>You may purchase the
         widget(s)in 12 monthly installments
         of $");
28       printf ("%01.2f", $Payments);
29       print (" each.\n<P>");
30   } else {
31       print ("Please make sure that you
         have entered both a quantity and
         an applicable discount and then
         resubmit.\n"); }
32   ?>
33   </BODY>
34   </HTML>
```

# Creating and Using Functions that Return a Value

Once you've begun writing functions that take an argument, the next step is to have a function return an output or a value. To do so requires just two more steps. First, you use the **return** statement within the function. Second, you must assign the output somehow when you call the function. Commonly you would assign the returned value to a variable, but you could also, for example, directly print the output. Here is the basic format for a function that takes an argument and returns a value:

```
function FunctionName ($Argument) {
    statement(s);
    return $Value;
}
```

Normally this function would be used with a line of code such as:

```
$Value = FunctionName($Variable);
```

Note that I've assigned the returned value of the function to a variable. To best demonstrate this concept and its various uses, you'll create two functions based upon the numbers.php page started in Chapter 4, *Using Numbers*, and later modified in Chapter 6, *Control Structures*.

## To create and use a function that returns a value:

1. Open numbers.php in your text editor (**Script 9.5**).

   *continues on next page*

**2.** Open the initial PHP section and start the first function, `CalculateTotal()`, that contains lines 14-21 from the original page (**Script 9.6**):

```php
<?php
function CalculateTotal ($HowMany,
    $Price, $TaxRate, $Savings) {
    $TaxRate++; // $TaxRate is now
        worth 1.06.
    $TheCost = ($Price * $HowMany);
    if ( ($TheCost < 50) AND
        ($Savings) ) {
        print ("Your \$$Savings
            will not apply because
            the total value of the
            sale is under $50!\n<P>");
    }
    if ($TheCost >= 50) {
        $TheCost = $TheCost -
            $Savings;
    }
    $TheCost = $TheCost * $TaxRate;
    return $TheCost;
}
```

This function takes four arguments—the number of widgets purchased, the price of each widget, the applicable tax rate, and the discount the customer may have—then makes the necessary calculations to determine the total cost which it returns.

**3.** Now create a second function:

```php
function CalculatePayments
    ($Amount, $NumberPayments) {
    $Payments = round($Amount, 2) /
        $NumberPayments;
    $Payments = sprintf ("%01.2f",
        $Payments);
    return $Payments;
}
```

The `CalculatePayments()` function will take two arguments—a total amount and the number of payments—and perform a simple calculation. First, the function determines the payment amount using

**Script 9.6** Both functions in this script return a value. When the CalculateTotal function is called, the returned value is assigned to a variable. When the CalculatePayments function is called, the returned value is printed to the browser.

```
script
1   <?php
2   function CalculateTotal ($HowMany,
    $Price, $TaxRate, $Savings) {
3       $TaxRate++; // $TaxRate is now worth
    1.06.
4       $TheCost = ($Price * $HowMany);
5       if ( ($TheCost < 50) AND ($Savings) ) {
6           print ("Your \$$Savings will not
    apply because the total value of
    the sale is under $50!\n<P>");
7       }
8       if ($TheCost >= 50) {
9           $TheCost = $TheCost - $Savings;
10      }
11      $TheCost = $TheCost * $TaxRate;
12      return $TheCost;
13  } // End of the CalculateTotal function.
14  function CalculatePayments ($Amount,
    $NumberPayments) {
15      $Payments = round($Amount, 2) /
    $NumberPayments;
16      $Payments = sprintf ("%01.2f",
    $Payments);
17      return $Payments;
18  } // End of the CalculatePayments function.
19  ?>
20  <HTML>
21  <HEAD>
22  <TITLE>Calculation Functions</TITLE>
23  </HEAD>
24  <BODY>
25  <?php
26  $Cost = 20.00;
27  $Tax = 0.06;
28  if ($Quantity) {
29      $Quantity = abs($Quantity);
30      $Discount = abs($Discount);
31      $TotalCost = CalculateTotal
    ($Quantity, $Cost, $Tax, $Discount);
32      // Print the results.
33      print ("You requested to purchase
    $Quantity widget(s) at \$$Cost
    each.\n<P>");
34      print ("The total with tax, minus
    your \$$Discount, comes to $");
```

*Script continues on next page*

**Script 9.6** *continued*

```
                    script
35      printf ("%01.2f", $TotalCost);
36      print (".\n<P>You may purchase the
        widget(s) in 12 monthly installments
        of $");
37      print (CalculatePayments($TotalCost,
        "12"));
38      print (" each.\n<P>");
39  } else {
40      print ("Please make sure that you
        have entered both a quantity and an
        applicable discount and then
        resubmit.\n");
41  }
42  ?>
43  </BODY>
44  </HTML>
```

the same formula that `numbers.php` orginally used. Then, the $Payments value is formatted using the `sprintf()` function, which, as I said in Chapter 4, *Using Numbers*, works exactly like `printf()` only it does not print anything to the browser, it just alters the variable accordingly. Finally, the value of $Payments is returned.

The benefits of putting even a one-step calculation into a function are twofold: first, it will be easier to find and modify at a later date with your function located at the beginning of your script instead of hidden in the rest of the code; and, second, should you want to repeat the action again in a script, you can do so without duplicating code.

4. Close the initial PHP section, then create the basic HTML header.

```
?><HTML><HEAD><TITLE>Calculation
→ Functions</TITLE></HEAD><BODY>
```

5. Open a new PHP section and set your variables:

```
<?php
$Cost = 20.00;
$Tax = 0.06;
```

I've not changed the value of the $Cost variable, but you can set it, as well as $Tax, to whatever value you prefer.

6. Now write the heart of the PHP script.

```
if ($Quantity) {
    $Quantity = abs($Quantity);
    $Discount = abs($Discount);
    $TotalCost = CalculateTotal
→ ($Quantity, $Cost, $Tax,
→ $Discount);
    // Print the results.
    print ("You requested to purchase
→ $Quantity widget(s) at \$$Cost
→ each.\n<P>");
```

*continues on next page*

```
    print ("The total with tax, minus
    → your \$$Discount, comes to $");
    printf ("%01.2f", $TotalCost);
    print (".\n<P>You may purchase
    → the widget(s)in 12 monthly
    → installments of $");
    print (CalculatePayments
    → ($TotalCost, "12"));
    print (" each.\n<P>");
} else {
    print ("Please make sure that
    → you have entered both a
    → quantity and an applicable
    → discount and then resubmit.\n");
}
```

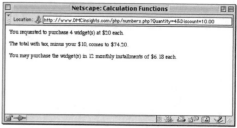

**Figure 9.4** Again, although the actual results are like those you had without functions, these functions can be universally applied across an entire Web site. Creating functions such as these two as you work also expedites future programming projects by building up a strong library of reusable code.

Except for the calls to the functions, this section is exactly as it was when you wrote it in Chapter 6, but now you've increased the efficiency of the page by separating out the calculations into their own functions. This section of code also demonstrates the two ways of using functions that return a value. On line 31 a variable is set to the returned value of the CalculateTotal() function and on line 37 the result of calling the CalculatePayment() function is immediately printed.

7. Close this last PHP section and then finish the HTML.

   ?></BODY></HTML>

8. Save your script, upload it to the server, and test it in your Web browser (**Figure 9.4**). Remember to send the script a Quantity value (and a Discount value, if you want)—by appending it to the URL or via an HTML form. If the script does not receive a Quantity value you'll see the "Please make sure ..." error message generated by line 40.

## ✔ Tips

■ In the CalculatePayments() function you could change the sprintf() line to printf(), immediately printing the result and just remove the return statement altogether. Although I haven't done so here, it's perfectly reasonable to have your function directly print out any results.

■ You can only have one return statement executed in a function but the same function can have multiple return statements. As an example, you may want to write a function that checks for a condition and returns whether or not the condition was satisfied. In such a case you would code, in your function:

```
if (condition) {
    return TRUE;
} else {
    return FALSE;
}
```

The result returned by the function then is either TRUE or FALSE indicating whether or not the stated condition was met.

■ A return statement can only return one value. In order to return multiple values, you'll need to make use of arrays. See Appendix C, *PHP Resources*, for more on where you can learn about returning multiple values.

# Variables and Functions

I did not introduce the concept of variable scope in Chapter 2, *Variables*, because without an understanding of functions, scope makes little sense. Now that you have a reasonable familiarity with functions, I'll revisit the topic of variables and discuss in some detail how exactly variables and functions work together.

## Variable scope and the *global* statement

As you saw in the second section of this chapter, *Creating and Calling Functions that Take Arguments*, you can send variables to a function by passing them as arguments. However, you can also call a variable from within a function using the `global` statement. This is possible because of variable scope. The scope of a variable is essentially the realm in which it exists. By default, the variables you write in a script exist for the life of that script. Conversely, environment variables (such as $PHP_SELF) exist throughout the server.

Functions, though, create a new level of scope. Function variables—the arguments of a function as well as any variables defined within the function—only exist within that function and are not accessible outside of it (i.e. they are local variables with local scope). Likewise a variable from outside of a function can only be referenced by passing it to the function as an argument or by using the `global` statement. The `global` statement roughly means "I want this variable within the function to be the same as it is outside of the function." In other words, the `global` statement turns a local variable with local scope into a global variable with global scope. Any changes made to the variable within the function are also passed on to the variable when it is outside of the function (assuming the function is called, that is), without using the **return** command. The syntax of the **global** statement is as follows:

```
function FunctionName ($Argument) {
    global $Variable;
statement(s);
}
```

As long as $Variable exists outside of the function, it will also have the same value within the function. This leads to a parallel topic regarding functions and variables: because of variable scope, a variable within a function is a different entity (perhaps with a different value) than a variable outside of the function, *even if the two variables use the exact same name* (and assuming you do not use the **global** statement within the function). I'll go over this more explicitly.

Frequently you use a function call line like **FunctionName ($Value1);** in which case the function (here, **FunctionName ($Argument1)**) then equates the value of $Argument1 to that of $Value1, so their values are the same but their names are different. However, if the name of the argument in the function was also $Value1 (so the function creation line reads **FunctionName ($Value1)**), the $Value1 variable within the function assumes the same value as the original $Value1 outside of the function but they are still two separate variables. The one has a scope within the function and the other outside of it. For this reason, I have been careful, when writing functions, to use different variable names in the function defining line than I did in the function call line in order to avoid confusion.

*continues on next page*

**VARIABLES AND FUNCTIONS**

I mention this topic because you do not actually have to come up with different names. You could use the exact same name in the function and the call line for convenience sake (it becomes very easy to remember what arguments are passed that way), but remember that they are not the same variable. What happens to a variable's value within a function stays within the function, unless you use the global statement, which does make the two variables the same.

In order to better understand this concept, you'll rework the numbers.php script using the global statement.

## To use the global statement:

1. Open numbers.php in your text editor (Script 9.6).

2. Remove the $Price and $TaxRate arguments from the CalculateTotal function (**Script 9.7**) so that line 2 now looks like so:

   ```
   function CalculateTotal ($HowMany,
   → $Savings) {
   ```

   The $Price and $TaxRate variables will be brought into the function as $Cost and $Tax using the global statement so it will no longer be necessary to pass them as arguments.

3. Add two global statements:

   ```
   global $Cost;
   global $Tax;
   ```

   These two statements tell the function to incorporate the exact same $Cost and $Tax variables as the ones that exist outside of the function.

**Script 9.7** Since the $Cost and $Tax values are required by the CalculateTotal function, that can be brought in just as easily using the global statement. When making this change, remember to no longer pass them as arguments, which could confuse the programmer and create peculiar errors.

```
script
1   <?php
2   function CalculateTotal ($HowMany,
    $Savings) {
3       global $Cost;
4       global $Tax;
5       $Tax++; // $Tax is now worth 1.06.
6       $TotalCost = ($Cost * $HowMany);
7       if ( ($TotalCost < 50) AND
        ($Savings) ) {
8           print ("Your \$$Savings will not
            apply because the total value of
            the sale is under $50!\n<P>");
9       }
10      if ($TotalCost >= 50) {
11          $TotalCost = $TotalCost -
            $Savings;
12      }
13      $TotalCost = $TotalCost * $Tax;
14      return $TotalCost;
15  } // End of the CalculateTotal function.
16  function CalculatePayments ($Amount,
    $NumberPayments) {
17      $Payments = round($Amount, 2) /
        $NumberPayments;
18      $Payments = sprintf ("%01.2f",
        $Payments);
19      return $Payments;
20  } // End of the CalculatePayments
    function.
21  ?>
22  <HTML>
23  <HEAD>
24  <TITLE>Calculation Functions</TITLE>
25  </HEAD>
26  <BODY>
27  <?php
28  $Cost = 20.00;
29  $Tax = 0.06;
30  print ("The tax value is currently
    \$$Tax .\n<P>");
31  if ($Quantity) {
```

*Script continues on next page*

**Script 9.7** *continued*

```
                    script
32    $Quantity = abs($Quantity);
33    $Discount = abs($Discount);
34    $TotalCost = CalculateTotal
      ($Quantity, $Discount);
35    print ("After calling the function,
      the tax value is now \$$Tax .\n<P>");
36    // Print the results.
37    print ("You requested to purchase
      $Quantity widget(s) at \$$Cost
      each.\n<P>");
38    print ("The total with tax, minus
      your \$$Discount, comes to $");
39    printf ("%01.2f", $TotalCost);
40    print (".\n<P>You may purchase the
      widget(s) in 12 monthly installments
      of $");
41    print (CalculatePayments($TotalCost,
      "12"));
42    print (" each.\n<P>");
43  } else {
44    print ("Please make sure that you
      have entered both a quantity and an
      applicable discount and then
      resubmit.\n");
45  }
46  ?>
47  </BODY>
48  </HTML>
```

**4.** Edit the rest of the function using $Cost in place of $Price, $Tax instead of $TaxRate, and $TotalCost in lieu of $TheCost:

```
$Tax++; // $Tax is now worth 1.06.
$TotalCost = ($Cost * $HowMany);
if ( ($TotalCost < 50) AND
→ ($Savings) ) {
    print ("Your \$$Savings will
    → not apply because the
    → total value of the sale
    → is under $50!\n<P>");
}
if ($TotalCost >= 50) {
    $TotalCost = $TotalCost -
    → $Savings;
}
$TotalCost = $TotalCost * $Tax;
return $TotalCost;
```

Since the function is now using different variable names, the calculations must be changed accordingly. To get an understanding of variable scope, I've also changed the $TheCost variable to be called $TotalCost. Remember that the $TotalCost variable within the function is a different variable than the same one referred to outside of the function, even though, in the end they will both have the same value.

**5.** Further down the script, after the line $Tax = 0.06; (line 29), print out the current value of the variable to monitor how it changes over the course of the page.

```
print ("The tax value is currently
→ \$$Tax .\n<P>");
```

To demonstrate that the global statement brings the $Tax variable into the function and that any changes made within the function apply globally, you'll print out the value of $Tax before and after the function is called.

*continues on next page*

**6.** Change the `CalculateTotal()` function call so that $Tax and $Cost are no longer passed as arguments.

```
$TotalCost = CalculateTotal
→ ($Quantity, $Discount);
```

Since the function now only takes two arguments, passing four arguments as the script used to do would cause a error.

**7.** Once again print out the value of $Tax.

```
print ("After calling the function,
→ the tax value is now \$$Tax .\
→ n<P>");
```

Without the `global` statement, the value printed here and the value printed above would be the same. Since the global $Tax was modified in the function, though, you will see different values printed.

**8.** Save your script, upload it to the server, and test it in your Web browser (**Figure 9.5**). Remember to send the script a Quantity value (and a Discount value, if you want)—by appending it to the URL or via an HTML form.

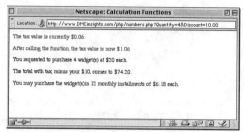

**Figure 9.5** Because the $Tax variable within the function is the same variable as the similarly-named $Tax variable outside of the function (on account of the `global` statement), every change made to its value within the function is applied universally.

## Setting default argument values

While writing functions, PHP allows you to preset a value for your arguments. The function will use this default value unless it receives an argument which would then overwrite the default. In other words, by setting a default value for an argument, you have rendered that particular argument optional when calling the function.

Using the `CalculatePayments()` function as an example (Script 9.7), you could set 12 as the number of monthly payments by creating your function like this:

```
function CalculatePayments ($Amount,
→ $NumberPayments = "12") {
```

VARIABLES AND FUNCTIONS

Calling the function with the code `CalculatePayments ($Amounts);` would still work without a problem but coding `CalculatePayments ($Amounts, "24");` would set the $NumberPayments variable equal to 24, not the default 12.

You would set an argument's default value if you wanted to assume a certain value but still allow for other possibilities. However, keep in mind that the default arguments should always be written after the other standard arguments (those without defaults). This is because PHP directly assigns values to arguments in the order they are received from the call line. Thus, it is not possible to omit a value for the first argument but include one for the second (which would therefore mean that you sent one value which would automatically be equated to the first argument, not the second).For example, if a function was written as this:

```
function CalculateTotal ($HowMany,
→ $Price = "20.00", $TaxRate = "0.06") {
```

and you called the function with this line:

```
CalculateTotal (3, "0.07");
```

with the intention of setting $HowMany to 3, leaving $Price at 20.00 and changing the $TaxRate to 0.07, there would be problems. The end result would be that $HowMany gets set to 3, $Price gets set to 0.07 and $TaxRate remains at 0.06 which is not the desired result. The proper way to achieve that affect would be to code:

```
CalculateTotal (3, "20.00", "0.07");
```

Let's rework the `numbers.php` page (Script 9.7) to incorporate the notion of setting default argument values.

## To write a function that uses default values:

1. Open numbers.php (Script 9.7) in your text editor, if it is not already.

2. Add a default value to the $Savings variable in the CalculateTotal() function (**Script 9.8**):

   ```
   function CalculateTotal ($HowMany,
   → $Savings = "0") {
   ```

3. You have now set the value of $Savings to be 0, as a default. If no argument is passed to the function, it will be assumed that no discount applies. Edit the second function, setting the $NumberPayments argument to the default of 12.

   ```
   function CalculatePayments ($Amount,
   → $NumberPayments = "12") {
   ```

   If two arguments are sent to the CalculatePayments() function, the $NumberPayments will be set to the second value instead of the default.

4. Delete the two lines in the main body of the script that printed out the value of $Tax, since they are no longer relevant.

5. Alter the call to the CalculatePayments function so that it no longer sends along an argument for the number of payments.

   ```
   print (CalculatePayments
   → ($TotalCost));
   ```

   The CalculatePayments() call now only passes the $TotalCost value as an argument, since $NumberPayments has a default value. You could pass a $NumberPayments value here if you wanted to set a different number than 12 as the number of monthly payments.

**Script 9.8** The numbers.php page is now written as you commonly would write a function. Setting the default value within a function makes an argument optional.

```
1   <?php
2   function CalculateTotal ($HowMany,
        $Savings = "0") {
3       global $Cost;
4       global $Tax;
5       $Tax++; // $Tax is now worth 1.06.
6       $TotalCost = ($Cost * $HowMany);
7       if ( ($TotalCost < 50) AND
           ($Savings) ) {
8           print ("Your \$$Savings will not
               apply because the total value of
               the sale is under $50!\n<P>");
9       }
10      if ($TotalCost >= 50) {
11          $TotalCost = $TotalCost -
               $Savings;
12      }
13      $TotalCost = $TotalCost * $Tax;
14      return $TotalCost;
15  } // End of the CalculateTotal function.
16  function CalculatePayments ($Amount,
        $NumberPayments = "12") {
17      $Payments = round($Amount, 2) /
           $NumberPayments;
18      $Payments = sprintf ("%01.2f",
           $Payments);
19      return $Payments;
20  } // End of the CalculatePayments
        function.
21  ?>
22  <HTML>
23  <HEAD>
24  <TITLE>Calculation Functions</TITLE>
25  </HEAD>
26  <BODY>
27  <?php
28  $Cost = 20.00;
29  $Tax = 0.06;
30  if ($Quantity) {
31      $Quantity = abs($Quantity);
32      $Discount = abs($Discount);
33      $TotalCost = CalculateTotal
           ($Quantity, $Discount);
```

*Script continues on next page*

**Script 9.8** *continued*

```
         script
34    // Print the results.
35    print ("You requested to purchase
      $Quantity widget(s) at \$$Cost
      each.\n<P>");
36    print ("The total with tax, minus
      your \$$Discount, comes to $");
37    printf ("%01.2f", $TotalCost);
38    print (".\n<P>You may purchase the
      widget(s) in 12 monthly installments
      of $");
39    print (CalculatePayments($TotalCost));
40    print (" each.\n<P>");
41  } else {
42    print ("Please make sure that you
      have entered both a quantity and an
      applicable discount and then
      resubmit.\n");
43  }
44  ?>
45  </BODY>
46  </HTML>
```

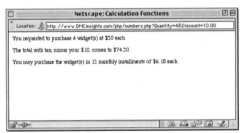

**Figure 9.6** Even though the end user, viewing your pages in their browser, will never be able to tell the difference between scripts which use functions and those which do not (compare this to Figure 9.4), you've increased the usability of your programming tenfold.

6. Save your script, upload it to the server, and test it in your Web browser (**Figure 9.6**). Remember to send the script a Quantity value (and a Discount value, if you want)—by appending it to the URL or via an HTML form.

## ✔ Tips

■ In every example in this chapter, I pass arguments to functions by value, which means that a copy of the value of a variable is sent to the function, not the actual variable itself. You can also pass arguments by reference, which allows you to modify a variable in a function, but that's too complex a topic for this book. See Appendix C, *PHP Resources*, for more on where you can learn about this subject.

■ When it comes to naming conventions for function arguments, there are different schools of thought. On the one hand, using the same name in the function as a variable outside of the function makes it easy to remember how values match up. On the other hand, using generic argument names in your function makes it less script-specific. You could also use a hybrid method by appending a lower case *f* to the beginning of function names such as $fHowMany and $fTaxRate. Some programmers identify global variables as $gVariable. Again, the key is to remain consistent to your naming policy.

**VARIABLES AND FUNCTIONS**

**153**

# FILES AND
# DIRECTORIES

To truly take your Web applications to the next level, you'll need a method of storing and retrieving data. E-commerce sites, Internet portals, and template-driven content providers all make use of writing and reading information to the server.

There are two primary ways of storing data with PHP: using files (and directories) or databases. In this chapter, I will discuss the former, and in the next chapter, I will introduce the latter. It is worth your time to comprehend both methods.

At the very least, there are two benefits to using files and directories to store data instead of databases: one, they don't require knowledge of databases (a complicated subject), and, two, most Web hosts charge extra for database access with your account, whereas file access is a given. While a database will inevitably be more powerful than a file-based system, you may be surprised at how much you can do just sending and retrieving information from simple text documents on the server!

In this chapter, you'll learn about file permissions, then learn to: write to and read from files; create directories; handle file uploads from an HTML form; and, perform other common tasks with both files and directories (renaming, deleting, etc.).

# File Permissions

Before I go through the examples of writing to, and reading from, a file, I should briefly mention file permissions. This is another topic (like security and regular expressions) which is large enough that you may want to pursue it further—in which case see Appendix C, *PHP Resources*—but I'll cover enough to get you started.

File and directory permissions identify who can do what to the file or directory. The options are: *read*, *write*, and *execute* (actually, files can be designated *executable* whereas directories are made *searchable*). On top of that, these options can be set differently for three unique types of users: the *owner* of the file, i.e., the person who put it on the server; members of a particular *group*, which a server administrator sets; and, *others*, i.e., those who don't fall into the previous two categories. There is also the implied *everyone* level which includes all of the above users.

Normally a file's *owner* is given read and write permissions by default, while *others* are able to read a file (*groups* don't really come into play here). Execution of a file is a major security issue and fortunately doesn't affect PHP scripts (Perl can write an executable file but PHP generally cannot, since it is a scripting language, not a programming language). Being able to write to a file can also be a security issue and should only be designated an option when absolutely necessary.

In this chapter, you will be working with a text file on the server named **data.txt**. Depending upon your server configuration (e.g., if you are working on an ISP's server or your own home computer), you may want to set the permissions on this file ahead of time. If the file does not have the correct permissions to do what your PHP script is asking it to, you will see an error message similar to that in **Figure 10.1**.

Before proceeding through this chapter, you should create **data.txt** on the server.

**Figure 10.1** The "permission denied..." message is the result of attempting to do something to a file which is not allowed by the server. Here the server is denying the fopen() function which is attempting to open data.txt for the purposes of writing to it.

```
$ chmod 0666 data.txt
$ ls -l
-rw-rw-rw-  ullman  375   data.txt
```

**Figure 10.2** At the shell prompt in the directory where `data.txt` is located, the line `chmod 0666 data.txt` changes the permissions for the file. You can check the permissions by typing `ls -l`. This command reveals that: `data.txt` has read and write permissions for all three categories of users; the file's owner is *ullman*; and the file's size is 375 bytes.

**Figure 10.3** The Fetch FTP application for the Macintosh uses this pop-up window to allow you to set a file's permissions.

### ✔ Tip

■ If you are already familiar with telnet and *chmod*, you probably also understand what the `0666` number means (Figure 10.2), but I'll explain for those of you who aren't familiar with it. The `0` is a necessary prefix and then each `6` corresponds to write (4) plus read (2) permission—first assigning `6` to the *owner*, then to the *group*, then to *others*. Comparatively, `0777` allows write (4) plus read (2) plus execute (1) permission to all three types of user. This is applicable for Unix variant operating systems only (e.g. Linux and Solaris).

### To create `data.txt`:

1. Open your text editor and create a new document.

2. Without typing anything into the file, save it as `data.txt`.

3. Upload the file to your server.

This may seem like an odd series of steps, but in order to set the permissions on a file, it must exist first. You do want the file to be blank, though, as you'll use PHP to write data to it later.

Depending upon your situation, there are a number of ways you can set a file's permissions. The desired end result for this example is to give either *others* or *everyone* permission to *read* and *write* (but not *execute*) `data.txt`. You will need to check with your ISP as to how to set file permissions, but most likely it will involve one of the following options:

### To set a file's permissions:

◆ Some ISPs offer their users a Web-based control panel where they can set file permissions, as well set other hosting parameters.

◆ If you have telnet access to the server, navigate to the directory where `data.txt` is located and use the *chmod* command (on a Unix server) to alter its permissions (**Figure 10.2**). See the tip below for more information about setting permissions using *chmod* on Unix servers.

◆ You may be able to change a file's permissions using your FTP client (**Figure 10.3**).

◆ If you are working on your own Windows NT server, you can alter a file's permissions by right-clicking on the file and selecting "Properties," then clicking on the "Security" tab.

**FILE PERMISSIONS**

# Writing to Files

Since you need to write something to a file in order to read something from it, we'll I'll explore writing first. Writing to a file on the server is a three-step process: first, you open the file; second, write your data to it; and, third, close the file. Fortunately PHP's built-in functions for doing these steps are quite obvious:

```
$FileName = "data.txt";
$FilePointer = fopen ($FileName, "mode");
fwrite ($FilePointer, "data to be
→ written");
fclose ($FilePointer);
```

When handling files, the first thing I do is assign the filename and path (where it is on the server) to a variable, for convenience sake. Use common path conventions when assigning the value (e.g., if the file was in the `files` directory which is a subset of the current directory, the filename would be `files/data.txt`).

Once you've identified the file, you must create a file pointer when opening it. This file pointer, assigned to the appropriately-named $FilePointer variable, is used by PHP to refer to the open file.

The most important consideration when opening the file is what *mode* you use. Depending upon what you intend to do with the file, the mode dictates how to open it. The most forgiving mode is *a+*, which allows you to read or write to a file. It will create the file if it doesn't exist and it will append—hence *a*—new data to the end of the file automatically. Conversely *r* will only allow you to read from a file. **Table 10.1** lists all of the possible modes.

The `fwrite()` function will write the new data, sent as the second argument in the function call, to the file in accordance with the selected mode. Finally, you close the file by once again referring to the file pointer.

Let's create a form that stores user-submitted URLs in a separate file.

## File Modes

| MODE | ALLOWS FOR |
|---|---|
| r | Read from the file only. |
| w | Write to the file only, but it will create the file if it doesn't exist or discard existing contents before writing if the file does exist. |
| a | Append new data to the end of the file and create the file if it doesn't exist. |
| r+ | Read and write to the file. |
| w+ | Read and write to the file, but it will create the file if it doesn't exist or discard existing contents before writing if the file does exist. |
| a+ | Read from and write to the file and create the file if it doesn't exist. New data will be appended to the end of file. |

**Table 10.1** Which mode to use when opening a file is rather self-evident. The most important things to keep in mind are: whether you will be reading, writing, or both, and what to do with any existing contents (append to or overwrite).

**Script 10.1** This is the existing version of form.html. You can remove the first and last name lines, if you want to, as they won't be needed here (see **Script 10.2**).

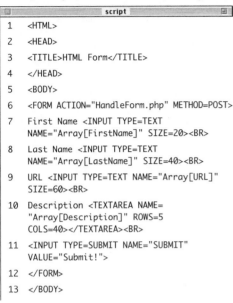

```
1   <HTML>
2   <HEAD>
3   <TITLE>HTML Form</TITLE>
4   </HEAD>
5   <BODY>
6   <FORM ACTION="HandleForm.php" METHOD=POST>
7   First Name <INPUT TYPE=TEXT
    NAME="Array[FirstName]" SIZE=20><BR>
8   Last Name <INPUT TYPE=TEXT
    NAME="Array[LastName]" SIZE=40><BR>
9   URL <INPUT TYPE=TEXT NAME="Array[URL]"
    SIZE=60><BR>
10  Description <TEXTAREA NAME=
    "Array[Description]" ROWS=5
    COLS=40></TEXTAREA><BR>
11  <INPUT TYPE=SUBMIT NAME="SUBMIT"
    VALUE="Submit!">
12  </FORM>
13  </BODY>
```

## To write to an external file:

**1.** If you wish, open form.html from Chapter 8, *Regular Expressions*, (**Script 10.1**) in your text editor.

I'll make some minor changes to the form, but you can skip this step, if you wish, without affecting the end result.

**2.** Remove the first and last name lines (**Script 10.2**).

**3.** Save your page and upload it to the server.

Now you'll write a new HandleForm.php script to process the data generated by form.html.

**4.** Create a new PHP document in your text editor.

*continues on next page*

**Script 10.2** In order to keep things orderly, I have cut out the unnecessary first and last name lines from form.html. However, since I did not alter the name of the two important inputs—Array[URL] and Array[Description]—leaving the page as it was would not be a problem either.

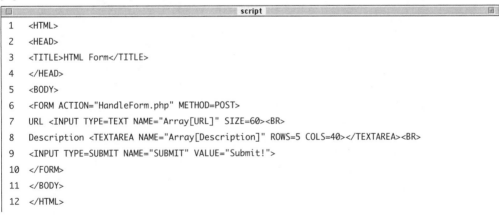

```
1   <HTML>
2   <HEAD>
3   <TITLE>HTML Form</TITLE>
4   </HEAD>
5   <BODY>
6   <FORM ACTION="HandleForm.php" METHOD=POST>
7   URL <INPUT TYPE=TEXT NAME="Array[URL]" SIZE=60><BR>
8   Description <TEXTAREA NAME="Array[Description]" ROWS=5 COLS=40></TEXTAREA><BR>
9   <INPUT TYPE=SUBMIT NAME="SUBMIT" VALUE="Submit!">
10  </FORM>
11  </BODY>
12  </HTML>
```

WRITING TO FILES

**5.** Begin by defining the PHP function (**Script 10.3**):

```
<?
function WriteToFile ($URL,
→ $Description) {
```

The `WriteToFile()` function takes two arguments—the URL and the description of the URL which the user entered in `form.html`.

**6.** Identify and open the file.

```
$TheFile = "data.txt";
$Open = fopen ($TheFile, "a");
```

These two lines identify the file and open it for writing only (creating, if necessary, and writing the new data to the end of the file if the file does exist). The `data.txt` file referred to here should be the same one that was created and had its proper permissions set in the previous section of this chapter.

**7.** Now, you'll create a conditional based upon the success of the `fopen()` function.

```
if ($Open) {
    fwrite ($Open, "$URL\
    → t$Description\n");fclose
    → ($Open);
    $Worked = TRUE;
} else {
    $Worked = FALSE;
}
```

If the file is successfully opened, the function will then append the new data to the old. The format for the data is the URL followed by a tab character (created using an escaped *t*), then the description followed by a new line character (created by an escaped *n*). The file is then closed.

**Script 10.3** This script demonstrates a number of techniques learned to this point which you ought to consider using when programming. First, the function is written as the first element of the script. Second, the user-submitted data is checked for accuracy using regular expressions. Third, messages are sent to the browser in case of problems.

```
script
1   <?
2   function WriteToFile ($URL, $Description) {
3   /* Function WriteToFile takes two
    arguments--URL and Description--which
    will be written to an external file. */
4       $TheFile = "data.txt";
5       $Open = fopen ($TheFile, "a");
6       if ($Open) {
7           fwrite ($Open,
            "$URL\t$Description\n");
8           fclose ($Open);
9           $Worked = TRUE;
10      } else {
11          $Worked = FALSE;
12      }
13      return $Worked;
14  } // End of WriteToFile Function.
15  ?>
16  <HTML>
17  <HEAD>
18  <TITLE>Using Files</TITLE>
19  <BODY>
20  <?php
21  /* This page receives and handles the
    data generated by "form.html". */
22  $Pattern = "(http://)?([^[:space:]]+)
    ([[:alnum:]\.,-_?/&=])";
23  if (eregi($Pattern, $Array["URL"])) {
24      $Replace = "<a href=\"http://\\2\\3\"
        target=\"_new\">\\2\\3</a>";
25      $Array["URL"] = eregi_replace($Pattern,
        $Replace, $Array["URL"]);
26      $CallFunction = WriteToFile
        ($Array["URL"], $Array["Description"]);
27      if ($CallFunction) {
28          print ("Your submission--
            $Array[URL]--has been
            received!<BR>\n");
29      } else {
```

*Script continues on next page*

**Script 10.3** *continued*

```
                     script
30        print ("Your submission was
          not processed due to a system
          error!<BR>\n");
31     }
32  } else {
33     print ("Please enter a valid Web
          address!\n");
34  }
35  ?>
36  </BODY>
37  </HTML>
```

**8.** Return the $Worked value and close the function.

```
    return $Worked;
} // End of WriteToFile Function.
```

If the file was successfully opened, the $Worked variable is set to TRUE and returned in order to indicate the success of the function.

**9.** Close the initial PHP code and create the standard HTML header.

```
?>
<HTML><HEAD><TITLE>Using Files
→ </TITLE><BODY>
```

**10.** Open the main PHP section.

```
<?php
```

**11.** Now define the regular expression pattern:

```
$Pattern =
"(http://)?([^[:space:]]+)
→ ([[:alnum:]\.,-_?/&=])";
```

Once again, regular expressions will be used to confirm a valid URL and then turn it into a clickable link.

**12.** Create a conditional based upon successful execution of the regular expression.

```
if (eregi($Pattern, $Array["URL"]))
{
    $Replace = "<a href=\"http://
    → \\2\\3\" target=\"_new\">
    → \\2\\3</a>";
    $Array["URL"] = eregi_replace
    → ($Pattern, $Replace,
    → $Array["URL"]);
    $CallFunction = WriteToFile
    → ($Array["URL"],
    → $Array["Description"]);
```

If the user-submitted URL matches the regular expression, it will then be changed using eregi_replace() and the concept of back referencing. Then, the WriteToFile() function is called.

*continues on next page*

**13.** Now, PHP will print a message based upon the results of the function call.

```
if ($CallFunction) {
    print ("Your submission-
    → $Array[URL]-has been
    → received!<BR>\n");
} else {
    print ("Your submission was not
    → processed due to a system
    → error!<BR>\n");
}
```

The $CallFunction variable will be equal to the returned value of $Worked from the function. If PHP could open the file, $Worked, and therefore $CallFunction will be TRUE, else it will be FALSE. Accordingly, a message will be displayed to the user indicating the result.

**14.** Close the if statement, the PHP, and the HTML.

```
} else {
print ("Please enter a valid Web
→ address!\n");
}
?>
</BODY></HTML>
```

**15.** Save your script as HandleForm.php, upload it to the server (in the same location as form.html and data.txt), and test both in your Web browser (**Figures 10.4, 10.5,** and **10.6**).

## ✔ Tips

■ As an extra step of safe-checking, you can use the is_writeable() function to determine if the server will allow you to write data to the file before attempting to open it. Here is how you would begin to incorporate it (this is only the beginning of the script):

```
$TheFile = "data.txt";
if (is_writeable ($TheFile)) {
$Open = fopen ($TheFile, "a");
```

**Figure 10.4** As long as the user enters a valid Web address and the script is able to write the data to the file, all the user should see is this.

**Figure 10.5** After running the form.html and HandleForm.php pages at least once, you can download data.txt to your computer and view it in your text editor. Notice that the HTML A HREF tag, generated with the eregi_replace() function, is written to the file as well.

**Figure 10.6** For each additional submission of form.html, another line of information will be added to data.txt. This particular text editor (BBEdit) also indicates tabs (with the triangle) and new lines (the last character on lines 2 and 4).

■ On Windows servers, be sure to escape the backslashes in a filename path or use forward slashes instead. For example, you could say either c:\\php\\data.txt or c:/php/data.txt but not c:\php\data.txt since the backslash is the escape character. Unix servers use the forward slash as the standard so this is not an issue on those servers.

**Script 10.4** The script is rendered easier to understand by creating four functions: one to read from the file, one to write to it, one to create a form, and one to handle the form. Thus, the main body of the page is a simple conditional with calls to the functions.

```
script
1   <HTML>
2   <HEAD>
3   <TITLE>Storing URLs in an External
    File</TITLE>
4   </HEAD>
5   <BODY>
6   <?php
7   function WriteToFile ($URL, $Description) {
8   /* Function WriteToFile takes two
    arguments--URL and Description--which
    will be written to an external file. */
9       $TheFile = "data.txt";
10      $Open = fopen ($TheFile, "a");
11      if ($Open) {
12          fwrite ($Open, "$URL\
            t$Description\n");
13          fclose ($Open);
14          $Worked = TRUE;
15      } else {
16          $Worked = FALSE;
17  }
18      return $Worked;
19  } // End of WriteToFile Function.
20
21  function ReadFromFile () {
22  /* Function ReadFromFile displays all the
    information stored in an external file. */
23      $TheFile = "data.txt";
24      $Open = fopen ($TheFile, "r");
25      if ($Open) {
26          print ("URLs currently listed in
            the data file:<P>\n");
27          $Data = file ($TheFile);
28          for ($n = 0; $n < count($Data);
            $n++) {
29              $GetLine = explode("\t",
                $Data[$n]);
30              print ("$GetLine[0]<BR>
                \n$GetLine[1]<P>\n");
31          }
```

*Script continues on next page*

# Reading from Files

Now that you've coded a script that writes data to a file, it's time to create one that can read that information. Reading data from a file is almost as easy as its writing counterpart. There are, again, three steps. First you open the file, then you read from the file, finally you close the file.

```
$FileName = "data.txt";
$FilePointer = fopen ($FileName, "mode");
$Array = file ($FileName);
fclose ($FilePointer);
```

The file() function is a valuable built-in tool in PHP. It reads everything from a file and places that information into an array, with each array element being delineated by a carriage return or new line. If data.txt contains two lines of information, each of which ends with a new line (see Figure 10.6, but do not be confused by the fact that each line appears to spill over onto a second line), the corresponding array will contain two elements. The first element will be equal to the first line of data.txt and the second element equal to the second line. Once the data is stored into an array, it can be easily manipulated or printed.

Now you'll use this knowledge to create a script that both collects URLs from a user as well as displays previously submitted URLs—all in one page!

## To read from a file:

1. Create a new document in your text editor.

2. Begin with the standard HTML header (**Script 10.4**):
```
<HTML><HEAD>
<TITLE>Storing URLs in an External
→ File</TITLE>
</HEAD><BODY>
```

*continues on next page*

Because this page will both act as the form itself and handle the results of the form, I'll write this script a little differently than I have heretofore, which is why I do not begin the page itself with the functions as I otherwise would.

3. Open a PHP code section and duplicate the WriteToFile() function from HandleForm.php (Script 10.3).

```php
<?php
function WriteToFile ($URL,
→ $Description) {
$TheFile = "data.txt";
$Open = fopen ($TheFile, "a");
if ($Open) {
fwrite ($Open, "$URL\
→ t$Description\n");
fclose ($Open);
$Worked = TRUE;
} else {
$Worked = FALSE;
}
return $Worked;
} // End of WriteToFile Function.
```

You shouldn't have had to change any of the lines here—one of the benefits of programming with functions!

4. Create a new function that will retrieve data from the file.

```php
function ReadFromFile () {
$TheFile = "data.txt";
$Open = fopen ($TheFile, "r");
if ($Open) {
print ("URLs currently listed in the
→ data file:<P>\n");
$Data = file ($TheFile);
for ($n = 0; $n < count($Data);
→ $n++) {
$GetLine = explode("\t", $Data[$n]);
print ("$GetLine[0]<BR>
→ \n$GetLine[1]<P>\n");
}
fclose ($Open);
print ("<HR><P>\n");
```

**Script 10.4** continued

```
32          fclose ($Open);
33          print ("<HR><P>\n");
34      } else {
35          print ("Unable to read from
            data.txt!<BR>\n");
36      }
37  } // End of ReadFromFile Function.
38
39  function CreateForm () {
40  /* Function CreateForm will display the
    HTML form. */
41      print ("Add a URL to the data file:\n");
42      print ("<FORM ACTION=\"urls.php\"
            METHOD=POST>\n");
43      print ("URL <INPUT TYPE=TEXT NAME=
            \"Array[URL]\" SIZE=60><BR>\n");
44      print ("Description <TEXTAREA
            NAME=\"Array[Description]\" ROWS=5
            COLS=40></TEXTAREA><BR>\n");
45      print ("<INPUT TYPE=HIDDEN
            NAME=\"BeenSubmitted\"
            VALUE=\"TRUE\">\n");
46      print ("<INPUT TYPE=SUBMIT
            NAME=\"SUBMIT\" VALUE=\"Submit!\">
            </FORM>\n");
47  } // End of the CreateForm function.
48
49  function HandleForm () {
50      global $Array;
51      $Pattern = "(http://)?([^[:space:]]+)
            ([[:alnum:]\.,-_?/&=])";
52      if (eregi($Pattern, $Array["URL"])) {
53          $Replace = "<a href=
                \"http://\\2\\3\"
                target=\"_new\">\\2\\3</a>";
54          $Array["URL"] = eregi_replace
                ($Pattern, $Replace, $Array["URL"]);
55          $CallFunction = WriteToFile
                ($Array["URL"],
                $Array["Description"]);
56          if ($CallFunction) {
57              print ("Your submission--
                    $Array[URL]--has been
                    received!<P><HR><P>\n");
58          } else {
59              print ("Your submission
                    was not processed due to a
                    system error!<BR>\n");
```

*Script continues on next page*

**Script 10.4** *continued*

```
                    script
60          }
61      } else {
62          print ("Please enter a valid Web
            address!\n");
63      }
64  } // End of the HandleForm function.
65
66  /* This next conditional determines
    whether to handle the form, depending
    upon whether or not $BeenSubmitted is
    TRUE. */
67  if ($BeenSubmitted) {
68      HandleForm();
69  }
70  ReadFromFile();
71  CreateForm();
72  ?>
73  </BODY>
74  </HTML>
```

```
} else {
print ("Unable to read from data.txt!
→ <BR>\n");
}
} // End of ReadFromFile Function.
```

This function begins like `WriteToFile()` with the identification of the file, the attempt to open it (using r as the mode so that the PHP can read the data), and then continues on, assuming it successfully opened the file.

The function will then print a caption and read the file data into an array called $Data. Each element of $Data is a string (in the format of the URL, followed by a tab, followed by its description, followed by the new line). You'll turn each string into a new array, called $GetLine, by looping through $Data one element at a time. Within the loop, the `explode()` function will create that $GetLine from the string by separating out the elements based upon the location of the tab. Using this new variable, you can print the pieces of the original string individually.

Finally, the file is closed, some HTML formatting is sent to the browser, and then the conditional is completed, generating an error message if PHP cannot open the file.

5. Now write a third function, which will create the HTML submission form with each call.

```
function CreateForm () {
    print ("Add a URL to the data
    → file:\n");
    print ("<FORM ACTION=\"urls.php\"
    → METHOD=POST>\n");
    print ("URL <INPUT TYPE=TEXT NAME=
    → \"Array[URL]\" SIZE=60><BR>\n");
    print ("Description <TEXTAREA
    → NAME=\"Array[Description]\"
    → ROWS=5 COLS=40></TEXTAREA>
    → <BR>\n");
```

*continues on next page*

```
print ("<INPUT TYPE=HIDDEN NAME=
→ \"BeenSubmitted\" VALUE=
→ \"TRUE\">\n");
print ("<INPUT TYPE=SUBMIT NAME=
→ \"SUBMIT\" VALUE=\"Submit!\">
→ </FORM>\n");
} // End of the CreateForm function.
```

This function is mostly just the `form.html` page with two major changes. First, the form's ACTION tag now sends the form data to `urls.php`, which will be the name of this script. Second, I have added a hidden field which sets the value of $BeenSubmitted to TRUE. You'll see why I do this shortly.

**6.** Write a fourth function for the purposes of handling the form.

```
function HandleForm () {
    global $Array;
```

This function is based upon the previous `HandleForm.php` script. The first thing it will do is bring in the $Array variable, by using the *global* statement, which holds the form data.

**7.** The bulk of this function is from the main body of the previous `HandleForm.php` page (Script 10.4).

```
$Pattern = "(http://)?
→ ([^[:space:]]+)([[:alnum:]
→ \.,-_?/&=])";
if (eregi($Pattern, $Array
→ ["URL"])) {
    $Replace = "<a href=\"http://
    → \\2\\3\" target=\"_new\">
    → \\2\\3</a>";
    $Array["URL"] =
    → eregi_replace($Pattern,
    → $Replace, $Array["URL"]);
    $CallFunction = WriteToFile
    → ($Array["URL"],
    → $Array["Description"]);
    if ($CallFunction) {
```

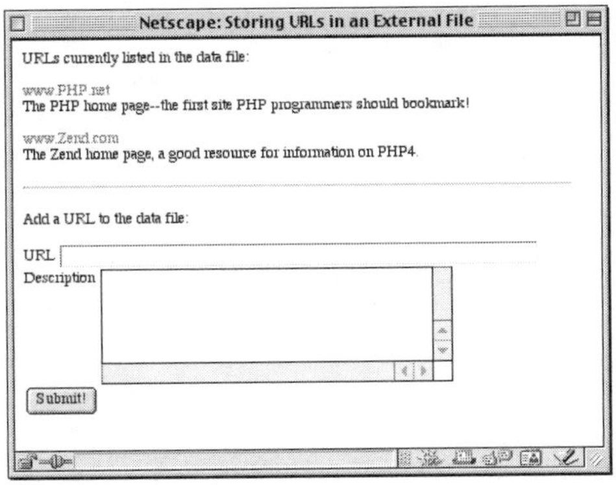

**Figure 10.7** The first time the user comes to the page, $BeenSubmitted is not equal to TRUE, so HandleForm() is never called (see Script 10.4). Once the form has been submitted, the PHP will handle the results and print a response as in Figure 10.8.

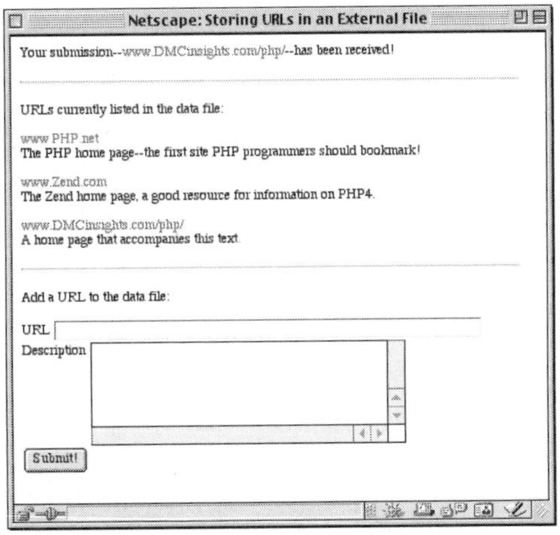

**Figure 10.8** After the user submits the form, urls.php will first handle the data then display the information from the file and create a new form.

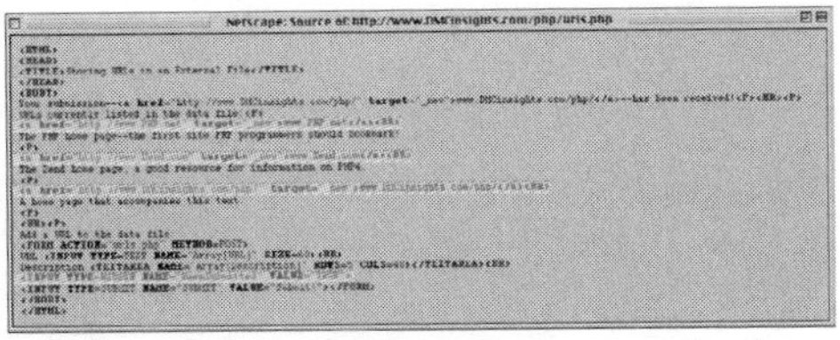

**Figure 10.9** This is the source of urls.php, after the form has been submitted. Notice that all URLs are made clickable and that the form uses a hidden value, which the user is oblivious to, that adds functionality to the design.

```
      print ("Your submission-
→ $Array[URL]-has been
→ received!<P><HR><P>
→ \n");
   } else {
      print ("Your submission
→ was not processed due
→ to a system error!
→ <BR>\n");
   }
   } else {
      print ("Please enter a
→ valid Web address!\n");
   }
} // End of the HandleForm function.
```

The function goes through the regular expression processes and will print out an error message if an invalid URL is entered. Assuming a valid URL has been submitted, the $CallFunction line and its corresponding conditional comes next.

8. Finally, create the conditional that decides whether or not to handle the form.

```
if ($BeenSubmitted){
   HandleForm();
}
ReadFromFile();
CreateForm();
```

If the value of $BeenSubmitted is TRUE (which means that the form has been submitted), the data will be processed. If the value of $BeenSubmitted is FALSE, which means the user has not submitted anything, then the HandleForm() function is not called. In either case, the existing data is displayed from the file and then a form is created so that the user may enter another URL.

9. Close the PHP and HTML.

```
?></BODY></HTML>
```

10. Save the page as urls.php, upload it to the server, and test it in your Web browser (**Figures 10.7**, **10.8**, and **10.9**).

**READING FROM FILES**

# Directories

Understanding how to read and write to files on the server is only part of the data storage process. It's likely you will also want to use directories at the same time. A directory is the same thing you might think of as a folder—it's a subsection of the hard drive which can store other files and directories. By default all your Web pages go within a specific directory (frequently called www or html) and within this directory you can create more directories for storing images, data, and so forth.

The command for creating a directory in PHP is:

```
mkdir ("path", "permissions");
```

The path will constitute the name and location of the directory while the permissions (in the form of a zero followed by three digits, such as 0666) will assign access rights to the directory.

Let's create a script that, when a new user logs in, creates a new directory for them.

## To create a new directory:

1. First you'll create a simple registration page that takes a Username and password. Open your text editor and begin a new HTML document (**Script 10.5**).

   ```
   <HTML><HEAD><TITLE>Registration
   → Form</TITLE></HEAD><BODY>
   ```

2. Create a form whose ACTION attribute is HandleNewUser.php and whose METHOD is POST.

   ```
   <FORM ACTION="HandleNewUser.php"
   → METHOD=POST>
   ```

   Since the form will take a password, be sure to use POST and not GET, as the latter is less secure.

**Script 10.5** This is a very simple registration form, requiring only two fields. The form in your applications will most likely be more involved, but the processes will be the same.

```
script
1   <HTML>
2   <HEAD>
3   <TITLE>Registration Form</TITLE>
4   </HEAD>
5   <BODY>
6   <FORM ACTION="HandleNewUser.php"
    METHOD=POST>
7   Username <INPUT TYPE=TEXT NAME=
    "Array[Username]" SIZE=15><BR>
8   Password <INPUT TYPE=PASSWORD
    NAME="Array[Password]" SIZE=15><BR>
9   <INPUT TYPE=SUBMIT NAME="SUBMIT"
    VALUE="Submit!">
10  </FORM>
11  </BODY>
12  </HTML>
```

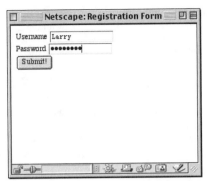

**Figure 10.10** This is the very basic registration form. The PASSWORD form INPUT TYPE hides the user entered information typed there.

3. Create two inputs—one TEXT for the Username and one PASSWORD for the Password.

   ```
   Username <INPUT TYPE=TEXT NAME=
   → "Array[Username]" SIZE=15><BR>
   Password <INPUT TYPE=PASSWORD NAME=
   → "Array[Password]" SIZE=15><BR>
   ```

   Be sure to make the TYPE equal to PASSWORD for the Password field so that the entered text is not visible (**Figure 10.10**).

4. Create a Submit button, then close the form and the HTML document.

   ```
   <INPUT TYPE=SUBMIT NAME="SUBMIT"
   → VALUE="Submit!">
   </FORM></BODY></HTML>
   ```

5. Save the page as NewUser.html and upload it to your server.

   Now you'll need to make a blank data file called users.txt and set the proper permissions for it, just as you did with data.txt.

6. Create a new, blank document in your text editor.

7. Save the document as users.txt and upload it to the server, in the same directory as NewUser.html.

8. Set the permissions of users.txt so that everyone can read to and write from it.

   The third step is to make a directory into which PHP will create all the other directories.

9. Using your FTP or telnet application (or Web-based control panel provided by your ISP), create a new directory called users, within the same directory as NewUser.html and users.txt.

   *continues on next page*

DIRECTORIES

**169**

**10.** Set the permissions on the users directory so that everyone can read from, write to, and search through it.

Finally, you'll write the HandleNewUser.php script which will process the information from the form and create the new directory.

**11.** Open your text editor and create a new PHP document.

**12.** Begin by opening up the PHP and then write the first function (**Script 10.6**).

```
<?
function MakeDirectoryName
→ ($Username) {
    srand ((double) microtime() *
    → 1000000);
    $Name = rand() . $Username;
    return $Name;
} // End of MakeDirectoryName
→ Function.
```

The directory name will be made using the Username and a random number. The name is generated by seeding the srand() function with a timestamp and then randomly picking a number based upon that. The concatenation of this number to the $Username should insure a unique directory name every time, which is then returned by the function.

**13.** Copy the WriteToFile() function from Script 10.4 and slightly alter it:

```
function WriteToFile ($Username,
→ $Password) {
    $TheFile = "users.txt";
    $Open = fopen ($TheFile, "a");
    if ($Open) {
        $Password = md5 ($Password);
```

One of the things you'll want to change here is the name of the text file (now users.txt). You'll also add a line encrypting the password before being stored (you generally always want to store an encrypted version for security reasons).

**Script 10.6** Although I wrote it as two functions here, you could create a third function explicitly for the purposes of creating the directory. To do so you would need to separate out the mkdir() conditional from the WriteToFile() function.

```
     ┌─────────────────── script ───────────────────┐
1    <?
2    function MakeDirectoryName ($Username) {
3    /* Function MakeDirectoryName takes one
     argument--usersname--which will be used
     to create and return a directory name. */
4        srand ((double) microtime() *
         1000000);
5        $Name = rand() . $Username;
6    return $Name;
7    } // End of MakeDirectoryName Function.
8
9    function WriteToFile ($Username,
     $Password) {
10   /* Function WriteToFile takes two
     arguments--Username and Password--which
     will be written to an external file. */
11   $TheFile = "users.txt";
12   $Open = fopen ($TheFile, "a");
13   if ($Open) {
14   $Password = md5 ($Password);
15   $Directory = "users/" .
     MakeDirectoryName ($Username);
16   fwrite ($Open, "$Username\t$Password\
     t$Directory\n");
17   fclose ($Open);
18   if (!(mkdir ($Directory, "0777"))) {
19   $Directory = FALSE;
20   }
21   } else {
22   $Directory = FALSE;
23   }
24   return $Directory;
25   } // End of WriteToFile Function.
26   ?>
27   <HTML>
28   <HEAD>
29   <TITLE>Using Directories</TITLE>
30   <BODY>
31   <?php
32   /* This page receives and handles the
     data generated by "NewUser.html". */
33
```

*Script continues on next page*

**Script 10.6** *continued*

```
                  script
34  if (($Array[Username]) &&
    ($Array[Password])) {
35      $Check = WriteToFile
        ($Array[Username], $Array[Password]);
36      if ($Check) {
37          print ("Your request was
            successfully processed!<BR>\n");
38      } else {
39          print ("Your request was not
            processed due to a system
            error!<BR>\n");
40      }
41  } else {
42      print ("Please enter a Username and
        Password!\n");
43  }
44  ?>
45  </BODY>
46  </HTML>
```

**14.** Create the directory name.

```
$Directory = "users/" .
→ MakeDirectoryName ($Username);
```

The new directory's name is created by calling the MakeDirectoryName function and stating that the directory will be a sub-directory of users.

**15.** Add the new data to the file.

```
fwrite ($Open, "$Username\t$Password\
→ t$Directory\n");
fclose ($Open);
```

**16.** Attempt to create a directory and write a conditional to handle the success of the action.

```
if (!(mkdir ($Directory, "0777"))) {
$Directory = FALSE;
}
} else {
$Directory = FALSE;
}
return $Directory;
} // End of WriteToFile Function.
```

The $Directory variable is assigned a value of the new directory name only if the file is successfully opened. If the file cannot be opened or if the directory cannot be made, $Directory is equal to FALSE, indicating that the function failed to perform its duties as requested, so this variable will be returned.

**17.** Close the PHP code area and create the HTML header.

```
?><HTML><HEAD><TITLE>Using
→ Directories</TITLE><BODY>
```

**18.** Open a second PHP section and then create the main conditional.

```
<?php
if (($Array[Username]) &&
→ ($Array[Password])) {
    $Check = WriteToFile
        → ($Array[Username],
        → $Array[Password]);
```

*continues on next page*

**DIRECTORIES**

```
if ($Check) {
    print ("Your request was
    → successfully processed!
    → <BR>\n");
} else {
    print ("Your request was
    → not processed due to a
    → system error!<BR>\n");
}
} else {
    print ("Please enter a Username
    → and Password!\n");

}
```

This part should be straightforward to you by now. There is a check to see if both form fields were filled in and, if so, it proceeds to write the data to the file and create the new directory. An appropriate message is sent based upon the returned value from the function.

19. Close this last PHP section and the HTML page itself.

?></BODY></HTML>

20. Save the page as HandleNewUser.php, upload it to the server (in the same location as the users directory, the users.txt file, and the NewUser.html page), and test it in your Web browser (**Figures 10.11** and **10.12**).

**Figure 10.11** If everything worked according to design, the only message the user will see is this one.

**Figure 10.12** The users.txt file lists three tab-delineated fields of information: the username, an encrypted version of the password, and the user's directory name.

✔ **Tips**

■ You can also insure that the page worked as it should by looking within the users directory on the server for the new sub-directories (either via telnet or FTP).

■ At some point, although not for the purposes here, you may want to create a system to guarantee unique usernames. The process for doing so is simple enough: before attempting to create the directory, use PHP to check your list of existing usernames for a match to the just-registered name. If no match is found, the new name is acceptable. If the username is already in use, the PHP can create an error message requesting a new username.

**Script 10.7** The simplicity of this script should also indicate how naturally PHP handles HTML forms. There are three steps to uploading files: change the HTML form accordingly, use copy() to move the file to the desired location, then delete the file using unlink().

```
script
1    <HTML>
2    <HEAD>
3    <TITLE>Handling File Uploads</TITLE>
4    </HEAD>
5    <BODY>                      .
6    <?php
7    /* This next conditional determines
     whether or not to handle the form,
     depending upon whether or not $File
     exists. */
8    if ($File) {
9        print ("File name: $File_name<P>\n");
10       print ("File size: $File_size<P>\n");
11       if (copy ($File, "users/$File_name")) {
12           print ("Your file was successfully
             uploaded!<P>\n");
13       } else {
14           print ("Your file could not be
             copied.<P>\n");
15       }
16       unlink ($File);
17   }
18
19   print ("Upload a file to the server:\n");
20   print ("<FORM ACTION=\"FileUpload.php\"
     METHOD=POST ENCTYPE=\"multipart/form-
     data\">\n");
21   print ("File <INPUT TYPE=FILE
     NAME=\"File\" SIZE=20><BR>\n");
22   print ("<INPUT TYPE=SUBMIT NAME=
     \"SUBMIT\" VALUE=\"Submit!\"></FORM>\n");
23   ?>
24   </BODY>
25   </HTML>
```

# Handling File Uploads

As I've hopefully demonstrated, handling HTML forms using PHP is a remarkably easy achievement. Regardless of the data being submitted, PHP can handle it easily and directly. The same is true when the user uploads a file via an HTML form.

In order to give the user the option of uploading a file, two changes must be made to the standard HTML form. First, the initial FORM line must include the code ENCTYPE = "multipart/form-data", which lets the HTML know to expect a file as well other data. Second, the <INPUT TYPE=FILE NAME=NAME> element is used to create the necessary field.

The INPUT TYPE=FILE in forms allows the user to specify a file on the user's computer which, upon submission, will be uploaded to the server. Once this has occurred, you can then use PHP to handle the file.

When a file is uploaded, the server places it in a temporary directory. Your first responsibility is to save that file in a permanent location. The copy() function is used to duplicate a copy of the file in a new location.

```
copy ("SourceName", "DestinationName");
```

Then, you should delete the temporary file, as a matter of formality, using unlink().

You'll write a very basic script that uploads a file and stores it in the users directory. Like the urls.php script, this example will also both create the HTML form and process it, all in one page.

## To use PHP for file uploads:

1. Create a new PHP document in your text editor.

2. Begin with the standard HTML header (**Script 10.7**):

   <HTML><HEAD><TITLE>Handling File
   → Uploads</TITLE></HEAD><BODY>

*continues on next page*

3. Open the PHP section and create a conditional to test whether or not to handle the file upload.

```php
<?php
if ($File) {
```

The information for the uploaded file will be stored in a variable appropriately called $File. If this variable exists (i.e., it has a value), you'll know to process it.

4. Print the file name and file size, just for confirmation.

```php
print ("File name: $File_name<P>\n");
print ("File size: $File_size<P>\n");
```

When a file is uploaded, several variables are set. By taking the name of the main variable (in this case, $File) and appending _name and_size, you can retrieve that information for the file as well.

5. Attempt to copy the file to the users directory and print out a message based upon the success.

```php
if (copy ($File, "users/
→ $File_name")) {
print ("Your file was successfully
→ uploaded!<P>\n");
} else {
print ("Your file could not be
→ copied.<P>\n");
}
```

When copying the file, the source is stored in the $File variable and the destination is either absolute (e.g., c:/php/data.txt) or relative to the location of this file (e.g., "php/data.txt"). Here I've used a relative reference, requesting to put the file within the users directory which is located in the same directory as this page.

6. Now unlink the file and close the conditional.

```php
    unlink ($File);
}
```

**Figure 10.13** The FILE type of input creates a button which, once clicked, allows the user to navigate through their computer until they've located the desired file. Upon selection of the file, its name will then automatically be listed in the window.

**Figure 10.14** Successful handling of the file is reflected with a corresponding message. You can also access the file's name and size in bytes at the same time.

Most likely the file will automatically be unlinked by the server at some later time, but it is better to keep things tidy as you go, so you'll immediately delete the file once you are done with it.

**7.** Print out the HTML form for uploading the file.

```
print ("Upload a file to the
→ server:\n");
print ("<FORM ACTION=
→ \"FileUpload.php\" METHOD=POST
→ ENCTYPE=\"multipart/form-
→ data\">\n");
print ("File <INPUT TYPE=FILE
→ NAME=\"File\"><BR>\n");
print ("<INPUT TYPE=SUBMIT NAME=
→ \"SUBMIT\" VALUE=\"Submit!\">
→ </FORM>\n");
```

Be sure to add the ENCTYPE code to the opening FORM tag. The INPUT TYPE=FILE line is self-evident.

**8.** Close the PHP and the HTML.

```
?></BODY></HTML>
```

**9.** Save the file as FileUpload.php, upload it to the server (in the same directory as the users directory), and test it in your Web browser (**Figures 10.13** and **10.14**).

*continues on next page*

## ✔ Tips

■ I've decide to use the previously created users directory because I know that its permissions allow anyone to write to it. Should you try to copy a file to a directory that does not have the proper write permissions the results would be like those shown in **Figure 10.15**.

■ The maximum uploadable file size is determined by several factors. First, the server may have a limit set. Second, PHP itself can impose a limit (in the php.ini configuration file). Third, you can determine a maximum file size by coding `<INPUT TYPE=HIDDEN`
→ `NAME="MAX_FILE_SIZE" VALUE="2048">` in your form before the FILE input. The value field is in byte units.

■ A file's type, which is assigned to the $File_type variable when $File is uploaded, is the same thing as its MIME (*Multipurpose Internet Mail Extensions*) type, which e-mail applications and Web browsers use to know how to treat a file. A MIME type could be image/jpeg or text/html.

**Figure 10.15** Attempting to copy the file to a location which does not have the proper permissions generates this error message. You know that the file was successfully uploaded, though, as it accurately displays the file's name and size. The PHP just cannot copy the file to the suggested destination.

# Renaming and Deleting Files and Directories

There are a few useful file and directory functions built-in to PHP which I'll cover in brief here. They include renaming and deleting files as well as listing files located in a directory. I'll review the syntax for some of them first and then demonstrate how they function within the context of a very useful PHP script.

First, there is the `rename()` function, which works as you would expect it to:

```
rename ("old name", "new name");
```

It can be used on either files or directories.

Another function which will be used in this section is `filesize()`, which determines how large a file is in bytes. This value can be assigned to a variable or printed.

```
$Number = filesize ("filename");
```

One important concept that I'll demonstrate in the following script involves listing all of the files found within a directory.Such a script allows you to view directories without FTP access and can be used for creating an online document repository. Reading through a directory is quite similar to reading from a file. First you open the directory, then you look at the files one at a time, and lastly you close the directory. Instead of using a file pointer, as you did when reading files, you use a directory handle, but the concept is the same.

```
$Handle = opendir ("path");
readdir ($Handle);
closedir ($Handle);
```

*continues on next page*

Since the `readdir()` function identifies one file at a time, you'll need to place it in a loop, like this:

```
while (readdir ($Handle)) {
   statements;
}
```

You'll put all of these capabilities together into one page which will constitute a Web-based control panel for viewing and managing directories.

## To create the directory control panel:

1. Open your text editor and begin a new PHP document.

2. Create the standard HTML header (**Script 10.8**).

   ```
   <HTML><HEAD><TITLE>Viewing Files in
   → a Directory</TITLE></HEAD><BODY>
   ```

3. Begin a table and then start the PHP section.

   ```
   <TABLE BORDER=0 WIDTH="60%"
   → CELLSPACING=2 CELLPADDING=2
   → ALIGN=CENTER>
   <?php
   ```

   In the interest of making the page more attractive and orderly, the data will be formatted within a table.

4. Write a series of conditionals testing whether or not to perform certain acts based upon the existence of certain variables: $Upload (uploading files), $Rename (renaming files), and $Delete (deleting files).

   ```
   if ($Upload) {
   print ("<TR><TD COLSPAN=4
   → ALIGN=CENTER>Uploaded file name:
   → $File_name</TD></TR>\n");
   print ("<TR><TD COLSPAN=4
   → ALIGN=CENTER>Uploaded file size:
   → $File_size</TD></TR>\n");
   ```

**Script 10.8** Instead of using functions, this page uses conditionals, but the results are comparable. To test your knowledge, you might want to rewrite this using functions, especially the section that displays the files within a directory.

```
                        script
1    <HTML>
2    <HEAD>
3    <TITLE>Viewing Files in a Directory</TITLE>
4    </HEAD>
5    <BODY>
6    <TABLE BORDER=0 WIDTH="60%"
     CELLSPACING=2 CELLPADDING=2
     ALIGN=CENTER>
7    <?php
8    /* This file lists all the information for
     files in a directory and allows the user
     to delete, upload and rename files. */
9
10   if ($Upload) { // Handle file uploads.
11       print ("<TR><TD COLSPAN=4
         ALIGN=CENTER>Uploaded file name:
         $File_name</TD></TR>\n");
12       print ("<TR><TD COLSPAN=4
         ALIGN=CENTER>Uploaded file size:
         $File_size</TD></TR>\n");
13       if (copy ($File, "users/$File_name")) {
14           print ("<TR><TD COLSPAN=4
             ALIGN=CENTER>Your file,
             $File_name, was successfully
             uploaded!</TD></TR>\n");
15       } else {
16           print ("<TR><TD COLSPAN=4
             ALIGN=CENTER>Your file,
             $File_name, could not be
             copied.</TD></TR>\n");
17       }
18       unlink ($File);
19       print ("<TR><TD COLSPAN=4
         ALIGN=CENTER> </TD></TR>\n");
20   }
21
22   if ($Delete) { // Handle file deletions.
23       for ($i = 0; $i < count ($Delete);
         $i++) {
24           if ( unlink ("users/$Delete
             [$i]") ) {
25               print ("<TR><TD COLSPAN=4
                 ALIGN=CENTER>Your file,
                 $Delete[$i], was successfully
                 deleted!</TD></TR>\n");
```

*Script continues on next page*

Script 10.8 *continued*

```
                    script

26          } else {
27                  print ("<TR><TD COLSPAN=4
                    ALIGN=CENTER>Your file,
                    $Delete[$i], could not be
                    deleted.</TD></TR>\n");
28          }
29      }
30      print ("<TR><TD COLSPAN=4
        ALIGN=CENTER> </TD></TR>\n");
31  }
32
33  if ($Rename) { // Handle file renaming.
34      for ($n = 0; $n < count ($Rename);
        $n++) {
35          $OldFilename = $Rename[$n];
36          $Old = "users/$OldFilename";
37          $New = "users/$NewName
            [$OldFilename]";
38          if ( rename ($Old, $New) ) {
39                  print ("<TR><TD COLSPAN=4
                    ALIGN=CENTER>Your file,
                    $Rename[$n], was successfully
                    renamed!</TD></TR>\n");
40          } else {
41  print ("<TR><TD COLSPAN=4 ALIGN=CENTER>
    Your file, $Rename[$n], could not be
    renamed.</TD></TR>\n");
42          }
43      }
44      print ("<TR><TD COLSPAN=4
        ALIGN=CENTER> </TD></TR>\n");
45  }
46
47  // Start the form.
48  print ("<FORM ACTION=\"files.php\"
    METHOD=POST ENCTYPE=\"multipart/form-
    data\">\n");
49  print ("<TR><TD><B>File Name</B></TD>
    <TD><B>File Size</B></TD>
    <TD><B>Delete</B></TD>
    <TD><B>Rename</B> (Enter the New Name
    in the Box)</TD></TR>\n");
50
51  // Read the files from the directory.
52  $Open = opendir ("users");
53  while ($Files = readdir ($Open)) {
54      $Filename = "users/" . $Files;
55      if (is_file ($Filename)) {
```

*Script continues on next page*

```
if (copy ($File,
→ "users/$File_name")) {
print ("<TR><TD COLSPAN=4
→ ALIGN=CENTER>Your file, $File_name,
→ was successfully uploaded!
→ </TD></TR>\n");
} else {
print ("<TR><TD COLSPAN=4
→ ALIGN=CENTER>Your file, $File_name,
→ could not be copied.
→ </TD></TR>\n");
}
unlink ($File);
print ("<TR><TD COLSPAN=4
→ ALIGN=CENTER> </TD></TR>\n");
}
```

The $Upload variable will be set if the user uploaded a file. Hence, if $Upload exists, the uploaded file will be handled as you've seen previously.

The last **print** statement, which will create a blank table row, is there just for aesthetic purposes only, a theme which is continued through the next two conditionals as well. The extra space that line of code creates will make a more visually appealing Web page.

5. ```
   if ($Delete) {
   for ($i = 0; $i < count ($Delete);
   → $i++) {
   if ( unlink ("users/$Delete[$i]") ) {
   print ("<TR><TD COLSPAN=4
   → ALIGN=CENTER>Your file, $Delete[$i],
   → was successfully deleted!</TD>
   → </TR>\n");
   } else {
   print ("<TR><TD COLSPAN=4
   → ALIGN=CENTER>Your file, $Delete[$i],
   → could not be deleted.</TD>
   → </TR>\n");
   }
   }
   print ("<TR><TD COLSPAN=4
   → ALIGN=CENTER> </TD></TR>\n");
   }
   ```

*continues on next page*
   ```

You'll use a variable to identify whether or not any files need to be deleted, as you did with uploaded files. Since multiple files could be deleted, an array has been created and the loop will handle each array element by unlinking them in turn.

**6.** 
```
if ($Rename) {
for ($n = 0; $n < count ($Rename);
→ $n++) {
$OldFilename = $Rename[$n];
$Old = "users/$OldFilename";
$New = "users/$NewName
→ [$OldFilename]";
if ( rename ($Old, $New) ) {
print ("<TR><TD COLSPAN=4
→ ALIGN=CENTER>Your file, $Rename[$n],
→ was successfully renamed!</TD>
→ </TR>\n");
} else {
print ("<TR><TD COLSPAN=4
→ ALIGN=CENTER>Your file, $Rename[$n],
→ could not be renamed.</TD>
→ </TR>\n");
}
}
print ("<TR><TD COLSPAN=4
→ ALIGN=CENTER> </TD></TR>\n");
}
```

The same is true for renaming files as it is for deleting with respect to walking through the array elements. Once you've assigned the file's new and old names, a call to **rename()** will handle the alterations.

**7.** Create the HTML form, being sure to include the ENCTYPE code to allow for file uploads.

```
print ("<FORM ACTION=\"files.php\"
→ METHOD=POST ENCTYPE=\"multipart/
→ form-data\">\n");
```

**Script 10.8** *continued*

```
┌──────────────── script ──────────────────┐
56          $Size = filesize ("users/$Files");
57          print ("<TR><TD>$Files</TD>
            <TD>$Size</TD><TD><INPUT
            TYPE=CHECKBOX NAME=\"Delete[]\"
            VALUE=\"$Files\"></TD><TD><INPUT
            TYPE=CHECKBOX NAME=\"Rename[]\"
            VALUE=\"$Files\"><INPUT TYPE=TEXT
            NAME=\"NewName[$Files]\"></TD>
            </TR>\n");
58      }
59 }
60 closedir ($Open);
61
62 // Give the upload option.
63 print ("<TR><TD COLSPAN=4
   ALIGN=CENTER> </TD></TR>\n");
64 print ("<TR><TD COLSPAN=4
   ALIGN=CENTER><INPUT TYPE=CHECKBOX
   NAME=\"Upload\" VALUE=\"Yes\">Upload a
   file to the server:<INPUT TYPE=FILE
   NAME=\"File\" SIZE=20></TD></TR>\n");
65 print ("<TR><TD COLSPAN=4
   ALIGN=CENTER><INPUT TYPE=SUBMIT
   NAME=\"SUBMIT\" VALUE=\"Submit!\">
   </FORM></TD></TR>\n");
66 ?>
67 </TABLE>
68 </BODY>
69 </HTML>
```

8. Print out the table headers.

```
print ("<TR><TD><B>File Name</B>
→ </TD><TD><B>File Size</B>
→ </TD><TD><B>Delete</B></TD><TD>
→ <B>Rename</B> (Enter the New Name
→ in the Box)</TD></TR>\n");
```

9. Write the code to read from the directory.

```
$Open = opendir ("users");
while ($Files = readdir ($Open)) {
$Filename = "users/" . $Files;
if (is_file ($Filename)) {
$Size = filesize ("users/$Files");
print ("<TR><TD>$Files</TD>
→ <TD>$Size</TD><TD><INPUT
→ TYPE=CHECKBOX NAME=\"Delete[]\"
→ VALUE=\"$Files\"></TD><TD><INPUT
→ TYPE=CHECKBOX NAME=\"Rename[]\"
→ VALUE=\"$Files\"><INPUT TYPE=TEXT
→ NAME=\"NewName[$Files]\"></TD>
→ </TR>\n");
}
}
closedir ($Open);
```

Here is how I've looped through every file (and directory) located within the users directory. For these purposes, I only want to deal with files, not directories, so the is_file() function is used to insure that files will be listed while directories will not be.

10. Create the upload option in the form.

```
print ("<TR><TD COLSPAN=4
→ ALIGN=CENTER> </TD></TR>\n");
print ("<TR><TD COLSPAN=4
→ ALIGN=CENTER><INPUT TYPE=CHECKBOX
→ NAME=\"Upload\" VALUE=\"Yes\">
→ Upload a file to the server:
→ <INPUT TYPE=FILE NAME=\"File\"
→ SIZE=20></TD></TR>\n");
print ("<TR><TD COLSPAN=4
→ ALIGN=CENTER><INPUT TYPE=SUBMIT
→ NAME=\"SUBMIT\"
VALUE=\"Submit!\">
→ </FORM></TD></TR>\n");
```

*continues on next page*

**11.** Close the PHP and the HTML.

```
?></TABLE></BODY></HTML>
```

**12.** Save your script as files.php, upload it to the server (in the same location as the users directory), and test it in your Web browser (**Figures 10.16** and **10.17**).

## ✔ Tips

■ If you wanted, using the NewUser.html and HandleNewUser.php pages, files.php (with some modifications) could be copied into each new user's directory. Then, when the user logged in, they could be sent to their control panel wherein they could manage stored files.

■ To find out about other file and directory functions, look in the PHP manual under *Directories* and *Filesystem*.

**Figure 10.16** Upon first arriving at the page, this is what the user sees. Checkboxes are displayed giving the user the option of deleting, renaming, and uploading files.

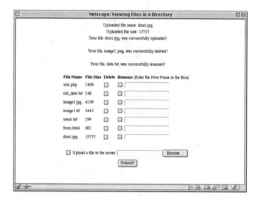

**Figure 10.17** Here I've uploaded one new file, deleted another, and renamed a third. Each successful operation is reported and an update list of the directory's contents is displayed.

# DATABASES

Strange as it may sound to say, the Internet would not be where it is today if not for the existence of databases. In fact, PHP itself would probably not be as popular or as useful if not for its built-in support for numerous types of databases. (PHP's degree of database support and its ease of use are things you won't find using CGI scripts, as a rule).

A database is a collection of tables (tables being made up of columns and rows) that stores information. Databases are used all over the Internet. E-commerce sites use databases to keep product specifications (such as price and color) as well as customer data, while content sites put articles and news stories into databases.

There are currently many existing database servers or Database Management Systems (DBMS), which function on different platforms. (Technically a DBMS is the software that interfaces with the database proper. However, more and more people are using the terms *database* and *DBMS* synonymously. I will continue to distinguish between the two to avoid confusion.) On any operating system, Oracle is generally considered the best DBMS, but its price puts it out of the running for all but the largest and best-financed applications. For Windows and Windows NT, you'll often encounter Access or SQL Server, both of which are very useful but not cross-platform compliant.

In this chapter, I'll use MySQL (**Figure 11.1**) as my example DBMS. Although MySQL, which is available for most platforms, is not as powerful as other database servers, it has enough speed and functionality for most purposes and its price—free for Unix servers—makes it the most common choice for Web development. If you are using a server provided by an ISP or Web host, check to see what DBMS they have available for you (most likely at an extra cost). If you are running your own server, you should consider installing MySQL (www.MySQL.com or another database server).

Databases are created, updated, and read using SQL (Structured Query Language). There are surprisingly few commands in SQL, which is both a blessing and a curse. SQL was designed to be written a lot like the English language, which makes it very user friendly, but it does take some thought to create more elaborate SQL statements with only the handful of available terms. Be aware that incorporating a database into your Web applications creates more potential for errors, so check and double-check your database work as you go.

I'll lead you through how to develop one simple database that records user feedback. Although you will learn enough here to get yourself started, you may want to visit Appendix C, *PHP Resources*, once you've finished this chapter to find some references where you can learn more about the topic.

Since I will be working with MySQL, all of the functions I use in this chapter will be MySQL specific. For example, to connect to a database in MySQL, the proper function is `mysql_connect()`, but if you are using PostgreSQL, you would instead write `pg_connect()`. If you are not using a MySQL DBMS, you will need to use the PHP manual (available through www.PHP.net) to find the appropriate function names.

**Figure 11.1** MySQL can be obtained from the MySQL home page (www.MySQL.com). Here you can also find documentation on installing and using MySQL as well as check for any applicable licensing fees.

# Connecting to and Creating a Database

When you worked with text files in Chapter 10, *Files and Directories*, you saw that you first had to create a file pointer while opening the file. This pointer then acted as a reference point to that open file. A similar process is used when working with databases. First, you have to establish a connection to the database server (in this case, MySQL). This connection will then be used as the access point for any future commands. The MySQL syntax for connecting to a database is:

```
$Link = mysql_connect ("host", "user",
   "password");
```

The link is established using three arguments: the host, which is almost always *localhost*; the user name; and, the password for that user name. These last two parameters will dictate what database permissions you have.

Database permissions is a bit more complicated than file permissions but you need to understand this: different types of users can be assigned different database capabilities. For example, a DBMS administrator can create new and delete old databases (within your DBMS you may have dozens of databases), but a lower-level administrator may only be able to create and modify tables within a single database. The most basic user may just be able to read from, but not modify, tables.

Your ISP will most likely give you the second type of access—control over a single database but not the DBMS itself—and will establish the initial database for you. If you are working on your own server or have administrative access, you have the capability to create new databases.

*continues on next page*

The code for creating a new database is:

```
mysql_create_db ("databasename", $Link);
```

Notice how the $Link value established when connecting to a database is used to continue working with the database, just as a file pointer is referenced to read from or write to the file.

After executing any command to the database it is considered good form to close the link, just as you would close an open file:

```
mysql_close ($Link);
```

For the first database example of this chapter, you will create a new database, which requires that you have administrator access. If your ISP restricts your access, they should create the initial database for you upon request, so you can skip ahead to the next section, *Creating a Table*.

## To connect to MySQL and create a new database:

1. Create a new PHP document in your text editor.

2. Begin with the standard HTML header (**Script 11.1**).

   ```
   <HTML><HEAD><TITLE>Creating a Database</TITLE><BODY>
   ```

3. Create a PHP section of the script and set the database variables.

   ```
   <?php
   $Host = "localhost";
   $User = "user";
   $Password = "password";
   $DBName = "NewDatabase";
   ```

   By assigning these values to variables, you can more easily alter the script to work with other databases at a later date. If you are working on an ISP's or Web host's server, they should provide you with the user name and password.

   When creating the database name, do not use spaces, just as you would not use spaces in variable or function names.

**Script 11.1** Creating a new database consists of three steps: linking to the database, using the `mysql_create_db()` function, and then closing the link. I make it a habit to establish all database dependencies — host, user name, password, database name — as their own variables to make them easier to change later.

```
                          script
1    <HTML>
2    <HEAD>
3    <TITLE>Creating a Database</TITLE>
4    <BODY>
5    <?php
6    // Set the variables for the database
     access:
7    $Host = "localhost";
8    $User = "user";
9    $Password = "password";
10   $DBName = "NewDatabase";
11
12   $Link = mysql_connect ($Host, $User,
     $Password);
13   if (mysql_create_db ($DBName, $Link)) {
14       print ("The database, $DBName, was
         successfully created!<BR>\n");
15   } else {
16       print ("The database, $DBName, could
         not be created!<BR>\n");
17   }
18   mysql_close ($Link);
19   ?>
20   </BODY>
21   </HTML>
```

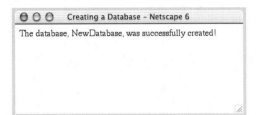

**Figure 11.2** If the script was able to create the new database, you will see this message in your Web browser.

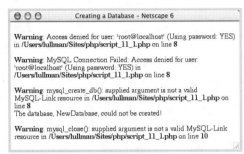

**Figure 11.3** If your PHP script is unable to create the new database, you will see several MySQL errors along with a PHP-generated one.

**4.** Connect to the database.

```
$Link = mysql_connect ($Host, $User,
→ $Password);
```

This script will attempt to connect to the MySQL DBMS on the server, using the host name, user name, and password. If the user name and password you entered do not match preset database privileges (for example, if you are using the wrong user name or password), you will get an error message at this point in the execution of the script.

**5.** Attempt to create the new database and print a message indicating the result of the attempt.

```
if (mysql_create_db ($DBName, $Link)) {
    print ("The database, $DBName, was
    → successfully created! <BR>\n");
} else {
    print ("The database, $DBName,
    → could not be created! <BR>\n");
}
```

If the script was successfully able to create the new database, you will only see the successful message (**Figure 11.2**). If, for some reason, it was not able to create the database, you will see a number of MySQL errors as well as the "could not be created!" error generated by this conditional (**Figure 11.3**).

*continues on next page*

CONNECTING TO AND CREATING A DATABASE

**6.** Close the MySQL link, then close the PHP section, and the HTML.

```
mysql_close ($Link);
?></BODY></HTML>
```

It is not strictly necessary to close the MySQL link as the server will automatically do so once the PHP script has stopped running, but I would recommend that you include this step anyway, as a matter of form and efficiency.

**7.** Save your script as `CreateDB.php`, upload it to the server, and test it in your Web browser.

## ✔ Tips

■ PHP has built-in support for most databases including: dBase, FilePro,mSQL, MySQL, Oracle, PostgreSQL, and Sybase. If you are using a type of database that does not have direct support—for example, Access or SQL Server—you'll need to use PHP's ODBC (Open Database Connectivity) functions along with that database's ODBC drivers to interface with the database. See the *Database Resources* section of Appendix C, *PHP Resources*, for more information.

■ The combination of using PHP and MySQL is so common now that there are two terms you may run across identifying servers configured with both PHP and MySQL: *LAMP* (*Linux* operating system, *Apache* Web server, *MySQL* DBMS, *PHP*) and *WAMP* (*Windows* operating system, *Apache* Web server, *MySQL* DBMS, *PHP*).

# Creating a Table

Once the initial database has been created, you can start to create individual tables within it. Remember that a database can consist of multiple tables, each of which has columns and rows. For this simple example you will create one table in which data will be stored.

To create a table within the database, you'll use SQL—the language that databases understand. The process of querying a database involves writing the SQL query and then querying the database using:

```
mysql_db_query ():
$Query = "text for the query goes here in
→ SQL format";
mysql_db_query ("DatabaseName", $Query,
→ $Link);
```

Because SQL is a lot like spoken English, the proper query to create a new table reads like so:

```
$Query = "CREATE table TABLENAME (column1,
→ column2, etc.)";
```

For each column, separated out by commas, you first indicate the column name and then the column type. Common types are TEXT and INT (integer). Because it is highly recommend to create a first column which acts as the *primary key* (a column used to refer to each row), a simple query could be:

```
$Query = "CREATE table NewTable (id INT
→ PRIMARY KEY, information TEXT)";
```

A table's primary key is a special column of unique values that is used to refer to the table's rows. The database makes an index of this column in order to more quickly navigate through the table. A table can have only one primary key which I normally set up as an automatically incremented column of integers. The first row will have a key of 1, the second will have a key of 2, and so forth. Referring back to the key will always retrieve the values for that row.

*continues on next page*

You can visit the MySQL Web site (Figure 11.1) for more information on SQL. By following my directions, though, you should be able to accomplish some basic database tasks.

For this example, you'll create a table that stores information submitted via an HTML form. In the next section of the chapter, you'll write the script that inserts the submitted data into the table created here.

## To create a new table:

1. Create a new PHP document in your text editor.

2. Code the standard HTML header (**Script 11.2**):

   ```
   <HTML><HEAD><TITLE>Creating a
   → Table</TITLE><BODY>
   ```

3. Open the PHP section of the script and set your database variables.

   ```
   <?php
   $Host = "localhost";
   $User = "user";
   $Password = "password";
   $DBName = "NewDatabase";
   $TableName = "Feedback";
   ```

   Note that I've added one more variable to the existing list from Script 11.1—$TableName. It helps to create relevant table names, so this table, intended to store user feedback, is called *Feedback*. Table names, as well as column names, in MySQL are case-sensitive.

4. Establish a link to the MySQL server.

   ```
   $Link = mysql_connect ($Host, $User,
   → $Password);
   ```

**Script 11.2** Creating a table, and most other database requests, are handled by writing the appropriate query and then using the mysql_db_query() function.

```
1   <HTML>
2   <HEAD>
3   <TITLE>Creating a Table</TITLE>
4   <BODY>
5   <?php
6   // Set the variables for the database
    access:
7   $Host = "localhost";
8   $User = "user";
9   $Password = "password";
10  $DBName = "NewDatabase";
11  $TableName = "Feedback";
12
13  $Link = mysql_connect ($Host, $User,
    $Password);
14  $Query = "CREATE table $TableName (id INT
    UNSIGNED NOT NULL AUTO_INCREMENT PRIMARY
    KEY, FirstName TEXT, LastName TEXT,
    EmailAddress TEXT, Comments TEXT)";
15  if (mysql_db_query ($DBName, $Query,
    $Link)) {
16      print ("The query was successfully
        executed!<BR>\n");
17  } else {
18      print ("The query could not be
        executed!<BR>\n");
19  }
20  mysql_close ($Link);
21  ?>
22  </BODY>
23  </HTML>
```

**5.** Write your query.

```
$Query = "CREATE table $TableName (id
→ INT UNSIGNED NOT NULL AUTO_INCREMENT
→ PRIMARY KEY, FirstName TEXT,
→ LastName TEXT, EmailAddress TEXT,
→ Comments TEXT)";
```

I'll break down the query to more recognizable parts. First, to create a new table, you write CREATE table $TableName (the $TableName variable name will be replaced by the value of $TableName upon execution). Then, within parentheses, you list every column you want with each column separated by a comma.

The first column in the table is called *id* and it will be an unsigned integer (INT UNSIGNED—which means that it can only be a positive integer). By including the words NOT NULL, you indicate that this column must have a value for each row. The values will automatically increase by one for each row (AUTO INCREMENT) and will stand as the *primary key*.

The next four columns will consist of TEXT, one called *FirstName*, the second *LastName*, the third *EmailAddress*, and the fourth *Comments*.

**6.** Query the database and print a message indicating the success of the query.

```
if (mysql_db_query ($DBName, $Query,
→ $Link)) {
    print ("The query was successfully
    → executed! <BR>\n");
} else {
    print ("The query could not be
    → executed! <BR>\n");
}
```

*continues on next page*

CREATING A TABLE

If the query is successfully created (hence, the conditional is TRUE), you will see only the "successfully executed" message (**Figure 11.4**). If the table was not created due to an SQL error, the result will be like that in **Figure 11.5**. However, if the table could not be created because of a database permission problem, you will see an error like those in Figure 11.3.

7. Close the MySQL link, then close the PHP section, and the HTML.

```
mysql_close ($Link);
?></BODY></HTML>
```

8. Save your script as CreateTable.php, upload it to the server, and test it in your Web browser.

## ✔ Tip

■ It is not necessary to write your SQL queries partially in all capital letters like I have here, but doing so does help to distinguish your SQL from the table and column names. The table and column names are case sensitive, whereas SQL in general is not.

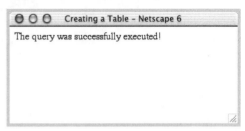

**Figure 11.4** If the script was able to create the new table, a simple message will be sent to the browser.

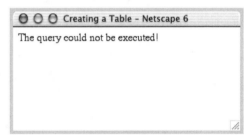

**Figure 11.5** If the script could not create the new table, it will state that the query could not be executed.

CREATING A TABLE

**Script 11.3** You've seen variants of this form in earlier chapters. As with all HTML forms the most important thing to remember is your INPUT field names so that you can refer back to them in your PHP.

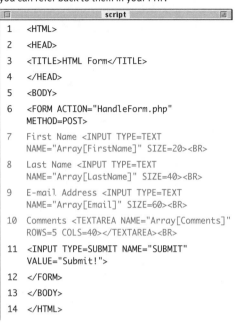

```
1    <HTML>
2    <HEAD>
3    <TITLE>HTML Form</TITLE>
4    </HEAD>
5    <BODY>
6    <FORM ACTION="HandleForm.php"
     METHOD=POST>
7    First Name <INPUT TYPE=TEXT
     NAME="Array[FirstName]" SIZE=20><BR>
8    Last Name <INPUT TYPE=TEXT
     NAME="Array[LastName]" SIZE=40><BR>
9    E-mail Address <INPUT TYPE=TEXT
     NAME="Array[Email]" SIZE=60><BR>
10   Comments <TEXTAREA NAME="Array[Comments]"
     ROWS=5 COLS=40></TEXTAREA><BR>
11   <INPUT TYPE=SUBMIT NAME="SUBMIT"
     VALUE="Submit!">
12   </FORM>
13   </BODY>
14   </HTML>
```

# Sending Data to a Database

As I have mentioned, this database will store user feedback in a table for future viewing. It's a simple but relevant use of a database. In the last section you created the table which consists of five columns: *id*, *FirstName*, *LastName*, *EmailAddress*, and *Comments*. The process of adding information to a table is similar to creating the table itself in terms of which functions you use, but the SQL query will be different.

```
$Query = "INSERT into $TableName values
→ ('value1', 'value2', 'value3', etc.)";
mysql_db_query ("DatabaseName", $Query,
→ $Link);
```

The query begins with `INSERT into $TableName values`. Then, within the parentheses, the value for each column should be put within single quotation marks with each value separated by a comma. There must be exactly as many values listed as there are columns in the table or else the query will not work! Then the query is submitted to the MySQL using `mysql_db_query()`.

To demonstrate this, you'll use an HTML form that takes the user's first name, last name, E-mail address, and comments. The PHP script that handles this form will put the submitted information into the database.

### To enter data into a database from an HTML form:

1. Create a new HTML document in your text editor that will create the HTML form.

2. Code the standard HTML header (**Script 11.3**):

   ```
   <HTML><HEAD><TITLE>HTML Form
   → </TITLE><BODY>
   ```

*continues on next page*

**3.** Create a form.

```
<FORM ACTION="HandleForm.php"
→ METHOD=POST>
```

**4.** Code for four text inputs.

```
First Name <INPUT TYPE=TEXT
→ NAME="Array[FirstName]"
→ SIZE=20><BR>
→ Last Name <INPUT TYPE=TEXT
→ NAME="Array[LastName]" SIZE=40><BR>
→ E-mail Address <INPUT TYPE=TEXT
→ NAME="Array[Email]" SIZE=60><BR>
→ Comments <TEXTAREA
→ NAME="Array[Comments]" ROWS=5
→ COLS=40></TEXTAREA><BR>
```

You can make your form more attractive than this one but be sure to make note of your input variable names, which you'll need in the HandleForm.php page.

**5.** Add the submit button, close the form, and close the HTML page.

```
<INPUT TYPE=SUBMIT NAME="SUBMIT"
→ VALUE="Submit!">
</FORM>
</BODY>
</HTML>
```

**6.** Save the page as form.html and upload it to the server.

Now you will write the HandleForm.php page, which takes the data generated by the form and puts it into the database.

**7.** Create a new PHP document in your text editor.

**8.** Begin with the standard HTML header (**Script 11.4**).

```
<HTML><HEAD><TITLE>Inserting Data
→ into a Database</TITLE><BODY>
```

**Script 11.4** The query statement for adding information to a database is straightforward enough, but be sure to match the number of values in parentheses to the number of columns in the database table.

```
1   <HTML>
2   <HEAD>
3   <TITLE>Inserting Data into a Database
    </TITLE>
4   <BODY>
5   <?php
6   /* This page receives and handles the
    data generated by "form.html". */
7   // Trim the incoming data.
8   $Array["FirstName"] = trim
    ($Array["FirstName"]);
9   $Array["LastName"] = trim
    ($Array["LastName"]);
10  $Array["Email"] = trim
    ($Array["Email"]);
11  $Array["Comments"] = trim
    ($Array["Comments"]);
12
13  // Set the variables for the database
    access:
14  $Host = "localhost";
15  $User = "user";
16  $Password = "password";
17  $DBName = "NewDatabase";
18  $TableName = "Feedback";
19
20  $Link = mysql_connect ($Host, $User,
    $Password);
21  $Query = "INSERT into $TableName values
    ('0', '$Array[FirstName]',
    '$Array[LastName]', '$Array[Email]',
    '$Array[Comments]')";
22  print ("The query is:<BR>$Query<P>\n");
23  if (mysql_db_query ($DBName, $Query,
    $Link)) {
24      print ("The query was successfully
        executed!<BR>\n");
25  } else {
26      print ("The query could not be
        executed!<BR>\n");
27  }
28  mysql_close ($Link);
29  ?>
30  </BODY>
31  </HTML>
```

**Figure 11.6** This is the HTML form I'm using to enter data into the database. The input here will be stored in the *Feedback* table in the *NewDatabase* database.

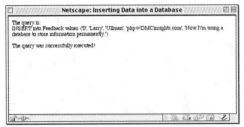

**Figure 11.7** Notice how PHP automatically escaped the apostrophe in my comment so that it won't cause troubles when submitting the query to the database. Without the apostrophe escaped, the SQL would think the last column consisted only of "Now I" and an error would result.

9. Start the PHP section of the page and trim all of the incoming data to rid it of extraneous spaces.

```
<?php
$Array["FirstName"] = trim
→ ($Array["FirstName"]);
$Array["LastName"] = trim
→ ($Array["LastName"]);
$Array["Email"] = trim
→ ($Array["Email"]);
$Array["Comments"] = trim
→ ($Array["Comments"]);
```

10. Set the variables for the database access.

```
$Host = "localhost";
$User = "user";
$Password = "password";
$DBName = "NewDatabase";
$TableName = "Feedback";
```

11. Connect to MySQL, then write the query.

```
$Link = mysql_connect ($Host, $User,
→ $Password);
$Query = "INSERT into $TableName values
→ ('0', '$Array[FirstName]',
'$Array[LastName]', '$Array[Email]',
→ '$Array[Comments]')";
```

The query begins with the necessary `INSERT into $TableName values` code, followed by five values (one for each column in order), within single quotation marks and separated by commas. Because the *id* column has been set to `AUTO_INCREMENT`, you can use 0 as the value and MySQL will automatically make that id the next logical value.

*continues on next page*

**12.** Just for the sake of error checking, print out the query to the browser.

```
print ("The query is:<BR>$Query<P>\n");
```

Whenever you are having difficulties with a database interaction, first check your query to make sure it is logical and valid. Although you wouldn't want the user to see the query, you can use this technique here while practicing or debugging (see the Tip below).

**13.** Create a conditional based upon the result of querying the database.

```
if (mysql_db_query ($DBName, $Query,
→ $Link)) {
    print ("The query was successfully
    → executed!<BR>\n");
} else {
    print ("The query could not be
    → executed!<BR>\n");
}
```

**14.** Close the MySQL link, then close the PHP section, and the HTML.

```
mysql_close ($Link);
?></BODY></HTML>
```

**15.** Save your script as HandleForm.php, upload it to the server in the same directory as form.html, and test both pages in your Web browser (Figures 11.2 and 11.3).

## ✔ Tip

■ If you want to be able to check your SQL statements, without making them obviously viewable to the user, add this line of code to your script: print ("<!–The query is $Query–>\n");. Now the PHP will write the query as an HTML comment, making it viewable by looking at the page source (Figures 11.8 and 11.9).

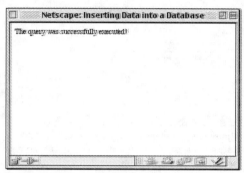

**Figure 11.8** This page, while designed with the user in mind, will not help you as you develop your site. However, by viewing the page source you can see what the exact SQL query was (Figure 11.5).

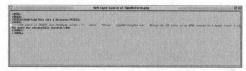

**Figure 11.9** During development of a Web site you can print your SQL queries as an HTML comment in order to double check exactly what the code is doing.

# Retrieving Data from a Database

The last process I'll demonstrate for working with databases is how to retrieve data from an established database. While you'll still use the `mysql_db_query()` function, retrieving data is slightly different than inserting data in that you have to assign the retrieved information to a variable in order to make use of it. I'll go through this one step at a time.

The easiest query to read data from a table is:

`$Query = "SELECT * from $TableName";`

The asterisk is the equivalent of saying *everything* (so this query states "select everything from $TableName"). This four-word statement will frequently be sufficient for data retrieval.

However, you could, in our example, limit the query by writing `SELECT FirstName, Comments from $TableName`. This query requests that only the information from those two columns (*FirstName* and *Comments*) be gathered.

Another way to restrict your query is to write something like `SELECT * from $Tablename where (FirstName='Larry')`. Here you want the information from every column in the table, but only from the rows where the *FirstName* column is equal to *Larry*. These are good examples of how SQL uses only a few terms effectively and flexibly.

The main difference in retrieving data from a database as opposed to inserting data into a database is that you need to handle the query differently. I prefer to assign the results of the query to a variable:

`$Result = mysql_db_query ($DBName,`
`→ $Query, $Link);`

*continues on next page*

In layman's terms, this variable now knows what the result of the query is. In order to access multiple rows of information retrieved, you should run the $Result variable through a loop.

```
while ($Row=mysql_fetch_array ($Result)) {
    statements;
}
```

With each iteration of the loop, the next row of information from the query (stored in $Result) will be turned into an array called $Row. This process will continue until there are no more rows of information to be found. The best way to comprehend this system is to try it out, so now you'll write a script that reads the information stored in the *Feedback* table (you may want to run through form.html a couple more times to build up the table).

## To retrieve data from a table:

1. Create a new PHP document in your text editor.

2. Begin with the standard HTML header (**Script 11.5**).

   ```
   <HTML><HEAD><TITLE>Retrieving Data
   → from a Database</TITLE><BODY>
   ```

3. Start the PHP section of the page and set the variables for the database.

   ```
   <?php
   $Host = "localhost";
   $User = "user";
   $Password = "password";
   $DBName = "NewDatabase";
   $TableName = "Feedback";
   ```

**Script 11.5** The SQL query for retrieving all data from a table is quite simple, but in order for PHP to access every item, you must loop through the results one row at a time.

```
1   <HTML>
2   <HEAD>
3   <TITLE>Retrieving Data from a
    Database</TITLE>
4   <BODY>
5   <?php
6   // Set the variables for the database
    access:
7   $Host = "localhost";
8   $User = "user";
9   $Password = "password";
10  $DBName = "NewDatabase";
11  $TableName = "Feedback";
12
13  $Link = mysql_connect ($Host, $User,
    $Password);
14
15  $Query = "SELECT * from $TableName";
16  $Result = mysql_db_query ($DBName,
    $Query, $Link);
17
18  // Create a table.
19  print ("<TABLE BORDER=1 WIDTH=\"75%\"
    CELLSPACING=2 CELLPADDING=2
    ALIGN=CENTER>\n");
20  print ("<TR ALIGN=CENTER
    VALIGN=TOP>\n");
21  print ("<TD ALIGN=CENTER
    VALIGN=TOP>Name</TD>\n");
22  print ("<TD ALIGN=CENTER
    VALIGN=TOP>Email Address</TD>\n");
23  print ("<TD ALIGN=CENTER
    VALIGN=TOP>Comments</TD>\n");
24  print ("</TR>\n");
25
26  // Fetch the results from the database.
27  while ($Row = mysql_fetch_array
    ($Result)) {
28      print ("<TR ALIGN=CENTER
        VALIGN=TOP>\n");
29      print ("<TD ALIGN=CENTER
        VALIGN=TOP>$Row[FirstName]
        $Row[LastName]</TD>\n");
```

*Script continues on next page*

Retrieving Data from a Database

**Script 11.5** *continued*

```
                  script
30    print ("<TD ALIGN=CENTER VALIGN=TOP>
      $Row[EmailAddress]</TD>\n");
31    print ("<TD ALIGN=CENTER
      VALIGN=TOP>$Row[Comments]</TD>\n");
32    print ("</TR>\n");
33  }
34  mysql_close ($Link);
35  print ("</TABLE>\n");
36  ?>
37  </BODY>
38  </HTML>
```

**4.** Connect to the database, write, and execute the query.

```
$Link = mysql_connect ($Host, $User,
→ $Password);
$Query = "SELECT * from $TableName";
$Result = mysql_db_query ($DBName,
→ $Query, $Link);
```

The query is straightforward and very useful. Then, as I indicated, earlier, the results of the query will be stored in a variable, which will be looped later in the script.

**5.** Start an HTML table to display the results of the query.

```
print ("<TABLE BORDER=1 WIDTH=\"75%\"
→ CELLSPACING=2 CELLPADDING=2
→ ALIGN=CENTER>\n");
print ("<TR ALIGN=CENTER
→ VALIGN=TOP>\n");
print ("<TD ALIGN=CENTER
→ VALIGN=TOP>Name</TD>\n");
print ("<TD ALIGN=CENTER
→ VALIGN=TOP>Email Address</TD>\n");
print ("<TD ALIGN=CENTER
→ VALIGN=TOP>Comments</TD>\n");
print ("</TR>\n");
```

Since you are retrieving information from a table and displaying it in an HTML form, it makes sense to create an HTML table to improve the appearance of the data.

**6.** Create a loop that retrieves each row from the database until there are no more rows.

```
while ($Row = mysql_fetch_array
→ ($Result)) {
```

What this loop is doing is setting the variable $Row to an array comprised of the first table row in $Result. The loop will then execute the following commands (step 7). Once the loop gets back to the beginning, it will assign the next row, if it exists. It will continue to do this until there are no more rows of information to be obtained.

*continues on next page*

**199**

7. Print out the database information in the HTML table.

```
print ("<TR ALIGN=CENTER
→ VALIGN=TOP>\n");
print ("<TD ALIGN=CENTER
→ VALIGN=TOP>$Row[FirstName]
→ $Row[LastName]</TD>\n");
print ("<TD ALIGN=CENTER
→ VALIGN=TOP>$Row[EmailAddress]
→ </TD>\n");
print ("<TD ALIGN=CENTER
→ VALIGN=TOP>$Row[Comments]
→ </TD>\n");
```

Because the `mysql_fetch_array()` function was used, you can refer to each individual column in the row as you would any other array. The array's keys are the names of the columns from the table, hence, *FirstName*, *LastName*, *EmailAddress*, and *Comments* (there's no need to print out the *id*).

8. Close the HTML row and close the while loop.

```
print ("</TR>\n");
}
```

Just to make sure that it is clear, this loop will assign a row of table data to the $Row array, then print out an HTML table row.

9. Close the MySQL link, close the HTML table, then close the PHP section, and the HTML page itself.

```
mysql_close ($Link);
print ("</TABLE>\n");
?></BODY></HTML>
```

10. Save your script as `DisplayDB.php`, upload it to the server, and test it in your Web browser (**Figure 11.10**).

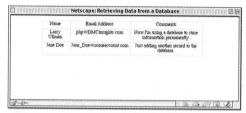

**Figure 11.10** Being able to pull out data from a database and create a dynamic Web page is a great use of PHP and something you'll never be able to accomplish with HTML alone.

# COOKIES

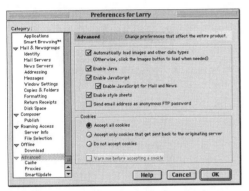

**Figure 12.1** In Netscape Navigator, you can set your cookie permissions through Edit > Preferences > Advanced. In Internet Explorer 5.0 (for Macintosh) you would go through Edit > Preferences > Cookies, although different versions of the browsers are organized differently especially on Windows compared to Macintosh.

Cookies are one of the lesser understood and most maligned tools for today's World Wide Web. While many users have concerns about the security issues cookies are rumored to create, few people realize what benefits cookies offer to the user.

Prior to the existence of cookies, traversing through a Web site was a trip without a history. Although your browser tracks the pages you visit, allowing you to use the *back* button to return to previously visited pages and indicating visited links in a different color, the server keeps no record of who has seen what. All of this is still true for sites that do not use cookies, as well as for users who have disabled cookies in their Web browsers (**Figure 12.1**).

Why is that a problem? Without the server being able to track a user, there can be no shopping carts for you to make purchases online. If cookies didn't exist or if they are disabled in your Web browser, people would not be able to use Hotmail, which requires user registration.

Cookies are a way for a server to store information about the user (on the user's machine) so that the server can remember the user over the course of the visit or through several visits. Think of a cookie like a name tag: you tell the server your name and it gives you a name tag. Then it can know who you are by referring back to the name tag.

This brings me to another point about the security issues involved with cookies. Cookies have gotten a bad rap because users believe that cookies allow a server to know too much about them. However, a cookie can only be used to store information that you give it, so it's as secure as you want it to be.

PHP has very good support for cookies. In this chapter you will learn how to set a cookie, retrieve information from a cookie, and then delete the cookie. You will also see some of the optional parameters you can use to apply limits to a cookie's existence.

**COOKIES**

**Figure 12.2** This friendly and informative message is what you'll see if the `setcookie()` function is called after anything, even a blank line, has already been sent to the Web browser.

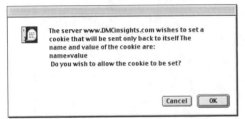

**Figure 12.3** If the user has the "Warn me before accepting a cookie" box checked in their Preferences (Figure 12.1), a prompt like this will appear for each cookie sent.

# Creating and Reading from Cookies

The most important thing to understand about cookies is that they must be sent from the server to the client prior to any other information. Should the server attempt to send a cookie after the Web browser has already received HTML, even an extraneous white space, an error message will result and the cookie will not be sent (**Figure 12.2**). This is by far the most common cookie-related error.

Cookies are sent using the `setcookie()` function:

```
setcookie ("name", "value");
```

That line of code will send a cookie to the browser with a name of *name* and a value of *value* (**Figure 12.3**).

You can continue to send more cookies to the browser with subsequent uses of the `setcookie()` function, although you are limited by Web protocols to sending at most 20 cookies from one server to one user:

```
setcookie ("name2", "value2");
setcookie ("name3", "value3");
```

To retrieve a value from a cookie, you only need to refer to the cookie name as a variable (the name preceded by a dollar sign), just as you would refer to an HTML form element as a variable on the handling page. For example, to retrieve the value of the cookie established with the line `setcookie ("UserName", "Larry");` you would use the variable $UserName.

For an example of setting cookies, let's create a page that allows the user to specify the text and background colors of a page.

## To send and retrieve cookies with PHP:

1. Create a new PHP document in your text editor by beginning with the standard opening PHP tag (**Script 12.1**).

   ```
   <?php
   ```

2. Write a conditional that will send the cookie if the form has been submitted.

   ```
   if ($BeenSubmitted) {
   ```

   Just as you've done before, the $BeenSubmitted variable will be used to determine whether or not the form has been submitted. If TRUE, then the PHP will process the form.

3. Set the cookies and then colors for the page itself.

   ```
   setcookie("BGColor",
   → "$NewBGColor");
   setcookie("TextColor",
   → "$NewTextColor");
   $BGColor = $NewBGColor;
   $TextColor = $NewTextColor;
   ```

   If the form has been submitted, the PHP will send two cookies with the values for the background and text colors. The script will then set the current values ($BGColor and $TextColor) to the preferred values ($NewBGColor and $NewTextColor) in order to reflect the change immediately.

4. Finish the conditional.

   ```
   } else {
       if (!$BGColor) {
           $BGColor = "WHITE";
       }
       if (!$TextColor) {
           $TextColor = "BLACK";
       }
   }
   ```

   If the form has not been submitted, the PHP will check to make sure that the background and text colors have not been assigned. If they have not been, they'll be assigned default values.

**Script 12.1** Two cookies will be used to store the user's choices for the background and text colors. The form-submitted values will also be assigned to the page so that the requested change is applied immediately.

```
                        script
1    <?php
2    if ($BeenSubmitted) {
3        setcookie("BGColor", "$NewBGColor");
4        setcookie("TextColor",
         "$NewTextColor");
5        $BGColor = $NewBGColor;
6        $TextColor = $NewTextColor;
7    } else {
8        if (!$BGColor) {
9            $BGColor = "WHITE";
10       }
11       if (!$TextColor) {
12           $TextColor = "BLACK";
13       }
14   }
15   ?>
16   <HEAD>
17   <TITLE>User Customization</TITLE>
18   </HEAD>
19   <?
20   print ("<BODY BGCOLOR=$BGColor
         TEXT=$TextColor\n");
21   ?>
22   Currently your page looks like this!
23   <FORM ACTION="cookies.php" METHOD=POST>
24   Select a new background color:
25   <SELECT NAME="NewBGColor">
26   <OPTION VALUE=WHITE>WHITE</OPTION>
27   <OPTION VALUE=BLACK>BLACK</OPTION>
28   <OPTION VALUE=BLUE>BLUE</OPTION>
29   <OPTION VALUE=RED>RED</OPTION>
30   <OPTION VALUE=GREEN>GREEN</OPTION>
31   </SELECT>
32   Select a new text color:
33   <SELECT NAME="NewTextColor">
34   <OPTION VALUE=WHITE>WHITE</OPTION>
35   <OPTION VALUE=BLACK>BLACK</OPTION>
36   <OPTION VALUE=BLUE>BLUE</OPTION>
37   <OPTION VALUE=RED>RED</OPTION>
38   <OPTION VALUE=GREEN>GREEN</OPTION>
```

*Script continues on next page*

**Script 12.1** *continued*

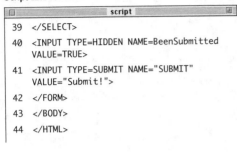

```
39  </SELECT>
40  <INPUT TYPE=HIDDEN NAME=BeenSubmitted
    VALUE=TRUE>
41  <INPUT TYPE=SUBMIT NAME="SUBMIT"
    VALUE="Submit!">
42  </FORM>
43  </BODY>
44  </HTML>
```

**5.** Close the initial PHP section then create the HTML head.

```
?>
<HEAD>
<TITLE>User Customization</TITLE>
</HEAD>
```

**6.** Establish another PHP section to print out the <BODY> tag with the proper values for the background color and text color.

```
<?
print ("<BODY BGCOLOR=$BGColor
→ TEXT=$TextColor>\n");
?>
```

**7.** Print a simple sentence that will reveal the text color.

```
Currently your page looks like this!
```

**8.** Create an HTML form that will be submitted back to itself.

```
<FORM ACTION="cookies.php"
→ METHOD=POST>
```

You could also have PHP print the value of $PHP_SELF which always refers to the page.

**9.** Make two pull-down menus for the user to select the background and text colors.

```
Select a new background color:
<SELECT NAME="NewBGColor">
<OPTION VALUE=WHITE>WHITE</OPTION>
<OPTION VALUE=BLACK>BLACK</OPTION>
<OPTION VALUE=BLUE>BLUE</OPTION>
<OPTION VALUE=RED>RED</OPTION>
<OPTION VALUE=GREEN>GREEN</OPTION>
</SELECT>
Select a new text color:
<SELECT NAME="NewTextColor">
<OPTION VALUE=WHITE>WHITE</OPTION>
<OPTION VALUE=BLACK>BLACK</OPTION>
<OPTION VALUE=BLUE>BLUE</OPTION>
<OPTION VALUE=RED>RED</OPTION>
<OPTION VALUE=GREEN>GREEN</OPTION>
</SELECT>
```

*continues on next page*

Each pull-down menu only gives 5 options, in word form. You can add more choices to these menus, if you want, as long as you restrict yourself to the valid HTML colors.

**10.** Code for a hidden variable that will indicate whether or not the form has been submitted.

```
<INPUT TYPE=HIDDEN
NAME=BeenSubmitted → VALUE=TRUE>
```

This is the variable that will tell the script that the form has been submitted.

**11.** Add the submit button, then close the form and the HTML page.

```
<INPUT TYPE=SUBMIT NAME="SUBMIT"
→ VALUE="Submit!">
</FORM>
</BODY>
</HTML>
```

**12.** Save the page as `cookies.php`, load it to the server, and test in your Web browser (**Figures 12.4**, **12.5**, **12.6**, **12.7** and **12.8**).

### ✔ Tips

■ The value of a cookie is automatically urlencoded when it is sent and urldecoded upon being received by the PHP page. As you know, the same is true of values sent by HTML forms.

■ It is important to remember that the value of a cookie will always take precedence over values passed by a form. In `cookies.php`, for example, if the form inputs were named BGColor and TextColor you would have problems because the BGColor and TextColor cookies would override the form values.

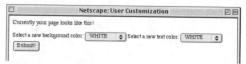

**Figure 12.4** Upon first coming to `cookies.php`, the page looks like this with the default colors being used: a white background and black text.

**Figure 12.5** This is the message the user will see when the first `setcookie()` call is made if they have opted to be warned before accepting a cookie. This cookie is storing the value of *BLUE* in a cookie named *BGColor*.

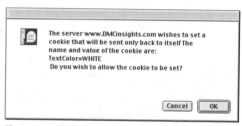

**Figure 12.6** The second cookie that gets sent is called *TextColor* and has a value of *WHITE*. If the "Warn me before accepting a cookie" box is not checked in the user's preferences, they will not see these messages.

**Figure 12.7** Upon receiving the values from the HTML form, the `cookies.php` page will send the two cookies to store the information and then reflect the changes in the page.

**Figure 12.8** By viewing the source code of the page, you can also track how the color values change.

# Adding Parameters to a Cookie

Although passing just the name and value arguments to the `setcookie()` function will suffice for most of your cookie uses, you ought to be aware of the other arguments available. The function can take up to four more arguments, each of which will limit the operation of the cookie.

```
setcookie ("name", "value", "expiration",
→ "path", "domain", "secure");
```

The expiration argument is used to set a specific length of time for a cookie to exist. If it is not specified, the cookie will continue to be functional until the user closes their browser. Normally the expiration time is set by adding a particular number of minutes or hours to the current time. This line of code will set the expiration time of the cookie to be one hour (60 seconds times 60 minutes) from the current moment:

```
setcookie ("name", "value", time()_+
→ "3600");
```

Because the expiration time will be calculated as the value of `time()` plus 3600, this particular argument is not put in quotes (as you do not want to literally pass *time() + 3600* as the expiration but rather the result of that calculation).

The path and domain arguments are used to limit a cookie to a specific folder within a Web site (the path) or to a specific domain. For example, you could limit the life of a cookie to exist only while a user is within their folder of the domain:

```
setcookie ("name", "value", time()_+ 3600,
→ "/user/");
```

*continues on next page*

The secure value dictates that a cookie should only be sent over a secure HTTPS connection. A 1 indicates that a secure connection must be used, a 0 indicates that a secure connection is not necessary. You would want to insure a secure connection for e-commerce sites.

```
setcookie ("name", "value", time()_+
→ "3600", "", "", "1");
```

As with all functions that take arguments, you must pass all the values in order. In the above example, I did not want to specify (or limit) the path and domain so I used empty quotes to indicate such. By doing so I maintained the proper number of arguments and was still able to indicate that a HTTPS connection was necessary.

Let's add an expiration date to the existing cookies.php page so that the user's preferences will remain even after they have closed their browser and returned to the site.

## To set a cookie's expiration date:

1. Open cookies.php in your text editor (Script 12.1).

2. Change the two setcookie() lines to include an expiration date that's several days or more away (**Script 12.2**):

   ```
   setcookie("BGColor", "$NewBGColor",
   → time()+"10000000");
   setcookie("TextColor",
   → "$NewTextColor", time()+
   → "10000000");
   ```

   By setting the expiration date to time() + "10000000", the cookie will continue to exist for approximately 116 days after it is set (60 seconds * 60 minutes * 24 hours * 115 days is approximately 10000000).

**Script 12.2** By adding the expiration arguments to the two cookies, the cookies will continue to persist even after the user has closed out of and returned to their browser.

```
1   <?php
2   if ($BeenSubmitted) {
3       setcookie("BGColor", "$NewBGColor",
        time()+ "10000000");
4       setcookie("TextColor",
        "$NewTextColor", time()+ "10000000");
5       $BGColor = $NewBGColor;
6       $TextColor = $NewTextColor;
7   } else {
8       if (!$BGColor) {
9           $BGColor = "WHITE";
10      }
11      if (!$TextColor) {
12          $TextColor = "BLACK";
13      }
14  }
15  ?>
16  <HEAD>
17  <TITLE>User Customization</TITLE>
18  </HEAD>
19  <?
20  print ("<BODY BGCOLOR=$BGColor
    TEXT=$TextColor>\n");
21  ?>
22  Currently your page looks like this!
23  <FORM ACTION="cookies.php" METHOD=POST>
24  Select a new background color:
25  <SELECT NAME="NewBGColor">
26  <OPTION VALUE=WHITE>WHITE</OPTION>
27  <OPTION VALUE=BLACK>BLACK</OPTION>
28  <OPTION VALUE=BLUE>BLUE</OPTION>
29  <OPTION VALUE=RED>RED</OPTION>
30  <OPTION VALUE=GREEN>GREEN</OPTION>
31  </SELECT>
32  Select a new text color:
33  <SELECT NAME="NewTextColor">
34  <OPTION VALUE=WHITE>WHITE</OPTION>
35  <OPTION VALUE=BLACK>BLACK</OPTION>
36  <OPTION VALUE=BLUE>BLUE</OPTION>
37  <OPTION VALUE=RED>RED</OPTION>
38  <OPTION VALUE=GREEN>GREEN</OPTION>
```

*Script continues on next page*

**Script 12.2** *continued*

```
                    script
39   </SELECT>
40   <INPUT TYPE=HIDDEN NAME=BeenSubmitted
     VALUE=TRUE>
41   <INPUT TYPE=SUBMIT NAME="SUBMIT"
     VALUE="Submit!">
42   </FORM>
43   </BODY>
44   </HTML>
```

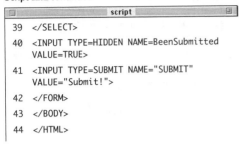

**Figure 12.9** The addition of the expiration argument is reflected in the message the user sees regarding the cookie.

**Figure 12.10** Because the expiration date of the cookies was set months into the future, the user's preferences, which are stored in the cookies, will still be valid even after the user has closed and reopened the browser as I've done here. Without this expiration date, the user would see the default colors and have to reassign their preferences with every new browser session.

3. Save the script, load it to the server, and test it in your Web browser (**Figures 12.9** and **12.10**).

## ✔ Tips

■ Some programmers report that specific versions of Netscape and Internet Explorer have difficulties with cookies that do not list every argument. If you think this is going to be an issue for your Web site, you can pass every argument by using empty quotation marks to represent default values:

```
setcookie("BGColor", "$NewBGColor",
→ time()+10000000, "", "", "");
```

■ There is really no rule of thumb for what kind of expiration date to use with your cookies. Here are some general guidelines, though: if the cookie should last as long as the session, do not set an expiration time; if the cookie should continue to exist after the user has closed and reopened their browser, set an expiration time months ahead; and, if the cookie can constitute a security risk, set an expiration time of an hour or fraction thereof so that the cookie does not continue to exist too long after a user has left their browser.

■ For security purposes, you could set a five or ten minute expiration time on a cookie and have the cookie resent with every new page the user visits. This way the cookie will continue to persist as long as the user is active but will automatically die five or ten minutes after the user's last action.

ADDING PARAMETERS TO A COOKIE

# Deleting a Cookie

The final thing to understand about using cookies is how to delete one. While a cookie will automatically expire when the user's browser is closed or when the expiration date/time is met, sometimes you'll want to manually delete the cookie as well. For example, Web sites that have registered users and login capabilities will probably want to delete any cookies when the user logs out.

Although the setcookie() function can take up to six arguments, only one is actually required—the name. If you send a cookie that consists of a name without a value it will have the same effect as deleting the existing cookie of the same name. For example, to create the cookie UserName, you use this line:

setcookie("UserName", "Larry");

To delete the UserName cookie, you would code:

setcookie("UserName", "");

As an added precaution, you can also set an expiration date that's in the past.

setcookie("UserName", "", time() - 60);

To demonstrate this feature, let's add a reset button to the cookies.php page that will destroy the sent cookies and display the default colors once again.

**Script 12.3** To reset all the values, blank cookies are sent with the same names as the existing cookies. A reset checkbox has also been added to the HTML form.

```
1   <?php
2   if ($BeenSubmitted) {
3       if ($Reset) {
4           setcookie("BGColor", "", time()-
            "100");
5           setcookie ("TextColor", "" ,
            time()-"100");
6           $BGColor = "WHITE";
7           $TextColor = "BLACK";
8       } else {
9           setcookie("BGColor",
            "$NewBGColor", time()+
            "1000000");
10          setcookie ("TextColor",
            "$NewTextColor", time()+
            "1000000");
11          $BGColor = $NewBGColor;
12          $TextColor = $NewTextColor;
13      }
14  } else {
15      if (!$BGColor) {
16          $BGColor = "WHITE";
17      }
18      if (!$TextColor) {
19          $TextColor = "BLACK";
20      }
21  }
22  ?>
23  <HEAD>
24  <TITLE>User Customization</TITLE>
25  </HEAD>
26  <?
27  print ("<BODY BGCOLOR=$BGColor
        TEXT=$TextColor>\n");
28  ?>
29  Currently your page looks like this!
30  <FORM ACTION="cookies.php" METHOD=POST>
31  Select a new background color:
32  <SELECT NAME="NewBGColor">
33  <OPTION VALUE=WHITE>WHITE</OPTION>
34  <OPTION VALUE=BLACK>BLACK</OPTION>
```

*Script continues on next page*

**Script 12.3** *continued*

```
                    script
35  <OPTION VALUE=BLUE>BLUE</OPTION>
36  <OPTION VALUE=RED>RED</OPTION>
37  <OPTION VALUE=GREEN>GREEN</OPTION>
38  </SELECT>
39  Select a new text color:
40  <SELECT NAME="NewTextColor">
41  <OPTION VALUE=WHITE>WHITE</OPTION>
42  <OPTION VALUE=BLACK>BLACK</OPTION>
43  <OPTION VALUE=BLUE>BLUE</OPTION>
44  <OPTION VALUE=RED>RED</OPTION>
45  <OPTION VALUE=GREEN>GREEN</OPTION>
46  </SELECT>
47  <P><INPUT TYPE=Checkbox NAME=Reset
    VALUE=TRUE> Check this box to reset the
    colors.<P>
48  <INPUT TYPE=HIDDEN NAME=BeenSubmitted
    VALUE=TRUE>
49  <INPUT TYPE=SUBMIT NAME="SUBMIT"
    VALUE="Submit!">
50  </FORM>
51  </BODY>
52  </HTML>
```

## To delete a cookie:

1. Open `cookies.php` in your text editor (Script 12.2).

2. Add another conditional within the existing `if ($BeenSubmitted)` conditional (**Script 12.3**, lines 3-8).

    ```
    if ($Reset) {
        setcookie("BGColor", "",
    → time()- "100");
        setcookie ("TextColor", "",
    → time()-"100");
        $BGColor = "WHITE";
        $TextColor = "BLACK";
    } else {
    ```

   If the form has been submitted, the PHP will first check to see if $Reset is TRUE. If it is, the script will delete the existing cookies by sending valueless cookies of the same name. The page will also reset the color values for the existing page.

3. Complete the if ($Reset) conditional.

    ```
    setcookie("BGColor", "$NewBGColor",
    → time()+ "1000000");
        setcookie ("TextColor",
    → "$NewTextColor", time()+
    → "1000000");
        $BGColor = $NewBGColor;
        $TextColor = $NewTextColor;
    }
    ```

   If the form has been submitted but $Reset is not TRUE, the form should be handled as it had been in Script 12.2.

   *continues on next page*

**4.** Within the HTML form, add a checkbox for the user to reset the colors (Script 12.3, line 47).

```
<P><INPUT TYPE=Checkbox NAME=Reset
→ VALUE=TRUE> Check this box to reset
→ the colors.<P>
```

This checkbox will tell the PHP whether or not to reset the values. I have added two paragraph tags to make the HTML form look nicer.

**5.** Save the script, load it to the server, and test it in your Web browser (**Figures 12.11**, **12.12** and **12.13**).

### ✔ Tips

■ To test that your setcookie() functions are working properly, be sure to check "Warn me before accepting a cookie" (in Netscape) or "Ask for each cookie" (in Internet Explorer) in your browser's preferences (Figure 12.1).

■ The setcookie() function is one of the few in PHP that could generate different results in different browsers, since browsers will treat cookies differently. Be sure to test your Web sites in multiple browsers on different platforms to insure consistency.

**Figure 12.11** A simple checkbox has been added to the HTML form giving the user the option of resetting the page. It will also delete the existing cookies.

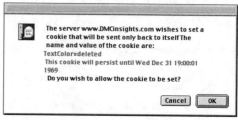

**Figure 12.12** When the setcookie() function is used with a name but no value, the existing cookie of that name will be deleted. The expiration date in the past also guarantees proper destruction of the existing cookie.

**Figure 12.13** If the user has checked the reset box and clicked Submit!, the PHP will destroy the cookies (Figure 12.12) and reset the form to its default colors.

# CREATING
# WEB APPLICATIONS

Now that you've learned the bulk of programming with PHP, it's time to tie it all together into professional-caliber Web applications. In this chapter you will learn about a number of functions and techniques that you can utilize to make your Web sites more professional, feature-rich, and easier to modify.

# Using include and require

Up to this point, you have written one page scripts which interface with databases, handle HTML forms, and send cookies. However, as you begin to develop multiple-page Web sites, it quickly becomes impractical to develop every attribute one script at a time. Certain features, such as the HTML design and PHP functions, will be used by every page within the site. You can put this common information into each individual page as you develop your site but when you need to make a change, you'll be required to make the change over and over again. You can save yourself time by creating separate pages for particular elements and then bringing them into the main PHP pages using one of two functions: include() or require().

```
include ("file.php");
require ("file.php");
```

Both functions work in the exact same way with only one significant difference. Regardless of where the require() function is within your script, it will always be called, even if it is the result of a conditional that is never true! The include() function, conversely, will only take effect if the function is called. Thus you should use require() if the file must be included and use include() if the file may or may not need to be included, depending upon the circumstances at hand.

But what do these two functions do? Both include() and require() will incorporate the file referenced  into the main file (for clarity's sake, I'll refer to the file that has the include() or require() line as the *parent* file). Any code within the included file will be treated as HTML unless it is within the PHP brackets in the included file itself. Any variables existing in the parent document before the include() or require() call will be available to the included file and any variables within the included file will be available to the parent document after the include() or require() call.

**Script 13.1** This is a basic included file which will create the HTML <HEAD> information as well as begin the layout table. Because each page will have a different title, a variable will be assigned to print the particular values.

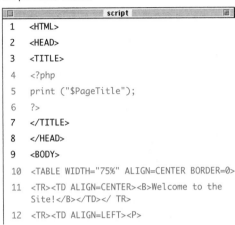

```
        script
1    <HTML>
2    <HEAD>
3    <TITLE>
4    <?php
5    print ("$PageTitle");
6    ?>
7    </TITLE>
8    </HEAD>
9    <BODY>
10   <TABLE WIDTH="75%" ALIGN=CENTER BORDER=0>
11   <TR><TD ALIGN=CENTER><B>Welcome to the
     Site!</B></TD></ TR>
12   <TR><TD ALIGN=LEFT><P>
```

**Figure 13.1** Although this isn't very fancy, it should adequately demonstrate how Web pages can be broken down into several components which are shared over multiple pages (see Figure 13.3).

There are any number of reasons to use included files. You could put your own defined functions into a common file. You might also want to place your database access information into a configuration file. First, however, let's place our HTML design into included files so that it can be used over several pages.

## To use include() or require():

1. Create a new PHP document in your text editor (**Script 13.1**).

   ```
   <HTML>
   <HEAD>
   <TITLE>
   ```

   Although this will be a `.php` file there is only one section of PHP so you'll code most of the page as you would a standard HTML script to avoid using numerous `print()` statements.

2. Use PHP to print out the title of the page.

   ```
   <?php
   print ("$PageTitle");
   ?>
   ```

   The $PageTitle variable will be assigned in the parent document and then used here to establish the page title which gets displayed at the top of the browser window (**Figure 13.1**).

3. Complete the HTML header information.

   ```
   </TITLE>
   </HEAD>
   <BODY>
   ```

4. Create a table to control the layout of the page.

   ```
   <TABLE WIDTH="75%" ALIGN=CENTER
   → BORDER=0>
   <TR><TD ALIGN=CENTER><B>Welcome to
   → the Site!</B></TD></ TR>
   <TR><TD ALIGN=LEFT><P>
   ```

   *continues on next page*

USING INCLUDE AND REQUIRE

**215**

The overall design of the site is going to use a table with three rows. The top row includes a welcome message, although it could also have a graphic. The second row will be for the page-specific content and the third row will contain a footer. You'll use the header include to make the top row and begin the second one.

**5.** Save the script as header.php and upload it to your server.

Now you'll write the corresponding footer file.

**6.** Create a new PHP document in your text editor (**Script 13.2**).

**7.** Close the second row of the layout table.

```
<P></TD></TR>
```

**8.** Code for the third and final row that contains the copyright.

```
<TR><TD ALIGN=CENTER><SMALL>
→ Copyright 2001</SMALL></TD></TR>
```

**9.** Close the table and the HTML page.

```
</TABLE>
</BODY>
</HTML>
```

**10.** Save the script as footer.php and upload it to your server.

Once the two included files are complete, you can start churning out the parent pages.

**11.** Create a new PHP document in your text editor (**Script 13.3**).

```
<?php
```

**12.** Assign the name of the page to the $PageTitle variable.

```
$PageTitle = "Home Page";
```

The value of $PageTitle will be used to create the title of the page which the browser displays at the top of the window. Because it will be different from parent page to parent page, I make it a variable that is used by the included file.

**Script 13.2** This is a basic included file which will complete the layout table and conclude the HTML page. I've also placed a copyright here.

```
1    <P></TD></TR>
2    <TR><TD ALIGN=CENTER><SMALL>Copyright
     2001</SMALL></TD></TR>
3    </TABLE>
4    </BODY>
5    </HTML>
```

**Script 13.3** Once the two included files have been created, the require() function will incorporate them into the parent file to create the entire page on the fly.

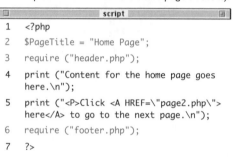

```
1    <?php
2    $PageTitle = "Home Page";
3    require ("header.php");
4    print ("Content for the home page goes
         here.\n");
5    print ("<P>Click <A HREF=\"page2.php\">
         here</A> to go to the next page.\n");
6    require ("footer.php");
7    ?>
```

**Script 13.4** This is another parent file and, except for line 4, it is exactly the same as Script 13.3. Whether your Web site has 10 pages or 100, they can all use this same basic template.

```
script
1    <?php
2    $PageTitle = "Second Page";
3    require ("header.php");
4    print ("Content for the second page goes
     here.\n");
5    require ("footer.php");
6    ?>
```

**13.** Include the header file.

```
require ("header.php");
```

In this case it won't matter if you use `include()` or `require()` but you'll use the latter to guarantee the inclusion occurs. This line of programming will bring all of the code from `header.php` into this page. Be sure to call this line after $PageTitle has been assigned or else the page will have no title.

**14.** Create the page-specific content.

```
print ("Content for the home page goes
→ here.\n");
print ("<P>Click <A HREF=\"page2.php\">
→ here</A> to go to the next page.\n");
```

For demonstration purposes, I'll only put in a simple message and a link to a second page. Any content you want could go here, though, including content dynamically generated by PHP.

**15.** Include the footer file and close the page.

```
require ("footer.php");
?>
```

**16.** Save the script as `index.php` and upload it to your server.

Finally, you'll write a second page that will also make use of the included design files.

**17.** Create a new PHP document in your text editor (**Script 13.4**).

```
<?php
$PageTitle = "Second Page";
require ("header.php");
print ("Content for the second page
→ goes here.\n");
require ("footer.php");
?>
```

To differentiate this page from `index.php`, give the $PageTitle variable a different value and then change the `print()` statement.

*continues on next page*

USING INCLUDE AND REQUIRE

**18.** Save the script as *page2.php*, upload it to your server, and test both it and `index.php` in your Web browser (**Figures 13.1**, **13.2**, and **13.3**).

### ✔ Tip

■ I would recommend that you use `.php` as your file extension and not `.inc`, which some people use for their included files. While it generally does not matter to the parent PHP file, a sneaky Web user could view the source of a `.inc` file but not the source of an included `.php` file (**Figures 13.4** and **13.5**).

**Figure 13.2** Nothing in the source of the page would indicate that this was compiled together on the fly. You can see how the two included files are brought in as if they were a part of the parent file itself.

**Figure 13.3** This page uses the same header and footer files as Figure 13.1 but the content and title are different.

**Figure 13.4** When your included files use a `.php` extension, users cannot necessarily view them directly because the server will try to execute the PHP, in some cases resulting in this blank page In other cases, the browser may also just reveal the beginning HTML, but, as a security measure you should use the `.php` extension!

**Figure 13.5** In comparison to Figure 13.4 where the file used the `.php` extension, when the `.inc` extension is used—which is a common enough occurrence—a sneaky user could see your source code by directly viewing the page. If passwords and database access information are stored in an included file, this could be a major security risk.

**Table 13.1** The list of formatting possibilities for the date() function is long and not easy to remember. I recommend keeping a copy of this list close at hand while you program.

### Format Options with the date() Function

| Character | Format |
|---|---|
| a | *am* or *pm* |
| A | *AM* or *PM* |
| d | day of the month as 2 digits with leading zeros: *01* to *31* |
| D | day of the week as 3 letters: *Sun, Mon*, etc. |
| F | month, long-form: *January* |
| g | hour of the day in 12-hour format without leading zeros: *1* to *12* |
| G | hour of the day in 24-hour format without leading zeros: *0* to *23* |
| h | hour of the day in 12-hour format: *01* to *12* |
| H | hour of the day in 24-hour format: *00* to *23* |
| i | minutes: *00* to *59* |
| j | day of the month without leading zeros: *1* to *31* |
| l (lowercase 'L') | day of the week, long-form: Sunday |
| m | month as 2 digits: *01* to *12* |
| M | month as 3 letters: *Jan* |
| n | month as digits without leading zeros: *1* to *12* |
| s | seconds: *00* to *59* |
| S | English ordinal suffix as 2 characters: *th, nd, rd*, etc. |
| t | number of days in the given month: *28* to *31* |
| U | seconds since the epoch |
| w | day of the week as a single digit: *0* (Sunday) to *6* (Saturday) |
| y | year as 2 digits: *01* |
| Y | year as 4 digits: *2001* |
| z | day of the year: *0* to *365* |

# Determining the Date and Time

Although you've used the `date()` function in various capacities throughout this book, it's a useful enough function to merit more specific coverage. The only thing the `date()` function does is return date and time information in a format based upon the arguments it is fed, but you would be surprised how useful that can be!

```
date("formatting");
```

In Chapter 6, *Control Structures*, you saw that `date ("A");` returned the values *AM* or *PM*. There are a long list of possible options for formatting as indicated in **Table 13.1**. These different parameters can also be combined, so that `date ("l F j, Y");` would return, for example, *Friday January 26, 2001*.

The `date()` function can take another argument called a timestamp. A timestamp is a number representing how many seconds it has been since midnight on January 1, 1970—a moment referred to as the epoch. As you saw in Chapter 12, *Cookies*, the `time()` function returns the timestamp for the current moment. The `mktime()` function can return a timestamp for a particular time and date.

```
mktime (hour, minute, second, month, day,
→ year);
```

So the code `$Timestamp = mktime (12, 30,
→ 0, 12, 27, 1997);` would assign to $Timestamp the number of seconds from the epoch to 12:30 on December 27, 1997. That number could then be fed into the date function like so: `date ("D", $Timestamp);`, returning *Sat*, which is the three-letter format of that day of the week.

Let's use the `date()` and `mktime()` functions to create an online calendar, where you'll see these two functions used multiple times.

## To use date():

1. Create a new PHP document in your text editor (**Script 13.5**).

   ```
   <?php
   ```

2. Assign the $PageTitle variable a value and include the header file.

   ```
   $PageTitle = "Calendar";
   require ("header.php");
   ```

   You'll go ahead and continue to develop more pages all as part of the same large scale Web site, so they'll use the same included files as those you created earlier in the chapter.

3. Assign default values to $Month and $Year, if they don't exist.

   ```
   if ((!$Month) && (!$Year)) {
       $Month = date ("m");
       $Year = date ("Y");
   }
   ```

   The first time the user comes to this page, no month or year values will be passed to the page. The PHP will go ahead and use the current month (e.g., *1*) and year (e.g., *2001*) if that is the case.

4. Create a timestamp referring to the specific month and year.

   ```
   $Timestamp = mktime (0, 0, 0, $Month, 1,
   → $Year);
   ```

   For the timestamp, you feed the mktime() function zeros for the hour, minutes and seconds and then one for the day of the month. The month and the year will be calculated based upon the page values.

5. Determine what month it is in written form.

   ```
   $MonthName = date("F", $Timestamp);
   ```

   Feeding the date() function a capital F returns the name of the month (e.g., *January*).

**Script 13.5** This fairly long script uses two of PHP's date and time functions—date() and mktime()— to generate an accurate calendar. The form at the bottom will allow the user to display different months and years.

```
script

1   <?php
2   $PageTitle = "Calendar";
3   require ("header.php");
4   // If the $Month and $Year values don't
    exist, make them the current month and
    year.
5   if ((!$Month) && (!$Year)) {
6       $Month = date ("m");
7       $Year = date ("Y");
8   }
9   // Calculate the viewed Month.
10  $Timestamp = mktime (0, 0, 0, $Month, 1,
    $Year);
11  $MonthName = date("F", $Timestamp);
12  // Make a table with the proper month.
13  print ("<TABLE BORDER=0 CELLPADDING=3
    CELLSPACING=0 ALIGN=CENTER>");
14  print ("<TR BGCOLOR=BLUE><TD COLSPAN=7
    ALIGN=CENTER><FONT COLOR=WHITE><B>
    $MonthName $Year</B></FONT></TD></TR>");
15  print ("<TR BGCOLOR=BLUE>
    <TD ALIGN=CENTER WIDTH=20><B>
    <FONT COLOR=WHITE>Su</FONT></B></TD>
    <TD ALIGN=CENTER WIDTH=20><B>
    <FONT COLOR=WHITE>M</FONT></B></TD>
    <TD ALIGN=CENTER WIDTH=20><B>
    <FONT COLOR=WHITE>Tu</FONT></B></TD>
    <TD ALIGN=CENTER WIDTH=20><B>
    <FONT COLOR=WHITE>W</FONT></B></TD>
    <TD ALIGN=CENTER WIDTH=20><B>
    <FONT COLOR=WHITE>Th</FONT></B></TD>
    <TD ALIGN=CENTER WIDTH=20><B>
    <FONT COLOR=WHITE>F</FONT></B></TD>
    <TD ALIGN=CENTER WIDTH=20><B>
    <FONT COLOR=WHITE>Sa</FONT></B></TD>
    </TR>\n");
16  $MonthStart = date("w", $Timestamp);
17  if ($MonthStart == 0) {
18      $MonthStart = 7;
19  }
20  $LastDay = date("d", mktime (0, 0, 0,
    $Month+1, 0, $Year));
21  $StartDate = -$MonthStart;
22  for ($k = 1; $k <= 6; $k++) { // Print 6
    rows.
```

*Script continues on next page*

**Script 13.5** *continued*

```
                    script
23    print ("<TR BGCOLOR=WHITE>");
24    for ($i = 1; $i <= 7; $i++) { // Use
      7 columns
25        $StartDate++;
26        if (($StartDate <= 0) ||
          ($StartDate > $LastDay)) {
27            print ("<TD BGCOLOR=GREEN>
               </TD>");
28        } elseif (($StartDate >= 1) &&
          ($StartDate <= $LastDay)) {
29            print ("<TD ALIGN=CENTER>
              $StartDate</TD>");
30        }
31    }
32    print ("</TR>\n");
33 }
34 print ("</TABLE>\n");
35 // Make the form.
36 print ("<FORM ACTION=\"calendar.php\"
   METHOD=GET>\n");
37 print ("Select a new month to view:\n");
38 print ("<SELECT NAME=Month>
   <OPTION VALUE=1>January</OPTION>\n
   <OPTION VALUE=2>February</OPTION>\n
   <OPTION VALUE=3>March</OPTION>\n
   <OPTION VALUE=4>April</OPTION>\n
   <OPTION VALUE=5>May</OPTION>\n
   <OPTION VALUE=6>June</OPTION>\n
   <OPTION VALUE=7>July</OPTION>\n
   <OPTION VALUE=8>August</OPTION>\n
   <OPTION VALUE=9>September</OPTION>\n
   <OPTION VALUE=10>October</OPTION>\n
   <OPTION VALUE=11>November</OPTION>\n
   <OPTION VALUE=12>December</OPTION>\n
   </SELECT>\n");
39 print ("<SELECT NAME=Year>
   <OPTION VALUE=2001>2001</OPTION>\n
   <OPTION VALUE=2002>2002</OPTION>\n
   <OPTION VALUE=2003>2003</OPTION>\n
   </SELECT>\n");
40 print ("<INPUT TYPE=SUBMIT NAME=SUBMIT
   VALUE=\"Submit!\">\n");
41 print ("</FORM>\n");
42 require ("footer.php");
43 ?>
```

**6.** Create a table to display the calendar.

```
print ("<TABLE BORDER=0 CELLPADDING=3
→ CELLSPACING=0 ALIGN=CENTER>");
```

**7.** Print a caption using the month and year.

```
print ("<TR BGCOLOR=BLUE>
→ <TD COLSPAN=7 ALIGN=CENTER>
→ <FONT COLOR=WHITE><B>$MonthName
→ $Year</B></FONT></TD></TR>");
```

**8.** Print out the days of the week.

```
print ("<TR BGCOLOR=BLUE>
→ <TD ALIGN=CENTER WIDTH=20>
→ <B><FONT COLOR=WHITE>Su</FONT></B>
→ </TD><TD ALIGN=CENTER WIDTH=20>
→ <B><FONT COLOR=WHITE>M</FONT></B>
→ </TD><TD ALIGN=CENTER WIDTH=20>
→ <B><FONT COLOR=WHITE>Tu</FONT></B>
→ </TD><TD ALIGN=CENTER WIDTH=20>
→ <B><FONT COLOR=WHITE>W</FONT></B>
→ </TD><TD ALIGN=CENTER WIDTH=20>
→ <B><FONT COLOR=WHITE>Th</FONT></B>
→ </TD><TD ALIGN=CENTER WIDTH=20>
→ <B><FONT COLOR=WHITE>F</FONT></B>
→ </TD><TD ALIGN=CENTER WIDTH=20>
→ <B><FONT COLOR=WHITE>Sa</FONT></B>
→ </TD></TR>\n");
```

**9.** Determine the first day of the week for that month.

```
$MonthStart = date("w", $Timestamp);
```

This line will assign the day of the week, in numerical form from 0 to 6, to the $MonthStart variable for the calendar's month and year. Because the first day of the month was used in establishing the timestamp, this code will identify that particular day. You need to do this in order to see if the month begins on a Monday, Tuesday, etc.

**10.** Make sure the $MonthStart value is usable.

```
if ($MonthStart == 0) {
    $MonthStart = 7;
}
```

*continues on next page*

DETERMINING THE DATE AND TIME

If $MonthStart is equal to 0, which means that the month begins on a Sunday, you'll run into problems using that number when the script executes, so you turn a 0 into a 7.

11. Determine the last day of the month.

```
$LastDay = date("d", mktime (0, 0, 0,
→ $Month+1, 0, $Year));
```

$LastDay will be assigned a value of a number such as *01*, *22*, or *30*, which is equal to the last day of that month. This is determined by using **0** as the day and the next month (`$Month + 1`) as the month in the `mktime()` function. Mathematically, the number of seconds to day 0 of the next month will be the same as the number of seconds to the last day of this month.

12. Choose a starting date based upon the first day of the month.

```
$StartDate = -$MonthStart;
```

Since the calendar is going to begin on a Sunday, you need to determine how many days to skip before the first day of the month occurs. If the first day of the month is a Tuesday, then $MonthStart is equal to 2, which means that $StartDate will be equal to negative 2, insuring that two blank days are created before the numbering starts.

13. Code a loop that will print out the calendar rows (weeks).

```
for ($k = 1; $k <= 6; $k++) {
→ print ("<TR BGCOLOR=WHITE>");
```

The calendar will use 6 rows, so the following section of code will be repeated 6 times by the for loop.

14. Create a second loop that will print out the calendar columns (days).

```
    for ($i = 1; $i <= 7; $i++) {
```

The calendar will have 7 columns, one for each day of the week.

**15.** Increase the value of $StartDate by one.

```
$StartDate++;
```

The value of $StartDate will be printed each day to create the date. So with each iteration of the loop, this value needs to be increased.

**16.** Code a conditional for when to print out the $StartDate.

```
if (($StartDate <= 0) ||
→ ($StartDate > $LastDay)) {
    print ("<TD
    → BGCOLOR=GREEN> 
    → </TD>");
} elseif (($StartDate >= 1) &&
→ ($StartDate <= $LastDay)) {
    print ("<TD ALIGN=CENTER>
    → $StartDate</TD>");
}
```

First, if $StartDate is less than 0 (in other words, the month hasn't begun yet) or greater than the number of days in the month ($LastDay), the page will print out a blank green space. If $StartDate is at least one but still not more than the number of days in the month ($LastDay), the page will print out the number itself.

**17.** Close the second for loop, close the table row, and then close the first for loop.

```
    }
    print ("</TR>\n");
}
```

**18.** Finish the table.

```
print ("</TABLE>\n");
```

**19.** Now you'll make a simple HTML form that submits the page back to itself.

```
print ("<FORM
ACTION=\"calendar.php\"
→ METHOD=GET>\n");
```

*continues on next page*

**20.** Create two pull-down menus: one for the month and one for the year.

```
print ("Select a new month to view:\n");
print ("<SELECT NAME=Month>
→ <OPTION VALUE=1>January</OPTION>\n
→ <OPTION VALUE=2>February</OPTION>\n
→ <OPTION VALUE=3>March</OPTION>\n
→ <OPTION VALUE=4>April</OPTION>\n
→ <OPTION VALUE=5>May</OPTION>\n
→ <OPTION VALUE=6>June</OPTION>\n
→ <OPTION VALUE=7>July</OPTION>\n
→ <OPTION VALUE=8>August</OPTION>\n
→ <OPTION VALUE=9>September</OPTION>\n
→ <OPTION VALUE=10>October</OPTION>\n
→ <OPTION VALUE=11>November</OPTION>\n
→ <OPTION VALUE=12>December</OPTION>\n
→ </SELECT>\n");
print ("<SELECT NAME=Year>
→ <OPTION VALUE=2001>2001</OPTION>\n
→ <OPTION VALUE=2002>2002</OPTION>\n
→ <OPTION VALUE=2003>2003</OPTION>\n
→ </SELECT>\n");
```

You can put whatever years you want here. Notice that these two menus will generate variables called $Month and $Year once the form is submitted. At that point in time, thanks to the conditional beginning on line 5, these new values will be used instead of the default.

**21.** Create a submit button and close the form.

```
print ("<INPUT TYPE=SUBMIT NAME=
→ SUBMIT VALUE=\"Submit!\">\n");
print ("</FORM>\n");
```

**22.** Include the footer file and close out the PHP.

```
require ("footer.php");
?>
```

**23.** Save the script as calendar.php, upload it to the server, and test it in your Web browser (**Figures 13.6** and **13.7**).

**Figure 13.6** Upon first coming to the calendar page, you will see the calendar displayed for the current month. Using the form at the bottom allows you to see other months (Figure 13.7).

**Figure 13.7** Regardless of what month and year is selected, this script will always display an accurate calendar.

✔ **Tip**

■ Instead of determining the last day of the month like I've done here on line 20 (by referring to the zero second of the first day of the next month), you could also use the date ("t"); format, which returns the number of days in a month. The rest of the script would need to be slightly altered then to use this new value.

# Using HTTP Headers

An HTTP (HyperText Transfer Protocol) header is used to send information back and forth between the server and the client (the Web browser). Normally this information is in the form of HTML, which is why the address for Web pages begins with `http://`.

But HTTP headers are a complicated enough subject to warrant a little more attention. There are actually dozens upon dozens of uses for HTTP headers, all of which you can take advantage of using PHP's `header()` function.. Here I'll demonstrate the most frequently used purpose—redirecting the user from one page to another—although the World Wide Web consortium's specifications on the subject are vast (`http://www.w3.org/Protocols/rfc2616/rfc2616`).

To redirect the user's browser with PHP, you would code:

```
header ("Location: page.php");
```

You can also use the header function to send cookies, which is a good backup to the `setcookie()` function which sometimes has inconsistent results from one browser to the next.

```
header ("Set-cookie: name=value;
→ expires=expiration");
```

The most important thing to understand about using `header()` is that it must be called before anything else is sent to the Web browser, just as you have to be careful when using the `setcookie()` function.

To demonstrate redirection, let's create a simple login script that sends a user to one page if they use the correct username and password or to another if they don't.

## To use the header() function:

1. Create a new PHP document in your text editor (**Script 13.6**):

```
<?php
```

2. Assign the page title and include the header file.

```
$PageTitle = "Login Page";
require ("header.php");
```

3. Create a conditional that will print a message if the user is not successfully logged in.

```
if ($Message == "Invalid") {
    print ("<B><CENTER><FONT COLOR=
→ RED>The username and password
→ you entered do not match what is
→ on file. Please try again!</FONT>
→ </CENTER></B>\n");
}
```

If the user-submitted name and password do not match those on file, the user will be sent back to this page with $Message equal to *Invalid*, prompting an error message.

4. Create an HTML form that takes a user name and a password.

```
print ("<FORM ACTION=
→ \"HandleLogin.php\"
→ METHOD=POST>\n");
print ("Username: <INPUT TYPE=TEXT
→ NAME=UserName><BR>\n");
print ("Password: <INPUT TYPE=PASSWORD
→ NAME=Password><BR>\n");
print ("<INPUT TYPE=SUBMIT
→ NAME=SUBMIT VALUE=\"Submit!\">\n");
```

5. Include the footer file and then close the PHP page.

```
require ("footer.php");
?>
```

6. Save the script as login.php and upload it to the server.

Now you'll need to create the page that will process login.php.

**Script 13.6** You might not ordinarily think to do so, but including the error message capacity in the login script makes sense because you'd most likely want to redirect your user back there if they are not authenticated.

```
script
1   <?php
2   $PageTitle = "Login Page";
3   require ("header.php");

4   if ($Message == "Invalid") {
5       print ("<B><CENTER><FONT COLOR=RED>
        The username and password you entered
        do not match what is on file. Please try
        again!</FONT></CENTER></B>\n");
6   }
7   print ("<FORM ACTION=\"HandleLogin.php\"
        METHOD=POST>\n");
8   print ("Username: <INPUT TYPE=TEXT
        NAME=UserName><BR>\n");
9   print ("Password: <INPUT TYPE=PASSWORD
        NAME=Password><BR>\n");
10  print ("<INPUT TYPE=SUBMIT NAME=SUBMIT
        VALUE=\"Submit!\">\n");
11  require ("footer.php");
12  ?>
```

**Script 13.7** This script will validate the user and password using predetermined values, and redirect the user accordingly. There should be no extraneous spaces outside of the PHP in this script or else the header() calls will not work.

```
script
1   <?php

2   if (($UserName == "Larry") &&
    ($Password == "LarryPass")) {
3   header ("Location:
    index.php?UserName=$UserName");
4   exit;
5   } else {
6   header ("Location: login.php?Message=
    Invalid");
7   exit;
8   }
9   ?>
```

7. Create a new PHP document in your text editor (**Script 13.7**):

   `<?php`

8. Create the conditional that will check for the proper match of UserName and Password.

   `if (($UserName == "Larry") &&`
   `→ ($Password == "LarryPass")) {`

   This conditional checks to make sure that both the username and the password match those on file. You could also write the script so that it checks a database to find the Password for the UserName, which will allow for many different combinations. Normally, for security reasons, you would not explicitly write these values in your script but rather retrieve them from a database or text file. For demonstration purposes here, you'll establish these values within the PHP though.

9. If the authentication works, redirect the user to the main page.

   `header ("Location: index.php?`
   `→ UserName=$UserName");`
   `exit;`

   This line of code will send the user out of this page and to `index.php`. It will also pass along the UserName to that page.

   The `exit;` statement tells the PHP to stop executing any line of code on this page, which you want to do now that they have been redirected.

10. Finish the conditional and redirect the user back to the login page.

    `} else {`
    `header ("Location: login.php?`
    `→ Message=Invalid");`
    `exit;`
    `}`

*continues on next page*

**USING HTTP HEADERS**

If the submitted values do not match, the user will be given another chance to log in by sending them back to `login.php`. The `?Message=Invalid` appended to the URL will tell `login.php` to print the error message as it was programmed to do in Script 13.6.

**11.** Close the PHP page.

`?>`

**12.** Save the script as `HandleLogin.php` and upload it to the server.

Now you'll modify the original `index.php` page to greet the user.

**13.** Open `index.php` in your text editor (Script 13.3):

**14.** Change line 4 to read (**Script 13.8**):

`print ("Greetings, $UserName!\n");`

**15.** Save the script as `index.php`, upload it to the server, and test all the pages, beginning with `login.php`, in your Web browser (**Figures 13.8**, **13.9**, and **13.10**).

**Script 13.8** I've added the user-specific greeting to this page to make it more dynamic and personalized. The $UserName value is being passed by the `header()` function in Script 13.7.

```
1   <?php
2   $PageTitle = "Home Page";
3   require ("header.php");
4   print ("Greetings, $UserName!\n");
5   print ("<P>Click <A HREF=\"page2.php\">
    here</A> to go to the next page.\n");
6   require ("footer.php");
7   ?>
```

**Figure 13.8** This is the simple login page that takes a username and password.

**Figure 13.9** Upon successfully logging in, the user will be redirected to the `index.php` page where they will be greeted by username.

**Figure 13.10** If either the username or the password does not match that on file, the user will be redirected back to the `login.php` page where they will see this error message.

**Script 13.9** In PHP you can send emails with only one function—mail(). I have wrapped the mail() call within different conditionals to make sure that the email is only sent when appropriate.

```
1   <?php
2   $PageTitle = "Sending Emails";
3   require ("header.php");
4   if ($BeenSubmitted) {
5       if ($MailTo) {
6           if (mail($MailTo, $Subject,
                $Body, "From: $MailFrom")) {
7               print ("<B><CENTER><FONT
                    COLOR=BLUE>Your email has
                    been successfully sent!
                    </FONT></CENTER></B>\n");
8           } else {
9               print ("<B><CENTER><FONT
                    COLOR=RED>Your email was
                    not successfully sent due
                    to a system error!</FONT>
                    </CENTER></B>\n");
10          }
11      } else {
12          print ("<B><CENTER><FONT COLOR=
                RED>Please enter the recipient's
                mail to address!</FONT></CENTER>
                </B>\n");
13      }
14  }
15  ?>
16  <FORM ACTION="email.php" METHOD=POST>
17  Recipient's Email Address: <INPUT TYPE=
    TEXT NAME="MailTo" SIZE="50"><BR>
18  Your Email Address: <INPUT TYPE=TEXT
    NAME="MailFrom" SIZE="50"><BR>
19  Email Subject: <INPUT TYPE=TEXT
    NAME="Subject" SIZE="80"><BR>
20  Email Body:<TEXTAREA NAME="Body"
    ROWS="10" COLS="50">
21  </TEXTAREA><P>
22  <INPUT TYPE=HIDDEN NAME=BeenSubmitted
    VALUE=TRUE>
23  <INPUT TYPE=SUBMIT NAME="SUBMIT"
    VALUE="Submit!">
24  </FORM>
25  <?
26  require ("footer.php");
27  ?>
```

# Sending Email

Among the numerous things you can do with great ease in PHP is send emails.

```
mail ("mailto", "subject", "body");
```

The mail() function uses the server's email application (such as *sendmail* on Unix) to send out the messages. This function can take another argument through which you can add more details to the email, including a *From* address, email priority, and carbon copy addresses.

```
mail ("mailto", "subject", "body",
 → "From: fromaddress");
```

## To send email with PHP:

1. Create a new PHP document in your text editor (**Script 13.9**):

    ```
    <?php
    ```

2. Assign the page title and include the header file.

    ```
    $PageTitle = "Sending Emails";
    require ("header.php");
    ```

3. Create a conditional to process the form if it has been submitted.

    ```
    if ($BeenSubmitted) {
    ```

    *continues on next page*

**4.** Check to make sure that a recipient's email address has been submitted and, if so, send the email.

```
if ($MailTo) {
    if (mail($MailTo, $Subject,
    → $Body, "From: $MailFrom")) {
        print ("<B><CENTER>
        → <FONT COLOR=BLUE>
        → Your email has been
        → successfully sent!
        → </FONT></CENTER>
        → </B>\n");
    } else {
        print ("<B><CENTER>
        → <FONT COLOR=RED>
        → Your email was not
        → successfully sent due
        → to a system error!
        → </FONT></CENTER>
        → </B>\n");
    }
```

I've put the `mail()` function within a conditional so that a message will be displayed indicating whether or not the mail was successfully sent.

**5.** Complete the conditionals.

```
    } else {
        print ("<B><CENTER>
        → <FONT COLOR=RED>Please
        → enter the recipient's mail
        → to address!</FONT>
        → </CENTER></B>\n");
    }
}
```

**Figure 13.11** This very simple HTML form, combined with the power of PHP, will allow you to send emails from your Web browser.

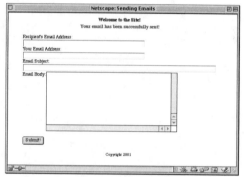

**Figure 13.12** If the PHP script was able to send the email, a message will be printed stating such.

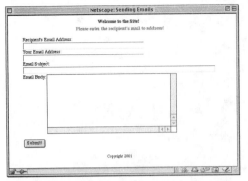

**Figure 13.13** If you forget to enter a recipient's email address, the script will not try to send the email and will just print an error message instead.

**Figure 13.14** This is the email I received in Eudora (an email client) after submitting the form in Figure 13.11.

6. Close the PHP section and create an HTML form that takes two email addresses, the subject, the body, and a hidden value to determine whether or not the form has been submitted.

```
?>
<FORM ACTION="email.php" METHOD=POST>
Recipient's Email Address:
→ <INPUT TYPE=TEXT NAME="MailTo"
→ SIZE="50"><BR>
Your Email Address: <INPUT TYPE=TEXT
→ NAME="MailFrom" SIZE="50"><BR>
Email Subject: <INPUT TYPE=TEXT
→ NAME="Subject" SIZE="80"><BR>
Email Body:<TEXTAREA NAME="Body"
→ ROWS="10" COLS="50">
</TEXTAREA><P>
<INPUT TYPE=HIDDEN NAME=BeenSubmitted
→ VALUE=TRUE>
<INPUT TYPE=SUBMIT NAME="SUBMIT"
→ VALUE="Submit!">
```

7. Close the form, then include the footer file.

```
</FORM>
<?
require ("footer.php");
?>
```

8. Save the script as `email.php`, upload it to the server, and test it in your Web browser (**Figures 13.11**, **13.12**, **13.13**, and **13.14**).

## ✔ Tip

■ It is possible to send emails with attachments, although that requires far more sophisticated coding (normally involving objects). Fortunately a number of programmers have already developed workable solutions which are available for use. See Appendix C, *PHP Resources*, for more information.

SENDING EMAIL

# 14

# DEBUGGING

It may seem ironic that the last chapter in the book deals with a subject you've probably been facing at every step of the way—debugging your code. However, because you've learned so much along the way, debugging will come more naturally to you now, and this chapter will help you learn some tricks of the trade. Unfortunately no matter how good you get as a programmer the occasional careless error will always catch you off guard, so it is best to be prepared when it does happen.

In this chapter you will learn a variety of techniques to reduce, report, and manage errors in your code. While avoiding errors is important in Web development, you also have to know how to deal with the errors that will inevitably occur when making Web sites.

# Common Errors

The most common type of error you'll run across is syntactical—failing to cross all your t's and dot all your i's, so to speak. Errors like this will result in error messages like the one in **Figure 14.1**. These are the first types of errors PHP will catch because the code is evaluated for syntax before execution takes place. In order to avoid making these sorts of mistakes when you program, be sure to:

**Figure 14.1** By now you've certainly seen your fair share of parse errors generated by syntactical mistakes in your scripts.

◆ End every executable line of code with a semi-colon.

◆ Use a closing quotation mark, parentheses, bracket, or brace for every opening quotation mark, parentheses, bracket, or brace.

◆ Escape, using the backslash, all single- and double-quotation marks within the `print()` statement.

One thing you should also understand about syntactical errors is that just because the PHP error message says the error is occurring on line 12, for example, doesn't mean that the mistake is actually on that line. It is not uncommon for there to be a difference between what PHP thinks is line 12 and what your text editor indicates is line 12. So while PHP's direction is useful in tracking down a problem, learn to treat the line number referenced as more of a starting point rather than an absolute.

**Figure 14.2** Warnings are created by PHP upon attempting to execute the script and are generally caused by misuse of or mis-reference to functions (e.g., misspelling a function's name or using the wrong number of arguments when calling a function).

The second type of error you'll encounter results from trying to do something which cannot be done. These errors occur, for example, when `setcookie()` or `header()` is called after the Web browser has already received HTML, when a function is called without the proper arguments, or when you try to write to a file that does not have the proper permissions. These errors are discovered by PHP when attempting to execute the code (**Figure 14.2**).

COMMON ERRORS

**Script 14.1** The original HandleLogin.php page was certainly acceptable but could be improved upon by making use of the headers_sent() function.

```
script
1   <?php
2   if (($UserName == "Larry") &&
    ($Password == "LarryPass")) {
3       header ("Location:
        index.php?UserName=$UserName");
4       exit;
5   } else {
6       header ("Location:
        login.php?Message=Invalid");
7       exit;
8   }
9   ?>
```

**Script 14.2** The headers_sent() function helps to avoid the common mistake of sending a header (or a cookie) after the Web browser has already received information (Figure 14.3).

```
script
1
2   <?php
3   if ( headers_sent() ) {
4       print ("Cannot process your request
        due to a system error!\n");
5   } else {
6       if (($UserName == "Larry") &&
        ($Password == "LarryPass")) {
7           header ("Location:
            index.php?UserName=$UserName");
8           exit;
9       } else {
10          header ("Location:
            login.php?Message=Invalid");
11          exit;
12      }
13  }
14  ?>
```

The third type of error you'll see—all too frequently—aren't PHP errors at all, but programmer errors, also called logic errors. (Some programmers would argue that all errors are programmer errors because PHP itself cannot make such mistakes.) One reason such errors happen is because you fail to use the proper variable name. If you do that, you will not see an error message like those in Figures 14.1 and 14.2, you will just witness odd or unpredictable results. These can be the hardest to discern because PHP will not give you a clue as to what the problem is or how to solve it. Nothing but accurate checking and smart detective work will fix them!

For the first exercise, let's add a safety check to the HandleLogin.php script from Chapter 13, *Creating Web Applications*, to avoid the commonplace occurrence of sending a header after the Web browser has already received some HTML or blank space.

## To prevent a common error:

1. Open HandleLogin.php in your text editor (**Script 14.1**).

2. Create a blank line by pressing Return before the initial PHP tag (**Script 14.2**).

*continues on next page*

**COMMON ERRORS**

This blank line, while it may seem insignificant, will generate the error message seen in **Figure 14.3**.

3. After the initial PHP tag, add the following conditional:

```
if ( headers_sent() ) {
    print ("Cannot process your request
    ⇢ due to a system error!\n");
} else {
```

The `headers_sent()` function returns the value TRUE if any HTML, blank space, etc. has been sent to the Web browser already. If this has occurred, attempting to use the `header()` function will create a harsh warning in the user's browser. Instead of having that happen, if the headers have been sent, this page will now show a generic system error.

If the headers have not been sent, then the `headers_sent()` function will be false and the rest of the page will be executed as normal.

4. Don't forget to close the `headers_sent()` conditional before the closing PHP tag!

```
}
```

5. Save your script as `HandleLogin.php`, upload it to the server in the same directory as `login.php`, and test both pages in your Web browser (**Figure 14.4**).

## ✔ Tip

■ Some text editors, such as BBEdit for the Macintosh, include utilities to check for balanced parenthesis, brackets, and quotation marks.

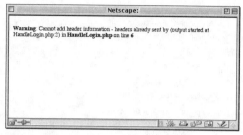

**Figure 14.3** Attempting to set a cookie or send a header after the Web browser has already received any information creates an error like this.

**Figure 14.4** By using the `headers_sent()` function, you can print a less perplexing message to the user. It still doesn't solve the problem, but it is better than having users see messages like that in Figure 14.3.

**Table 14.1**

| Error Reporting Levels | | |
|---|---|---|
| NUMBER | CONSTANT | MEANING |
| 1 | E_ERROR | Fatal run-time |
| 2 | E_WARNING | Non-fatal run-time warnings |
| 4 | E_PARSE | Compile-time parse |
| 8 | E_NOTICE | Run-time notices |
| 16 | E_CORE_ERROR | fatal errors that occur during PHP's initial startup (PHP 4 only) |
| 32 | E_CORE_WARNING | warnings (non fatal errors) that occur during PHP's initial startup (PHP 4 only) |
| 64 | E_COMPILE_ERROR | fatal compile-time errors (PHP 4 only) |
| 128 | E_COMPILE_WARNING | compile-time warnings (non fatal errors) (PHP 4 only) |
| 256 | E_USER_ERROR | user-generated error message (PHP 4 only) |
| 512 | E_USER_WARNING | user-generated warning message (PHP 4 only) |
| 1024 | E_USER_NOTICE | user-generated notice message (PHP 4 only) |
| | E_ALL | all of the above, as supported |

# Error Reporting and Logging

PHP has fairly good support built into it for both error reporting and handling. While these two concepts won't help you minimize your errors, they will give you another way of learning from them.

The error_reporting() function in PHP is used to establish what type of errors PHP should report on. The line error_report(0); turns error reporting off entirely. Errors will still occur; you just won't hear about them anymore. Conversely the line error_reporting(E_ALL); will report on every error that occurs, which PHP does not necessarily do. (The PHP manual lists all the possible levels of error reporting that can be set.) You'll use this function in the last section of the chapter, *Using the Die Statement*.

The error_reporting() tells PHP which errors to report upon while the error_log() function instructs PHP on how to file away error occurrences.

```
error_log("message", "type",
→ "destination");
```

When something goes awry, you can have PHP leave you a note in a file (i.e., record the errors in a log) or even email you directly. Prudent use of the error_log() function will allow Webmasters and programmers to keep better tabs on what the Web site is doing. To have PHP email you when an error occurs, add this line to your code:

```
error_log("message", "1",
→ "php@DMCinsights.com");
```

Let's alter the email.php script from Chapter 13, *Creating Web Applications*, so that it makes a note in a file every time it cannot successfully send an email.

## To use the error_log() function:

1. Open email.php in your text editor
   (**Script 14.3**).

2. After line 9, add (**Script 14.4**):

   ```
   error_log ("Unable to send an email to
   → $MailTo from $MailFrom at " . time() .
   → "\n", 3, "errors.txt");
   ```

**Script 14.3** This is the email.php script from Chapter 13, *Creating Web Applications*. Currently it has no error logging capability, which would make it more useful.

```
1   <?php
2   $PageTitle = "Sending Emails";
3   require ("header.php");
4   if ($BeenSubmitted) {
5       if ($MailTo) {
6           if (mail($MailTo, $Subject, $Body, "From: $MailFrom")) {
7               print ("<B><CENTER><FONT COLOR=BLUE>Your email has been successfully sent!
                </FONT></CENTER></B>\n");
8           } else {
9               print ("<B><CENTER><FONT COLOR=RED>Your email was not successfully sent due to a
                system error!</FONT></CENTER></B>\n");
10          }
11      } else {
12          print ("<B><CENTER><FONT COLOR=RED>Please enter the recipient's mail to
            address!</FONT></CENTER></B>\n");
13      }
14  }
15  ?>
16  <FORM ACTION="email.php" METHOD=POST>
17  Recipient's Email Address: <INPUT TYPE=TEXT NAME="MailTo" SIZE="50"><BR>
18  Your Email Address: <INPUT TYPE=TEXT NAME="MailFrom" SIZE="50"><BR>
19  Email Subject: <INPUT TYPE=TEXT NAME="Subject" SIZE="80"><BR>
20  Email Body:<TEXTAREA NAME="Body" ROWS="10" COLS="50">
21  </TEXTAREA><P>
22  <INPUT TYPE=HIDDEN NAME=BeenSubmitted VALUE=TRUE>
23  <INPUT TYPE=SUBMIT NAME="SUBMIT" VALUE="Submit!">
24  </FORM>
25  <?
26  require ("footer.php");
27  ?>
```

Every time the `mail()` function is unable to work, a simple message will be recorded to log file indicating that $MailFrom was unable to send a message to $MailTo at a particular time (established using the `time()` function). A savvy administrator could view this file and either follow up with the users who had trouble or determine when the `mail()` function stopped working properly.

*continues on next page*

**Script 14.4** The modified version of `email.php` uses the `error_log()` function to record any problems that occur in sending emails. You can use `error_log()` to email a message as well, although not if the problem is in sending mail!

```
1   <?php
2   $PageTitle = "Sending Emails";
3   require ("header.php");
4   if ($BeenSubmitted) {
5       if ($MailTo) {
6           if (mail($MailTo, $Subject, $Body, "From: $MailFrom")) {
7               print ("<B><CENTER><FONT COLOR=BLUE>Your email has been successfully sent!
                </FONT></CENTER></B>\n");
8           } else {
9               print ("<B><CENTER><FONT COLOR=RED>Your email was not successfully sent due to a
                system error!</FONT></CENTER></B>\n");
10              error_log ("Unable to send an email to $MailTo from $MailFrom at " . time() . "\n",
                3, "errors.txt");
11          }
12      } else {
13          print ("<B><CENTER><FONT COLOR=RED>Please enter the recipient's mail to
            address!</FONT></CENTER></B>\n");
14      }
15  }
16  ?>
17  <FORM ACTION="email.php" METHOD=POST>
18  Recipient's Email Address: <INPUT TYPE=TEXT NAME="MailTo" SIZE="50"><BR>
19  Your Email Address: <INPUT TYPE=TEXT NAME="MailFrom" SIZE="50"><BR>
20  Email Subject: <INPUT TYPE=TEXT NAME="Subject" SIZE="80"><BR>
21  Email Body:<TEXTAREA NAME="Body" ROWS="10" COLS="50">
22  </TEXTAREA><P>
23  <INPUT TYPE=HIDDEN NAME=BeenSubmitted VALUE=TRUE>
24  <INPUT TYPE=SUBMIT NAME="SUBMIT" VALUE="Submit!">
25  </FORM>
26  <?
27  require ("footer.php");
28  ?>
```

**ERROR REPORTING AND LOGGING**

**3.** Save your script as `email.php` and upload it to the server.

Now you'll need to create a blank document called `errors.txt` for the `error_log()` function to write to.

**4.** Create a new blank document in your text editor.

**5.** Save your document as `errors.txt` and upload it to the server in the same directory as `email.php`.

**6.** Set the permissions on `errors.txt` so that everyone has write privileges on it.

**7.** Test `email.php` in your Web browser (**Figure 14.5**, **14.6**, and **14.7**).

### ✔ Tip

■ If your email application that the server uses to send emails is functioning properly, this script will not log any errors. If you want to see what the script would do if it couldn't send a message, change line 6 to:

```
if (!mail($MailTo, $Subject, $Body,
→ "From: $MailFrom")) {
```

**Figure 14.5** I've rewritten the `email.php` page to log any problems it encounters. This will all occur unbeknownst to the user.

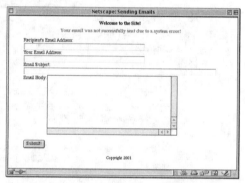

**Figure 14.6** All the user sees when a problem occurs is the simple message above the form. However, the system administrator can check the error log for more information (Figure 14.7).

**Figure 14.7** When making an error log, you can have it record whatever information you think is appropriate. This log lists the $MailTo and $MailFrom values along with a timestamp.

# Debugging Detective Work

When it comes to the more challenging type of errors—programmer errors, PHP won't help you out by telling you on what line to begin looking. In fact, all that you'll probably see is that the results weren't what you were expecting. In order to solve these riddles, you'll need to do a little detective work to see what mistakes were made and where.

There are three tools and techniques to help you in your cause:

◆ Using comments.

◆ Using the `print()` statement.

◆ Tracking variables.

Just as you can use comments to document your scripts, you can also use them to rule out problematic lines. If PHP is giving you an error on line 12, then commenting out that line should get rid of the error. If not, then you know the error is elsewhere.

In more complicated scripts, I frequently use the `print()` statement to leave myself notes as to what is happening as the script is executed. When a script has several steps, it may not be easy to tell if the problem is occurring in step two or step five. By using the `print()` statement you can narrow the problem down to the specific step.

Finally, it is pretty easy for a script not to work because you referred to the wrong variable or the right variable by the wrong name. To check for these possibilities, use the `print()` statement to let you know what the values are of the variables as the script progresses. Then you will know for sure if the variables are causing a problem.

I'll illustrate these techniques by modifying the `HandleLogin.php` page from earlier in the chapter to demonstrate how I would debug it if I were getting unpredictable results.

## To debug a script:

**1.** Open HandleLogin.php in your text editor (Script 14.2).

**2.** Delete the initial blank line created earlier making the initial PHP tag the first line of the page (**Script 14.5**).

```
<?php
```

**3.** After the headers_sent() conditional (line 2), add a print() statement:

```
if ( headers_sent() ) {
    print ("Headers have been sent. Not
→ attempting to verify. <P>\n");
    print ("Cannot process your request
→ due to a system error!\n");
```

If the problem is because the headers have already been sent, you'll make that clear to yourself while testing.

**4.** After the *else* (line 5), add three more print() statements.

```
} else {
    print ("Headers have not been sent.
→ Attempting to verify. <P>\n");
    print ("UserName is $UserName.
→ <P>");
    print ("Password is $Password.
→ <P>");
```

The first print() statement correlates to the one added above, indicating that the problem is not header() related.

The next two print statements will tell you exactly what values were received for $UserName and $Password. You can track the value of variables throughout a script by printing them out at key moments.

**Script 14.5** If the HandleLogin.php page was acting strangely and giving you results that you couldn't understand, you could modify it like this for debugging purposes. The combination of using print() statements, tracking variables, and commenting out lines of code will quickly help to solve any problems.

```
script

1   <?php
2   if ( headers_sent() ) {
3       print ("Headers have been sent.
        Not attempting to verify.<P>\n");
4       print ("Cannot process your request
        due to a system error!\n");
5   } else {
6       print ("Headers have not been sent.
        Attempting to verify.<P>\n");
7       print ("UserName is $UserName. <P>");
8       print ("Password is $Password. <P>");
9       if (($UserName == "Larry") &&
        ($Password == "LarryPass")) {
10          print ("<P>Match!");
11  // header ("Location: index.php?
        UserName=$UserName");
12          exit;
13      } else {
14          print ("<P>Not a Match!");
15  // header ("Location: login.php?
        Message=Invalid");
16          exit;
17      }
18  }
19  ?>
```

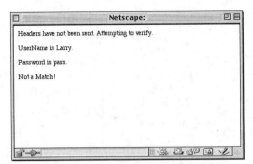

**Figure 14.8** In debugging a problem script, printing messages detailing the process that PHP is going through can be invaluable. Here you can determine that the problem is not caused by the headers or referring to the wrong variables.

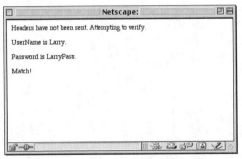

**Figure 14.9** Again, the specifics of what `HandleLogin.php` is doing is spelled out for you. If this page is causing any problems, you can now narrow it down to the `header()` lines.

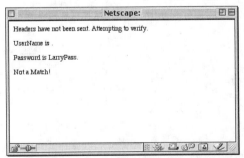

**Figure 14.10** This is all too-common of an occurrence. The reason that no match is being made is because the wrong variable name is being referred to. Notice that there is no value for UserName. This means there is a discrepancy between what `login.php` and `HandleLogin.php` use to refer to this value.

**5.** After the second *if* conditional (line 9), add another `print()` statement and comment out the `header()` line.

```
if (($UserName == "Larry") &&
→ ($Password == "LarryPass")) {
    print ("<P>Match!");
    // header ("Location: index.php?
    → UserName=$UserName");
    exit;
} else {
```

By printing the word *Match!* you'll know whether or not the system verified the username and password, which may let you rule that out as a possible cause of error.

Since you are debugging the script, you can eliminate the effect of the `header()` call by placing two slashes at the beginning of the line to comment it out. Simply removing the backslashes when you are ready uncomments the line and reinstates the command.

**6.** Again, add another `print()` statement and comment out the `header()` function after the *else* (line 13).

```
    print ("<P>Not a Match!");
    // header ("Location: login.php?
    → Message=Invalid");
    exit;
    }
}
?>
```

**7.** Save your script as `HandleLogin.php`, upload it to the server in the same directory as `login.php`, and test both pages in your Web browser (**Figures 14.8**, **14.9**, and **14.10**).

# Using the Die Statement

A final type of error you will encounter is the circumstantial error. These occur only when something else on the server goes wrong. Fortunately, they are more rare than programming errors. For example, if the MySQL database isn't running, every database-related function will generate an error. Or, as you saw with the `email.php` example, if the server's sendmail application isn't working (on a Unix server), that would cause a problem as well. Although these system errors are beyond the control of the programmer, you still ought keep their possible occurrence in mind as you code.

You can stop these errors in their tracks by using the `die` statement. The `die` statement tells the PHP to cease execution of a script when an error occurs. It can also print an error message to the browser or call a function. For example,

```
$Link = mysql_connect ($Host, $User,
→ $Password) or die ("Couldn't connect to
→ the database.");
```

If, for any reason, PHP is not able to connect to the database, the script will stop executing and the *Couldn't connect to the database* message will be printed.

```
$Link = mysql_connect ($Host, $User,
→ $Password) or die (mysql_error());
```

In this example, should PHP not be able to connect to the database, `die` will call the `mysql_error()` function. The `mysql_error()` function prints the actual error that the MySQL database generates.

Both of the above examples work because if PHP determines that the first part of the conditional (i.e., `mysql_connect`) is FALSE, it will enact the second part of the conditional (which is the `die` statement) to guarantee that the entire line evaluates to TRUE. In other words, the line says if the connection to the

**Script 14.6** For scripts that use several lines of code, each of which relies upon the successful completion of its predecessor, the die statement is invaluable in reducing and handling errors. Since die is managing potential errors, PHP's built-in error reporting has also been turned off (compare Figure 14.11 with Figure 14.13).

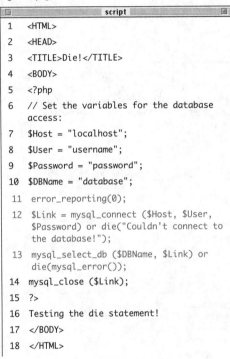

```
1   <HTML>
2   <HEAD>
3   <TITLE>Die!</TITLE>
4   <BODY>
5   <?php
6   // Set the variables for the database
    access:
7   $Host = "localhost";
8   $User = "username";
9   $Password = "password";
10  $DBName = "database";
11  error_reporting(0);
12  $Link = mysql_connect ($Host, $User,
    $Password) or die("Couldn't connect to
    the database!");
13  mysql_select_db ($DBName, $Link) or
    die(mysql_error());
14  mysql_close ($Link);
15  ?>
16  Testing the die statement!
17  </BODY>
18  </HTML>
```

database doesn't work, do this. If the connection to the database does go through, then that's all that is required.

As an example of this, you'll add the die statement to a very basic database script that connects to MySQL and then tries to select the database.

## To use the die statement:

1. Create a new PHP document in your text editor.

2. Begin with the standard HTML head (**Script 14.6**):
   ```
   <HTML>
   <HEAD>
   <TITLE>Die!</TITLE>
   <BODY>
   ```

3. Open the PHP section with the initial PHP tag and then set the variables for the database access.
   ```
   <?php
   $Host = "localhost";
   $User = "username";
   $Password = "password";
   $DBName = "database";
   ```

4. Turn off all error reporting.
   ```
   error_reporting(0);
   ```
   Since the die statement will manage the errors that occur, you'll turn off PHP's default method of reporting errors to avoid redundancy.

5. Connect to MySQL.
   ```
   $Link = mysql_connect ($Host, $User,
   → $Password) or die("Couldn't connect
   → to the database!");
   ```

*continues on next page*

This line of code tells PHP to attempt to connect to MySQL. If it cannot do so for any reason, it will print the *Couldn't connect to the database* message and stop execution of the script. It is important to stop the execution immediately, because if PHP cannot connect to the database, the next two lines of code, which rely on that connection, will also cause error messages. (In actuality, by turning `error_reporting` off, no error will be reported although errors will still occur. Regardless of this fact, it's best to stop problem scripts at the first possible instant.)

6. Select the database.

   ```
   mysql_select_db ($DBName, $Link) or
   → die(mysql_error());
   ```

   Here, if PHP cannot select the database (determined by $DBName), it will cease execution of the page and print the error generated by MySQL.

7. Close the MySQL link and the PHP section.

   ```
   mysql_close ($Link);
   ?>
   ```

8. Create a simple message and finish the HTML page.

   ```
   Testing the die statement!
   </BODY>
   </HTML>
   ```

   I have added this line of text so that the page has some content on it. This page could easily be modified to query a database as well.

9. Save your script as `die.php`, upload it to the server, and test in your Web browser (**Figures 14.11**, **14.12**, and **14.13**).

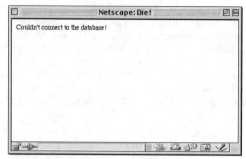

**Figure 14.11** By turning off error reporting and using the die statement, a more meaningful error message can be displayed to the user. Also, the script will cease execution of the page since it could not complete this first step.

**Figure 14.12** Here the die statement calls the `mysql_error()` function, which prints the actual error message the MySQL database generated.

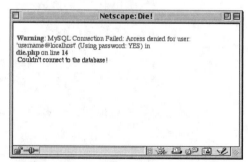

**Figure 14.13** If error reporting is not turned off, the end user would see both the PHP error message as well as the message created by the die statement. Compare this to Figure 14.11 where error reporting has been turned off.

## ✔ Tips

- You can also prevent error messages by using the *at* symbol (@) before any function call. Referred to as the *error-control operator*, the *at* symbol will disregard any errors caused by the function it precedes. It is used like so:

  ```
  $Link = @mysql_connect ($Host, $User,
  → $Password);
  ```

  Unlike `die`, @ does not give you the option of printing a message or calling a function.

- You can also use `die` to call your own functions. For example, if you have a function created for the purposes of printing error messages in a particular format, `die` could call it.

  ```
  $Link = mysql_connect ($Host, $User,
  → $Password) or die (print_message
  → ("Couldn't connect."));
  ```

# Installation and Configuration

Many PHP users, especially those just learning the language, never need learn how to install and configure PHP on a server. However, should you decide to take this route, rest assured that it is not necessarily that complicated and PHP's price—free—makes this an even more appealing option. When you create your own PHP install, you insure that the preferred version of PHP, supporting exactly those features you desire, is available for your programming use.

There are two primary questions to answer before beginning installation. First, what operating system will the server run? Second, what Web server application will you use? In this section I will demonstrate how to install PHP on Unix variant (e.g., Linux) and Windows servers. With respect to the Web server itself, Apache is by far the most common application for Unix servers and you'll most likely use it or IIS (Internet Information Server) on Windows machines.

After those two issues there are other considerations such as: which database(s) to support, ability to create images, PDF's or Shockwave files, XML interactivity and so forth. Any one of these capabilities should be considered before you begin installation.

The PHP manual, especially the online version, covers installation in a reasonable amount of detail. In this section I will list the basics of installing on either a Linux or Windows 2000 machine, which should suffice for most users, barring any unforeseen complications.

# Installing on a Linux Server

The popularity of Linux as an operating system, especially for use as a Web server, over the past couple of years has risen dramatically. The fact that it is free and very stable is a huge mark in its favor. However, the difficulty in setting up a Linux machine can still be a hurdle to overcome, although this is less of a problem now than it used to be.

In order to be able to do any installation on a Linux server, you must have the root password and access. The server does not necessarily need to be online though: you can work entirely on the one machine or create a mini-network by connecting another computer to it and "dialing-in."

## To install Apache and PHP:

1. Download the most current, stable versions of Apache and PHP to a common directory, such as /usr/local/ (**Figure A.1**).

   The Apache files can be found at http://www.Apache.org.

2. If the files have the .gz extension, use these lines to unzip each (press Return after typing each individual line):

   gunzip php-4.0.4pl1.tar.gz
   gunzip apache_1.3.14.tar.gz

   Although I will be referring to the specific versions of PHP and Apache that I installed for this demonstration, be sure to refer to the version you are using when you do your installation (e.g., *php-3.0.3pl1*).

3. Unpack the files:

   tar –xvf php-4.0.4pl1.tar
   tar –xvf apache_1.3.14.tar

   In order to get to the raw files, you'll need to run those two lines. This will change each package from one compressed version to a folder containing all of the specific files. You'll see a lot of information on the screen after typing each line (**Figure A.2**).

**Figure A.1** The ls command lists all the files within the current directory. PHP and Apache are in this folder along with a number of other libraries and applications.

**Figure A.2** When you use tar to expand a package, you'll see all the files it contains listed.

```
+---------------------------------------------+
| You now have successfully built and installed the    |
| Apache 1.3 HTTP server. To verify that Apache actually |
| works correctly you now should first check the   |
| (initially created or preserved) configuration files  |
|                                             |
|   /usr/local/apache/conf/httpd.conf          |
|                                             |
| and then you should be able to immediately fire up   |
| Apache the first time by running:             |
|                                             |
|   /usr/local/apache/bin/apachectl start      |
|                                             |
| Or when you want to run it with SSL enabled use:  |
|                                             |
|   /usr/local/apache/bin/apachectl startssl   |
|                                             |
| Thanks for using Apache.     The Apache Group    |
|                   http://www.apache.org/   |
+---------------------------------------------+
[root@server    apache_1.3.14]#
```

**Figure A.3** After configuring, making, and installing Apache, it will show you this message demonstrating that everything worked properly.

**Figure A.4** All the unpacked files and folders are now located within the PHP folder.

```
---------+
| License:
|
| This software is subject to the PHP License, available in
this  |
| distribution in the file LICENSE. By continuing this inst
allation |
| process, you are bound by the terms of this license agreem
ent.  |
| If you do not agree with the terms of this license, you mu
st abort |
| the installation process at this point.
|
+---------------------------------------------+
---------+

Thank you for using PHP.

[root@server   php-4.0.4pl1]#
```

**Figure A.5** Successful configuration, making, and installing of PHP will finish with the license and a thank you.

4. Move to the newly created Apache folder, then run the configuration (**Figure A.3**).

   `cd ../apache_1.3.14`

   `./configure –prefix=/www`

   The `cd` command allows you to change folders. Once you are within the Apache folder, you can preconfigure it.

5. Move to the PHP folder (**Figure A.4**) and run its configuration.

   `cd ../php-4.0.4pl1`

   `./configure --with-apache=../`
   `→ apache_1.3.14 --enable-track-vars`

   What configuration parameters you use depends upon which features you want PHP to support. Each configuration command of the sort –with requires you to indicate the directory where that particular item can be found. In this example, I want PHP to work with Apache and I state where the Apache folder is. The –enable-track-vars option is necessary for PHP to properly use HTML forms.

6. Make and install the PHP (**Figure A.5**).

   `make`
   `make install`

   These two lines of code install the configured PHP so that it is usable by Apache.

7. Move back to the Apache folder, run its configuration, then make and install it.

   `cd ../apache_1.3.14`

   `./configure --activate-module=`
   `→ src/modules/php4/libphp4.a`
   `make`
   `make install`

   Now that you have configured, made, and installed Apache, it is ready to run.

*continues on next page*

**INSTALLING ON A LINUX SERVER**

**8.** Copy the `php.ini` file to its new location.

`cp /usr/local/php-4.0.4pl1/`
`→ php.ini-dist /usr/local/lib/php.ini`

The php.ini file dictates how PHP operates. It comes with the package as php.ini-dist. In order for Apache to make use of it, it must be copied to the proper directory and renamed.

**9.** Start Apache.

`bin/apachect1 start`

Like any application, Apache must be running in order to work. If you are within the Apache folder, this line will start up the Web server.

**10.** Test to see if Apache and PHP is working by going to the proper URL with your Web browser (**Figure A.6**).

If the server is online, you can go to the URL such as `http://www.DMCinsights.com`. If the machine is not online, use either `http://localhost/` or an IP address assigned to the machine.

### ✔ Tips

■ You can test the PHP installation by using the `test.php` file created in Chapter 1, *Introduction*.

■ Because Linux can run on machines with very outdated hardware (I have one Linux machine with 16MB of RAM, a 1 GB hard drive, and a 90Mhz processor!), creating a Web server from an old Windows machine is a perfectly reasonable thing to do and is an excellent way to learn.

**Figure A.6** Apache uses this default page to indicate that it is running properly.

**Figure A.7** I downloaded the necessary files for installation on a Windows machine to my desktop.

**Figure A.8** Double-clicking on the Apache icon starts the installation process.

**Figure A.9** The unzipped PHP files have been placed within the C:\php folder.

# Installing on a Windows 2000 Server

Getting PHP and Apache to work on a Windows machine (it doesn't have to be Windows 2000) is easier in some ways than using Linux, as you have a graphical interface to make use of. Also, you do not need to necessarily be the server administrator and it is easier to install and test on the same machine.

You can install PHP on Windows 95, 98, ME, NT, or 2000, just be sure to download the proper files from the Apache and PHP Web sites. There are even specific Windows PHP files available to make installation easier.

## To install Apache and PHP:

1. Download the most current, stable versions of PHP and Apache to your computer (**Figure A.7**).

2. Unzip PHP to a logical folder (like C:/php). You'll need a zip utility to unzip the downloaded package.

3. Install Apache by running the installation application (**Figure A.8**).

4. Copy the php.ini-dist file from the PHP folder (**Figure A.9**) to the proper system folder (e.g. C:/windows). Save the file as php.ini.

5. Start the Apache server.
   The easiest way to start the Apache server is by going through the Start menu: Start > Programs > Apache Web Server > Start Apache.

6. Test to see if Apache and PHP is working with your Web browser.
   The easiest way to test Apache is by typing http://localhost/ in your Web browser window. Again, you can test the success of the PHP install by using the test.php file.

## ✔ Tip

■ You can also get PHP to run with other Web servers on a Windows machine such as IIS.

# Configuration

Although it is best to configure your PHP during installation, a number of parameters can be changed afterwards. The `php.ini` file which you copied to the proper directory during installation, contains a number of parameters for how PHP is run (**Figures A.10** and **A.11**). You can make changes by editing these parameters and restarting your Web server application. If you ever run into problems, you can reinstate the original `php.ini` file by copying the `php.ini-dist` file that came with the original package.

In order for PHP to support databases, generate images on the fly, use `mcrypt()` and so forth, you will need to download other libraries and packages and make these available to PHP by stating their location either during installation or by altering the `php.ini` file later. See the file itself and the PHP manual for more information on this topic.

**Figure A.10** The `php.ini` document is the most important file for determining how PHP functions.

**Figure A.11** Pages upon pages of parameters are listed in the `php.ini` file, as well as instructions on how to change them.

# SECURITY

Security is an aspect of the Web—from hardware to software to programming—that cannot be over pondered. Although there's no justification to assume that every site is a target for an attack, there's also no reason to leave your projects open to abuse. I mentioned a couple of security considerations both throughout the book and in Appendix A, *Installation and Configuration*. I will now quickly go over a few security measures you can take while programming as well as direct you to other security resources.

# Cryptography and SSL

Cryptography is the process of changing the format of data (i.e., encrypting it) so that it is more difficult to read. Some cryptography, such as PGP, available for free for public use from http://www.pgp.com, (**Figure B.1**), uses public and private keys in order to encode and decode information. Other cryptographic systems, like the `crypt()` function built into PHP will encrypt data but will not decrypt it. You can find out more about `crypt()` within the *Strings* section of the PHP manual.

In order to have a better level of cryptography available to your sites, you will need to download the mcrypt library from http://mcrypt.hellug.gr/ and then configure PHP with mcrypt support during installation. Inclusion of this library allows you to use the `mcrypt()` functions which can encrypt and decrypt information. See the above URL and the mcrypt section of the PHP manual for more information.

Cryptography is just a part of a secure solution as it can only be used once data has been received by the server. You may also need to take advantage of SSL connections in your Web sites. SSL, which stands for *Secure Sockets Layer*, is a method of securely transmitting information between a client (the Web browser) and the server. Utilization of SSL connections (indicated by the *https://* prefix in a URL) is a must for e-commerce applications. You can also specify that cookies are sent over a SSL connection by setting the proper parameters when using the `setcookie()` function. Check with your ISP or server administrator to see if SSL connections are supported on the machine you are using.

## ✔ Tip

■ Passwords used within your PHP application should always be encrypted. If the server you are using does not support `mcrypt()`, use `crypt()` to encrypt the password entered during the login, then check this against the stored encrypted password.

**Figure B.1** PGP is available in both free and commercial versions and allows you to send and receive encrypted data.

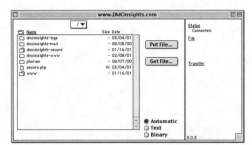

**Figure B.2** This folder is above the Web document root folder (www or dmcinsights-www) and is therefore unavailable to user via the Web browser. I can still use it to store and access sensitive documents such as secure.php, though.

# Writing Secure PHP

While PHP does not have the same security concerns that you might find using CGI scripts or ASP, they still exist. There are a several considerations to keep in mind while programming.

The first recommendation I would make is that files which contain sensitive information such as passwords be placed outside of the Web document root. Every Web server application uses a folder as the default root for Web documents. Items within the folder can be accessed via a URL but items located above the default folder cannot be. However, they can still be used within PHP with the line:

```
require ("../secure.php");
```

The above line of code will include the file **secure.php** which is located one folder above the current document (**Figure B.2**). The file cannot be directly accessed via the Web though as it is outside of the default Web document root.

My second recommendation is a two-parter involving getting user submitted data from HTML forms. First you should always remember to use the POST form method (as opposed to GET) when transferring sensitive information. This is because the GET method will append the submitted data to the URL, making it visible in the Web browser window.

Second, you should be wary of user-submitted data because it can be a common loophole through which malicious users can wreak havoc with your system. Clever people may be able to insert JavaScript or executable code into your site using an HTML form. This code could send them sensitive information, alter databases, and so forth. The easiest way to preempt this sort of malfeasance is to check all incoming data using regular expressions as you saw in Chapter 8, *Regular Expressions*. Appendix C, PHP Resources, will also direct you towards sites that contain articles on this specific topic as well as sources of example regular expression code.

# Security Resources

If you will be doing more than just basic Web development work, you ought to seriously consider learning more about Web security than the few points illustrated in this appendix.

There are literally dozens upon dozens of Web sites you can visit to keep yourself informed of pertinent security issues. The most prominent four, in my opinion, are:

- Computer Response Emergency Team (`http://www.cert.org`)
- Security Focus (`http://www.security-focus.com`)
- Packet Storm (`http://packetstorm.securify.com`)
- World Wide Web Consortium (`http://http://www.w3.org/Security/ Faq/www-security-faq.html`)

There are also any number of books available ranging from those that generically discuss security to those that will assist in establish secure Windows NT or Linux Web servers.

With respect to PHP, do not forget to read the PHP manual's section on security. Also review the security section of the documentation for the database you are using on the server. Some, such as MySQL's manual, includes tips specifically with respect to using PHP and MySQL.

# PHP RESOURCES

This book was written to give beginner and intermediate PHP programmers a good foundation on which to base their learning. A number of topics have either been omitted altogether or glossed over due to this book's focus. In this appendix I list a number of useful PHP-related Internet resources, briefly discuss where to obtain more information for databases and other advanced topics, and include a few tables, both old and new.

# The PHP Manual

Every PHP programmer should immediately acquire some version of the PHP manual before beginning to work with the language. The manual is available from the official PHP site—http://www.php.net/docs.php (**Figure C.1**)—as well as a number of other locations. You can download the manual in nearly a dozen languages in any of these formats: PDF, HTML, plain text, or Palm-compatible. The official Web site also has an annotated version of the manual available at `http://www.php.net/manual/en/` where other users have added helpful notes and comments that may solve some of the problems you encounter when using a particular function.

The manual begins with installation and security issues. It then continues with basic language constructs and some of PHP's features. The bulk of the manual details PHP's built-in functions, organized by topic. What is not apparent to the beginning PHP programmer is what the format that the manual uses to describe these functions means. Common lines are:

```
array file (string filename [, int
→ use_include_path])
int mysql_close ([int link_identifier])
void exit(void)
double round (double val)
```

It is important to understand that the first word on each line refers to what type of value the function will return. The `file()` function returns an array, `mysql_close()` returns an integer, `exit` returns nothing, and `round()` returns a floating-point (or double) number. The manual also lists the arguments (and argument types) that a function takes, with optional arguments listed within square brackets. For example, `exit` takes no arguments, `round()` takes a floating-point number and `mysql_close()` takes an optional link identifier.

**Figure C.1** The PHP home page has many different versions of the PHP manual available for download. I would recommend saving one version on your computer for quick reference and then checking the online annotated version if you are having problems with a specific function.

**Figure C.2** PHPBuilder has a long list of articles written explaining how to do certain things using PHP. They range from the most basic (e.g. documenting your code) to the more advanced (e.g. object oriented programming).

# Web sites and Newsgroups

I'll mention just a few of the many very useful Web sites you can turn to when programming and leave it up to you to discover the ones you like the best. Most of these also contain links to other PHP-related sites.

The first, and most obvious, site to bookmark is PHP.net (`http://www.php.net`), the official site for PHP.

Secondarily, you should familiarize yourself with Zend.com (`http://www.zend.com`), the home page for the creators of PHP version 4. The site contains numerous downloads plus a wealth of other resources, straight from the masters, so to speak.

For information on specific topics, PHPBuilder (`http://www.phpbuilder.com`) is a great place to turn. The site has dozens of articles explaining how to do particular tasks using PHP (**Figure C.2**). On top of that, PHPBuilder has support forums and a code library where programmers have uploaded sample scripts.

PHPstart4all (`http://php.start4all.com/`) is a good resource for those just beginning to use PHP. It contains links which redirect you to: PHP sites and tutorials, PHP hosts (including free hosts), available PHP books, PHP open source projects, and script libraries.

*continues on next page*

WEB SITES AND NEWSGROUPS

261

Similarly, the PHP Rescource Index (`http://php.resourceindex.com/`) will get you to online tutorials, available scripts and code libraries (**Figure C.3**). More code libraries can be found at:

♦ WeberDev (`http://www.weberdev.com/maincat.php3?categoryID=106&category=PHP`)

♦ HotScripts (`http://www.hotscripts.com/PHP/`).

One final Web reference I'll mention is the PHP Coding Standard, available at `http://utvikler.start.no/code/php_coding_standard.html`. The standard is a document making recommendations for programming in PHP in terms of proper format and syntax for variable names, control structures, and so forth. While you shouldn't feel obligated to abide by these rules, there are some solid and well-thought-out recommendations which can help minimize errors as you program.

If you have access to newsgroups, you can use these as a great sounding board for ideas, as well as a place to get your most difficult questions answered. Of course you can always give back to the group by offering your own expertise to those in need. The largest English language PHP newsgroup is alt.php. You may be able to access alt.php through your ISP or via a pay-for-use Usenet organization. There are newsgroups available in languages other than English too.

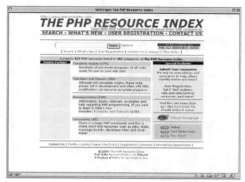

**Figure C.3** The PHP Resource Index, and other sites like it, have vast repositories of sample codes and scripts for you to use.

**Figure C.4** The MySQL Web site has most of the documentation you will need as well as the downloadable files of MySQL itself.

# Database Resources

Which database resources will be most useful to you depends, obviously, upon which database management system (DBMS) you are using. The most common database used with PHP is MySQL, although PostgreSQL may be a close second and PHP supports most of the standard ones.

To learn more about using MySQL, begin with the official MySQL (`http://www.mysql.com`) Web site (**Figure C.4**). You can download the MySQL manual from there to use as a reference while you work. There are also a handful of books available specifically on MySQL ranging from the entry-level *Sams' Teach Yourself MySQL in 21 Days* by Mark Maslakowski and Tony Butcher to the more technical *MySQL & mSQL* written by Randy Jay Yarger, George Reese, and Tim King, published by O'Reilly.

Information on using PostgreSQL databases can be gathered by first visiting their Web site (`http://www.postgresql.org`). One popular book about this database is *PostgreSQL: Introduction and Concepts* by Bruce Momjian.

You might also want to consider getting a general book on database design, such as Michael J. Hernandez's *Database Design for Mere Mortals*. While books such as this one will not go into the specifics of using MySQL or PostgreSQL, it will help you to better understand the underlying thinking behind creating and using databases. Since PHP can be used with many different databases, getting a broader sense of the topic can pay off in spades.

# Advanced Topics

While this book should adequately get you started using PHP there are still a few topics that you may want to investigate further.

The first such subject is creating objects and classes using PHP. As you improve upon your programming skills, and especially as you build a strong code library, being able to create and utilize objects can improve your programming speed and minimize runtime errors. Also, learning about objects using PHP can facilitate later acquisition of other programming languages which are object-oriented such as Java (despite the existence of objects within PHP, it is not an object-oriented language). You can find several good tutorials online regarding objects in PHP, including one at Zend.com, `http://www.zend.com/zend/tut/class-intro.php` (**Figure C.5**).

Two other subjects that I would recommend you investigate—using functions to return multiple values and variable variables—are discussed in the PHP manual. The former is demonstrated in the *Functions* section, explaining how you can use an array to return several values from within one function. The later can be found within the *Variables* area of the manual and shows how you can create, assign a value to, and retrieve a value from, variables on the fly. It's a complicated subject to understand and use but it can help take your programming to a much more sophisticated level.

**Figure C.5** The Zend.com tutorial on object-oriented programming in PHP is thorough and fairly easy to understand.

The topic of file permissions was briefly discussed in Chapter 10, *Files and Directories*. If you are using a Unix server and desire to know more, look to either the Unix manual (found with the *man* command) or to Elizabeth Castro's excellent book *PERL and CGI for the World Wide Web: Visual QuickStart Guide*. In her appendices, she covers permissions as well as security and some basic Unix information. Those of you using Windows servers can learn more about file permissions through Microsoft's Web site (http://www.microsoft.com) or the Windows Help files.

Finally, through the course of this book I recommended that you can expand your use of regular expressions and other PHP features by using existing codes. Check any of the Web sites listed earlier in this chapter for sample code which you can paste into your programming. Other programmers have already developed patterns for matching regular expressions and advanced scripts that allow you to do things such as send attachments in an email using PHP. Either outright using their work or merely building upon it can both save you time and teach you different ways of achieving your goals.

ADVANCED TOPICS

# Tables

Through the course of this book, I have included a handful of tables of useful information. In this appendix, I combine these tables in one location as a convenient reference, and I've included a new one, listing operator precedence (see **Tables C.1** through **C.6**).

**Table C.1** This is a partial list of operator precedence from highest to lowest (for example, multiplication takes precedence over addition).

| Operator Precedence |
| --- |
| ! ++ -- |
| * / % |
| + - . |
| < <= > >= |
| == != === |
| && |
| \|\| |
| = += -= *= /= .= %= |
| and |
| xor |
| or |

**Table C.2** This is a reprint of the list of special characters used for defining regular expression patterns as first revealed in Chapter 8, *Regular Expressions*.

| Special Characters for Regular Expression | |
| --- | --- |
| CHARACTER | MATCHES |
| . | any character |
| ^a | begins with *a* |
| a$ | ends with *a* |
| a+ | at least one *a* |
| a? | zero or one *a* |
| \n | new line |
| \t | tab |
| \ | escape |
| (ab) | *ab* grouped |
| a\|b | *a* or *b* |
| a{2} | *aa* |
| a{1,} | *a*, *aa*, *aaa*, etc. |
| a{1,3} | *a*, *aa*, *aaa* |
| [a-z] | any lowercase letter |
| [A-Z] | any uppercase letter |
| [0-9] | any digit |

**Table C.3** Don't forget that PHP has already defined several character classes for you to use when creating regular expression patterns. Here are the primary ones.

| Predefined Classes for Regular Expression | |
| --- | --- |
| CLASS | MATCHES |
| [[:alpha:]] | any letter |
| [[:digit:]] | any digit |
| [[:alnum:]] | any letter or digit |
| [[:space:]] | any white space |
| [[:upper:]] | any uppercase letter |
| [[:lower:]] | any lowercase letter |
| [[:punct:]] | any punctuation mark |

**Table C.4** Which parameter you use when opening a file determines what exactly the PHP can do with that file—write to, read from, and so forth.

| File Modes | |
| --- | --- |
| MODE | ALLOWS FOR |
| r | Read from the file only. |
| w | Write to the file only, but it will create the file if it doesn't exist or discard existing contents before writing (if the file does exist). |
| a | Append new data to the end of the file and create the file if it doesn't exist. |
| r+ | Read and write to the file. |
| w+ | Read and write to the file, but it will create the file if it doesn't exist or discard existing contents before writing (if the file does exist). |
| a+ | Read from and write to the file and create the file if it doesn't exist. New data will be appended to the end of file. |

**Table C.5** The various date formats may be the most common thing that I can never remember. Keep this table nearby when using the date() function.

## Format Options with the date() Function

| CHARACTER | FORMAT |
|---|---|
| a | *am* or *pm* |
| A | *AM* or *PM* |
| d | day of the month as 2 digits with leading zeros: *01* to *31* |
| D | day of the week as 3 letters: *Sun, Mon,* etc. |
| F | month, long-form: *January* |
| g | hour of the day in 12-hour format without leading zeros: *1* to *12* |
| G | hour of the day in 24-hour format without leading zeros: *0* to *23* |
| h | hour of the day in 12-hour format: *01* to *12* |
| H | hour of the day in 24-hour format: *00* to *23* |
| i | minutes: *00* to *59* |
| j | day of the month without leading zeros: *1* to *31* |
| l (lowercase 'L') | day of the week, long-form: Sunday |
| m | month as 2 digits: *01* to *12* |
| M | month as 3 letters: *Jan* |
| n | month as digits without leading zeros: *1* to *12* |
| s | seconds: *00* to *59* |
| S | English ordinal suffix as 2 characters: *th, nd, rd,* etc. |
| t | number of days in the given month: *28* to *31* |
| U | seconds since the epoch |
| w | day of the week as a single digit: *0* (Sunday) to *6* (Saturday) |
| y | year as 2 digits: *01* |
| Y | year as 4 digits: *2001* |
| z | day of the year: *0* to *365* |

**Table C.6** These error-reporting options come in handy both when you are initially developing a site and once it has gone live.

## Error Reporting Levels

| NUMBER | CONSTANT | MEANING |
|---|---|---|
| 1 | E_ERROR | Fatal run-time |
| 2 | E_WARNING | Non-fatal run-time warnings |
| 4 | E_PARSE | Compile-time parse |
| 8 | E_NOTICE | Run-time notices |
| 16 | E_CORE_ERROR | fatal errors that occur during PHP's initial startup PHP 4 only |
| 32 | E_CORE_WARNING | warnings (non fatal errors) that occur during PHP's initial startup PHP 4 only |
| 64 | E_COMPILE_ERROR | fatal compile-time errors PHP 4 only |
| 128 | E_COMPILE_WARNING | compile-time warnings (non fatal errors) PHP 4 only |
| 256 | E_USER_ERROR | user-generated error message PHP 4 only |
| 512 | E_USER_WARNING | user-generated warning message PHP 4 only |
| 1024 | E_USER_NOTICE | user-generated notice message PHP 4 only |
| | E_ALL | all of the above, as supported |

**TABLES**

# INDEX

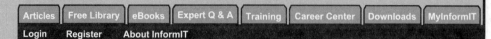